Henry Glapthorne

Plays and Poems of Henry Glapthorne

Henry Glapthorne

Plays and Poems of Henry Glapthorne

ISBN/EAN: 9783744710541

Printed in Europe, USA, Canada, Australia, Japan

Cover: Foto ©Thomas Meinert / pixelio.de

More available books at **www.hansebooks.com**

HENRY GLAPTHORNE'S
PLAYS AND POEMS.

THE PLAYS AND POEMS OF
HENRY GLAPTHORNE
NOW FIRST COLLECTED
WITH ILLUSTRATIVE NOTES
AND A MEMOIR OF THE
AUTHOR IN TWO VOLUMES

VOLUME THE FIRST

LONDON
JOHN PEARSON YORK STREET COVENT GARDEN
1874

CONTENTS OF

THE FIRST VOLUME

MEMOIR OF HENRY GLAPTHORNE

ARGALUS AND PARTHENIA

THE HOLLANDER A COMEDY

WIT IN A CONSTABLE

NOTES AND ILLUSTRATIONS

Memoir of

HENRY GLAPTHORNE

HENRY GLAPTHORNE (1) is one of the lateſt and one of the leaſt known of the great ſchool of Elizabethan dramatiſts. Indeed, ſtrictly ſpeaking, he can ſcarcely be ſaid to belong to that company at all, as he only began to write about midway in the reign of the firſt Charles, and fully thirty years after Elizabeth's death. But the term has always been uſed with ſuch latitude as to include that younger branch or offshoot of it, which wrote before the advent of the Commonwealth, an interregnum during which the drama ſlumbered for ſeveral years, and which ſerves to create a great and impaſſable gulf, ſeparating the leaſt of the Elizabethan dramatiſts, whether of the earlier or later branch,

---

(1) His name ſeems to have been ſpelt indifferently with and without the final *e*: it is *Glapthorn* in the Poems and *Glapthorne* in the Plays and *Whitehall*. We have adopted the latter and longer form, both from the greater frequency of its uſe and from its analogy to the ſpelling of the time.

from the greateſt of the Dramatiſts of the Reſtoration.

Like Nabbes, Brome, and Shirley (whom he greatly refembled in manner and ſtyle), Glapthorne's work was done in the later half of Charles I.'s reign.

"The affinity between the comedies which were produced immediately before the cloſing of the theatres under the Commonwealth and the ſubfequent taſte of the nation, involves," as a recent writer has remarked, " a queſtion of fome intereſt. Are there not ſigns in the work of our laſt playwrights of the Elizabethan ſucceſſion to make it probable that the drama of the Reſtoration would in the natural courſe of evolution, have been produced out of the elements already developed on the ſtage, even without the intervention of French models, and ſuppoſing that the Puritans had never got the upper hand?" (2)

Although one of the obſcureſt of a long-neglected claſs of writers, Glapthorne was, nevertheleſs, chofen fifty years ago as the ſubject of a lengthy article in the Retroſpective Review, (3) from which we extract the following paſſages:—

"Henry Glapthorne is one of the leaſt known of our neglected dramatiſts, one of the obſcureſt of an obſcure claſs. Although the author of nine plays, which

---

(2) Mr. J. A. Symonds, in *The Academy*, March 21, 1874.

(3) Vol. X., pp. 122—159. The quotations from his plays in this article are very inaccurately printed.

were received with approbation, or, as the phrase was, "with good allowance," in his own time, and a writer of no inconsiderable merit, he has not since been honoured with the slightest attention from the admirers of this species of literature. Dodsley's collection does not contain one of Glapthorne's plays, although it includes many far inferior to them; but one short quotation from him appears in *Lamb's Dramatic Specimens*; not a line in *Campbell's Specimens of English Poets*. We perceive, however, that two his plays (4) are announced for publication in the *Old English Drama*, a circumstance which has reminded us of a former intention of devoting a few pages to the investigation of his dramatic character, and has induced us now to afford him this tardy justice. Winstanley mentions him as 'one of the chiefest dramatic poets of that age;' (5) a judgment from which Langbaine, with his usual jealousy and contempt of his rival biographer, appeals, but, at the same time, 'presumes, that his plays passed with good approbation at the Globe and Cockpit Playhouses;' and the authors of the *Biographia Drama-*

---

(4) *Albertus Wallenstein* and *The Lady's Privilege*.

(5) "*Henry Glapthorn* was one well deserving of the English (*sic*), being one of the chiefest Dramatick Writers of this Age; deservingly commendable not so much for the quantity as the quality of his Plays; being, &c. In *Albertus Wallenstein* these lines are much commended:

This Law the Heavens inviolably keep,
Their Justice well may slumber, but ne'er sleep."
[Vol. II., p. 73.]

WILLIAM WINSTANLEY, *Lives of the most famous English Poets*. Lond. 1687.

tica allow him to have been a good writer, adding, however, that his plays are now entirely laid afide. For this total forgetfulnefs into which Glapthorne's plays have fallen, their extreme rarity will, in fome meafure, although not wholly, account. It may alfo be partly owing to his not having attained the higheft form in the dramatic art, and partly to that chance and change to which all things are liable. The biography of the author has experienced a fimilar fate to that of his plays, and we are confequently unable to fupply any particulars of it. With refpect to his character as an author, the opinion expreffed in the *Biographia Dramatica* is more correct than that of Winftanley. Glapthorne is certainly a better writer than a dramatift, more eloquent than impaffioned, more poetical than pathetic, infinitely better qualified to defcribe than to feel.

"Glapthorne belongs to an inferior order of genius : not being able to lay open the fprings of paffion, he covers them with flowers, in order that, as he cannot gratify us with their refrefhing waters, he may, at leaft, hide their exiftence. The confequence is, that, in thofe fituations in which we are prepared for our fympathies being called into exercife, we find poetry inftead of pathos, and elaborate fpeeches inftead of paffion. Almoft everything is good, well faid, eloquent, poetical ; but in fuch a profufion of rhetorical flourifhes, poetical images, and dazzling metaphors, it is not poffible that every thing fhould be in its proper place. Indeed it muft be admitted, that his imagery is not always appropriate, and is frequently but ill calculated to bear the teft of logic. In exuberance of ornament, he refembles George Peele, although he does not poffefs the fame richnefs of colouring, nor the fame ftately harmony of diction: in redundancy of fimiles he approaches the exquifite John Lilly, although he does not carry his fondnefs for them to quite fo extravagant a length ; nor are his compofitions diftinguifhed by fuch a laborious polifh and minute accuracy; nor do they contain the fame quantity of learned allufion as thofe of the witty Euphuift. The exceffive imagery in which Glapthorne indulges, completely fpoils the dramatic effect of his plays; but, although he frequently facrifices truth and nature to the utterance of a pretty fpeech, or the garnifh of a well expreffed fimilitude, there are paffages to which this cenfure does not apply, paffages of great poetical beauty, written with vigour of thought, and fervour of imagination.

Albertus Wallenftein, the firft in order of publication, and, probably, the firft which Glapthorne wrote, was originally printed in 1634.(6) This play, which is upon the whole a good one, is founded upon the revolt of that commander from the Emperor Ferdinand the Second. The chief intereft, however, centres in the fubfidiary ftory of Albert, the general's fon, and Ifabella, one of his wife's attendants. This part forms a fweet piece of dramatic hiftory, and is written with great beauty both of sentiment and diction: the characters of the two lovers are full of noblenefs ; that of Ifabella is a fine fpecimen of feminine perfection.

" The next production of our author was a comedy, called *The Hollander*, which was written in 1635, but not publifhed until 1640. This play contains fome fine writing, but very little comic power, except in the character of

---

(6) This is an error repeated by feveral writers. *Vide infrà.*

Captain Pirke, a very diminutive perfonage, who breathes nothing but big phrafes, and ftruts about with a moft valorous magniloquence. Sconce, the Dutchman, from whom the piece is named, is, we think, a failure.

The fcene between two quarrelling lovers, Freewit and Know-worth, exhibits that redundancy of imagery which we have cenfured in Glapthorne. It contains fome pretty images, but the whole paffage is fpoiled by the bad tafte and extravagance of the author.

"*Wit in a Conftable*, which was written in 1639, is an entertaining comedy, without poffeffing any paffages which are particularly worth extracting; it certainly does not fatisfy the expectations which the title is calculated to raife. If the conftable has much wit, he is like Hudibras, 'very fhy in ufing it.'

"*Argalus and Parthenia* is one of the many rhythmical verfions of the poetical profe of Sir Philip Sidney, and is diftinguifhed by all Glapthorne's extravagances without his beauties.

"The lateft and beft of our author's productions is *The Lady's Privilege*, a comedy abounding in poetry, and written with more feeling, more of the eloquence of real paffion, and lefs deformed with hyperbole than any of his plays. As a fpecimen of fervid and beautiful compofition, it might be quoted from the beginning to the end; but we muft at the fame time remark, that it is by no means free from that vicious redundancy of figure, for which we have cenfured the author. But even in this, the beft of his dramas, he does not arrive at any great degree of pathos, although the fubject is eminently fufceptible of it. The ftory is of a very dramatic caft, and yet the play is, as a whole, deficient in dramatic art: the character of Doria, however, is admirably conceived and well fuſtained. The plot is ſimple, and is in ſubſtance as follows:

"Chriſea, the niece of Trivulci, Duke of Genoa, ſurpriſes Doria, the victorious Genoeſe admiral, whom ſhe was engaged to marry, into a vow that he will not only renounce his own claim to her, but exert his utmoſt efforts to gain her the hand of his moſt intimate friend Vitelli. This arrangement of the faithleſs fair one, is as diſagreeable to Vitelli, who is in love with her ſiſter Eurione, as it is to Doria. The admiral, however, performs his vow with ſuch laudable zeal and ſincerity, that he prevails upon Vitelli, in the warmth of friendſhip, to ſacrifice his own wiſhes to thoſe of his friend. In the mean-time, this unexpected change in the ſituation of the parties, without any apparent cauſe, produces a quarrel between Doria and Bonivet, one of Chriſea's kinſmen, which terminates in the ſuppoſed death of the latter. Doria is brought to trial, and is about to be ſentenced to death, when the privilege which any virgin of Genoa has of redeeming a condemned perſon, on condition of her marrying him, is claimed by a young lady. Doria, at firſt, abſolutely refuſes to avail himſelf of the offer; but the lady, threatening to die with him if he perſiſt in his ungallant refuſal, he, at length, with extreme reluctance, yields his conſent, and is married. Chriſea had, notwithſtanding the urgent ſolicitations of Vitelli and Eurione, refuſed to claim the privilege, and ſave her former lover; but, at this period, ſhe makes her appearance in court, and, to her inexpreſſible grief, finds that Doria is married. It appears, that for the purpoſe of trying the conſtancy of Doria, ſhe had only feigned a paſſion for Vitelli, and, for the purpoſe of proving his fortitude, had ſecreted Bonivet, who ſuddenly appears amidſt the aſtoniſhed group. This, of courſe, annuls the ſentence; but as it does not annul the marriage, the lovers are ſtill in a dilemma ; fortunately, the bride relieves them from their painful difficulty, by announcing herſelf to be Sabelli, Doria's page.

"In this play the reader, beſides the qualities before deſcribed as characterizing Glapthorne's dramas, will frequently find great felicity of phraſe and expreſſion.

"The trial is a noble ſcene. The author riſes above his uſual tone, into a ſtrain of great dignity and energy. There are paſſages which almoſt approach the ſublime, particularly the one beginning 'Methinks, I'm like ſome aged mountain.'

"We have only to add in concluſion, that the remaining four plays, written by Glapthorne, were never printed (7); and that he was alſo the author of a book of poems."

The following remarks on Glapthorne's Plays, prefixed to a reprint of two of them publiſhed half-a-century ago, may alſo be worth quoting :—

"The biography of this author is unknown, and his productions almoſt forgotten. His plays were certainly received with approbation in his own time, and deſervedly ſo ; but their merit is rather of a poetical than a dramatic kind. They are not only ill calculated for repreſentation, from the declamatory and undramatic nature of the dialogue, but are deficient in intenſity and paſſion. The author only ſports on the ſurface of the heart ; he never penetrates into the ſanctuary. Indeed he is ſo intent on producing poetry, that he ſeldom even attempts to excite

---

(7) The four unprinted Plays were entitled, *The Parricide, or Revenge for Honour*; *The Veſtal*; *The Noble Trial*; and *The Dutcheſs of Fernandina*.

our fympathies: but in taking this courfe, he probably confulted his own powers, and fo far acted wifely. For pathos, therefore, he has fubftituted a highly ornamented ftyle of poetry, and the earneftnefs of the author for the paffion of the interlocutors. Amidft a great deal of redundant imagery, however, we frequently meet with paffages of exceeding beauty, particularly in *Albertus Wallenftein* and *The Lady's Privilege*.(8) This is the lateft and beft of Glapthorne's plays;—it is more dramatic and lefs extravagant, than *Albertus Wallenftein*, although by no means free from the hyperbole and vicious redundance of figure which diftinguifh the ftyle of this author. *The Lady's Privilege* is, however, altogether an eloquent compofition, and is written with more feeling than the author ufually difplays (9)."

We add fome obfervations on *The Tragedy of Albertus Wallenftein* by an accomplifhed living German critic :—

"The plot of Glapthorne's tragedy (10) partly turns on the intention of Wallenftein's younger fon Albertus to marry Ifabella, a virtuous chambermaid of his mother, which incites the father to difplay a moft tyrannical cruelty

---

(8) Preface to the Reprint of *Albertus Wallenftein* in The Old Englifh Drama (1824).

(9) *Ib.* Preface to the Reprint of *The Lady's Privilege* (1825).

(10) *Albertus Wallenftein, late Duke of Fridland and General to the Emperor Ferdinand II.* London, 1639 and 1640. Both editions are the fame impreffion, although the fecond contains a few corrections evidently made while the prefs was kept ftanding. Mr. Halliwell [Dictionary of

'in king Cambyſes' vein.' He is willing at length to allow the marriage, on condition that Albertus will engage to murder his young wife with his own hands on the morning after the wedding. At this moment the Ducheſs enters and accuſes ˌIſabella of having ſtolen a precious jewel, afterwards found in her own drawer. Wallenſtein, in ſpite of her proteſtations orders her to be hanged, and as the guards are laying hold of her, one of them is killed by Albertus in defence of his innocent bride. Wallenſtein in a rage ſtabs his ſon and Iſabella is hanged. Afterwards Wallenſtein alſo kills a page, who, ſent by the ducheſs, awakens him againſt his orders. In the fifth aćt Wallenſtein goes to Eger in order there to celebrate the wedding of his elder ſon Frederick with Emilia, daughter to Duke Saxon-Weimar, one of the Proteſtant leaders. Exaćtly as in Schiller's celebrated tragedy, the Earls of Tertzki and of Kintzki, Colonel Newman and Marſhal Illawe, are ſhot by ſome ſoldiers at a feaſt prepared for them by Gordon (governor of Eger), Leſlie, and Butler, upon which the conſpirators haſten to Wallenſtein's chamber, where Gordon inſtantly deſpatches him. How welcome a ſubjećt the life and death of Wallenſtein was to contemporary poets, is ſhown by the faćt, that it was likewiſe handled by the French poet Sarraſin (1603—1654) and by an Italian (Wallenſtein's Ermordung. Ed. by G. M. Thomas, Munich, 1858, 4to) (11).

Old Engliſh Plays, following Baker] erroneouſly gives 1634 as the date of the firſt edition; an error probably ariſing from the faćt that it was in that year Wallenſtein was murdered.

(11) KARL ELZE: *Introdućtion to George Chapman's Alphonſus*, Leipzig, 1867.

It is not only as a dramatift, however, that Glapthorne has claims on our efteem and admiration. In 1639 he publifhed a thin quarto volume of Poems, many of them of great fweetnefs and beauty.

"Glapthorne," fays Mr. W. Carew Hazlitt, (12) was an admirer of Lovelace. I do not know whether the admiration was reciprocal; but fome of the poems addreffed by Lovelace to *Lucafta* are fimilar in their fubjects to thofe addreffed by the earlier writer to *Lucinda*."

In the year 1641 Glapthorne edited and publifhed the Poems of his friend Thomas Beedome (13). To this little volume, befides two copies of commendatory verfes in Englifh and Latin, he prefixed the following Notice :—

"To the Reader.

"Bookes are the pictures of mens lives delineated, firft by fancy, and by judgement drawne to the life. Such is this piece, the living Idea of him that writ it, who though now dead, has a living Monument to his worth, His Booke, which defpight of fire, can never convert to afhes.

---

(12) Handbook of Poetical Literature *sub voce.*

(13) *Poems Divine and Humane.* By Thomas Beedome. London, Printed by E. P. for John Sweeting and are to be fold at his Shop, at the figne of the Angel in Popes-Head-Alley, neer Cornehill. 1641. Mr. Allibone afferts (*Dict. of Eng. Literature,* I. 158) that Beedome's Poems were reprinted in 1657, in a work called *Wit a Sporting.*

'Tis *Lentum Ilium*, flow *Troy*, that will not bee eafily confumed; he fhall live in Paper, which fhall make him live in's Marble. And in this, good Reader, his worth fhall bee Emergent, he has don many things well, and nothing ill. Therefore receive him as an abfolute teftimony of wit and fancy, or elfe deceive thy felfe, fince his workes are as excellent, as fingular.

"HEN. GLAPTHORNE."

Of Thomas Beedome, the fubject of all this hyperbolical laudation, nothing feems now to be known. His little volume of Poems has the merit of exceffive rarity, and, as far as I have examined it, very little other merit. He ofcillates between piety and indecency, and the favour of both is equally rank.

The laft production that we have from Glapthorne's pen is a fmall poetical pamphlet, dated 1643, ftill thinner than the firft, containing a Poem on Whitehall, and four Elegies, dedicated to "my noble Friend and Goffip, Captaine Richard Lovelace." After this he difappears from our view, both as an author and as a man.

Refpecting the life of Glapthorne, literally nothing is known with certainty. In a fmall collection of Elizabethan lyrics publifhed fome thirty years ago, (14) he is ftated to have been

---

(14) *The Helicon of Love, A Selection from the Poets of*

"born about 1608," though upon what authority beyond mere conjecture I am unable to afcertain. It may be noticed, however, that this fuppofition, if right, makes him the coeval of Milton.

That Glapthorne received a liberal education, and acquired fome facility in the art of Latin verfification, his elegy written in that language in memory of a friend (15) abundantly proves. Taken in connexion with the curious fact that there are prefixed to his *Tragedy of Albertus Wallenstein* fome Latin verfes by Alexander Gill, who was firft under and then head-mafter of St. Paul's School, there feems fome ground for fuppofing that Glapthorne may have received the rudiments of his education there (16); that he

---

the Sixteenth and Seventeenth Centuries. Lond. 1844, p. 98, where the exquifite fong, "Unclofe thofe eyelids," is quoted as a fpecimen of Glapthorne.

(15) *In obitum Lachrymabilem Thomas Beedome.* (See Vol. II. p. 231.)

(16) In anfwer to an application made to the prefent head-mafter to fearch the fchool records in order, if poffible, to confirm this conjecture, the following courteous communication was received:—

"St. Paul's, E.C.
"April 9, 1874.

"DEAR SIR.
"I wifh I could give you any information in the matter to which your inquiry refers.

may have been the contemporary there of Milton; and, like his greater fchool-fellow, have gained by his aptitude and proficiency the friendfhip of his mafter.

Of Alexander Gill fome account will be found in our Notes and Illuftrations: of Milton it may be remarked that his earlieft poetical publications, *Comus* (1637) and *Lycidas* (1638), almoft coincided in date with thofe of Glapthorne. (17).

" We have no record of the admiffions of fcholars prior to about 1750. In Knight's Life of Colet he gives us a lift of names of eminent Alumni in which that of *Henry Glapthorne* docs not appear. But this is not conclufive, as I could mention feveral eminent perfons whom he has not, for fome reafon or other, included.

" I fhould be glad to claim Glapthorne, whofe works you are editing you tell me. The proof, which I retain for the prefent, fhews a good amount of vigour. I fhall look out for the appearance of the book, which is, I fuppofe, one of a feries.

" I agree with you in thinking that Gill's Prefatory Iambics fuggeft the notion of the author of Wallenftein being a. Pauline. I judge you have collateral evidence in fupport of this opinion.

" I am, Dear Sir,
" Yours truly,
" H. KYNASTON, D.D."

(17) Edward Phillips, the nephew of Milton, in his *Theatrum Poetarum,* printed in the year of Milton's death

Henry Glapthorne.

We learn from one of his poems that he had a fifter named Prifcilla, whofe lofs he feems deeply to have deplored, and there can be little doubt that the George Glapthorne mentioned in a document to be prefently introduced was a relative of his. It feems moft probable, from the fmall number of his writings, that he muft have been ftill very young (18) when we lofe fight of him in 1643. From fome internal evidence gathered from his Dedications and Panegyrics (one of the former addreffed to the Earl of Strafford) we fhould judge him to have had a ftrong royalift feeling; and it feems more than probable that on the outbreak of the Civil Wars he may, like his friend Lovelace, have efpoufed the King's caufe, and have perifhed fighting for it. For twenty years after the date of Glapthorne's five extant plays, fcarcely a fingle new contribution was

---

(1674), chronicles "Henry Glaphthorn" (*fic*) as "a dramatic writer not altogether ill deferving of the Englifh Stage." (*Theatrum Poetarum*. By Edward Phillips. Lond 1675. Pt. 2, p. 66.) This, I fuppofe, is the origin of Winftanley's " well deferving of the Englifh [ftage ?]"

(18) His comedy of *The Hollander* (though not printed till 1640) is ftated on the title-page to have been "written 1635." All Glapthorne's plays appeared either in 1639 or 1640, and his Poems from 1639 to 1643.

made to the English drama; so that even if Glapthorne continued to live, he probably ceased to write. But as we hear nothing of him at the Restoration, we are inevitably led to the conclusion that he died before that event took place.

But he does not seem, nevertheless, to have been entirely forgotten. Two at least of his plays, *Argalus and Parthenia* and *Wit in a Constable*, were revived after the Restoration. The former especially seems to have been very successful. "The house was exceeding full," says Pepys, recording a visit to the theatre under date 31st January, 1661, "to see *Argalus and Parthenia*, the first time that it hath been acted: and indeed it is good, though wronged by my over great expectations, as all things else are." And on the 23rd May in the following year (1662) he and his wife "flunk away to the Opera, where we saw *Wit in a Constable*, the first time that it is acted; but so silly a play I never saw I think in my life."

The following document, sufficiently interesting and curious in itself (which we reprint entire from a pamphlet in the King's Library) may afford some clue to the family to which Glapthorne probably belonged :—

A brief Relation of the Proceedings before his Highnefs Councel concerning the Petitioners of the Ifle of Ely, *againft* George Glapthorne *Efquire; to take away the falfe report that is made touching the fame, and that the truth may plainly appear.*

Hereas *George Glapthorne* of *Wittlefey* in the Ifle of *Ely* Efquire, and chiefe Bailiff of the Liberty thereof, and Juftice of Peace of the fame; Hath feemed to cloud himfelf under this Shadow, and faith: *That his Highneffe Counfell had not heard him;* And faid further, *Surely, they would not judge him before they heard him.* Therefore to unvaile him, and take off that flander which he would feem to lay upon them, that dealt fo Honourably and Honeftly with him and the County: You may underftand there was a Petition with about foure hundred hands to it, out of the Ifle of *Ely* (a joyfull thing to fee fo many witneffes againft iniquity). Their complaint was againft the faid Mafter *Glapthorne*, that he was a common Swearer, a common Curfer, a frequenter of

Ale-houses, and an upholder of those of evill fame, that he was famed to be a companion of lewd Women; therefore they thought him not fit to be a Law-maker or Parliament man for them: Upon this complaint his Highnesse Councel gave Summons for Witnesses to appear to prove this charge; which was substantially proved by severall Witnesses, and they have left their testimonies behind them upon Oath. There was examined before the Councel and in the presence of Mr. *Glapthorne* and divers other persons and Mr. *Glapthorne* excepted (though without cause) but against one Witnesse, who did modestly forbear: There were examined Capt. *William Lane, William Head*, Mr. *William Marshall, George Bate* of *Wittlesey*, and *Roger Branham* of *Wisbich*; and there was *William Manesty*, and *Thomas Coney* came too late at that time to be examined before the Councel; but the Affidavits are here with some other of the Witnesses, which will like the Gyants foot set forth the whole stature: The Councel gave him liberty to say what he could for himself; and gave him also upon his desire a further day; but when he was called, he did not appear; he was called again the next morning, and in the afternoon, and the next day after, but, never appeared: Now let any honest man judge whether this man

hath caufe to complain, that he was not heard;
but, he hath done like himfelf: When you have
read thefe Affidavits annexed, then judge whe-
ther this man be fit to be a Parliament man or a
Juftice of Peace, or a chief Bailiff: for why
fhould honeft men ly under the power of him
that's a flave to his own lufts, an enemy to
fobriety and honeft living; Being the Laws are
made and Juftices ordained to keep men within
the rules of fobriety and honefty: This is of
publique concernment; For *if wickedneffe get
into high places mifery will be to the Common-
wealth.* Therefore it is defired fome ufe may be
made hereof, as may be to the publique good.

George Bate *of* Wittlefey *in the* Ifle *of* Ely *in the County of* Cambridge *Yeoman.*

Saith,

THat he hath known *George Glapthorn* of *Wittlefey* in the faid Ifle Efquire, for above twenty years laft paft; for all which time, he hath known him to be a common Swearer and Curfer, and a common frequenter of Alehoufes, his ufuall Oaths and Curfes being, *By Gods wounds, by Gods blood, by Jefus Chrift, by the eternall God, God confound me body and foule, God damme me, the Devill fetch me, God refufe me:* In or about Auguft 1653, he the faid *George Bate* heard the faid Oathes and Curfes: And fince the faid time (that is to fay) the Sunday before the Election for Knights for the faid Ifle, he the faid *George Bate*, heard him fweare, *By God*, and *by Gods wounds*; and the Tuefday after the Election he heard him Swear and Curfe bitterly, (viz.) *By Gods wounds, by Gods blood, God refufe him*, and the like. And further, he hath heard the faid Mafter Glapthorne, famed to be familiar with Women of evill fame (viz.) *Dorothy Fox* and *Anne Martin*, and *Elizabeth Mee.*

And further faith, he hath heard the faid Mafter *Glapthorne* doth ufually play at Cards on the Lords Day.

George Bate, *his mark.*
Sworn the 27. of October 1654.
before me,
Bent.

The Depofition of Captain William Lane.

Captain *William Lane* of *Wittlefey*, faith, That he hath known *George Glapthorn* of *Wittlefey* aforefaid Efquire for about 30 years, to be a common fwearer, his ufuall oathes being, *By Gods wounds, by Gods blood, God refufe my foule,* and fuch like. And in *Auguft* 1653. he the faid *George Glapthorne* did fwear the faid oaths: And fince the Election, which was the 12 of July 1654, he hath heard him fwear *by God:* he hath often by diverfe people heard him famed for the ufe of women, namely *Anne Mafon* and others; and that Mafter *Robert Compton* told him this Examinate, that there was a wench kept for the faid Mr. *Glapthorn* at *Wisbech* by one he did beftow a Bailiffs place on.

W. Lane.

The Information of Roger Branham *of* Wisbech *in the Iſle of* Ely *and County of* Cambridge *this* 26. *day of* October, 1654.

Saith, He hath known *George Glapthorne* of *Wittleſey*, in the ſaid Iſle Eſquire, about the ſpace of 20 years, from the date hereof; and that he hath known him all that time to be a common ſwearer and curſer, his ordinary oaths being theſe, *viz. Gods blood* and *by the eternal God*, and ſuch like; his curſes being, *God refuſe me*, and *God condemn me*, and curſes of that nature. And the ſaid *Roger Branham* further ſaith, That all the aforementioned time, that he hath known *George Glapthorne*, he hath known him to be a frequenter of women of evil fame, as in particular, the wife of *John Maſon* of *Wisbich*. And the ſaid *Roger Branham* ſaith, he going to *Wittleſey* upon a time with a company of Horſe, going into the houſe of one *William Martin* of *Wittleſey*, heard one *John Norman* pleaſant with the wife of *William Martin* profering her five ſhillings for a good turn; but ſhe the ſaid *Anne Martin* called him Puppily-foole, and ſaid the old Justice *Glapthorne* had offered her eighteen shillings for an occupying, and promised to make it up twenty shillings when he had more money.

Roger Branham   *Sworn the* 27 *of* October
   his mark.   1654 *before me.*
                                             Bent.

The Deposition of William Head.

WIlliam Head of Wittlesey aforesaid, saith, That he hath heard *George Glapthorne* of *Wittlesey* aforesaid Esquire, Swear and Curse, *By Gods wounds, by Gods blood, by the eternall God,* and the like; and that he hath often observed him to be in Alehouses both before and since the time of the said Election, and that he hath heard him much spoken of for women.

William Marshall *of* Wittlesey *in the Isle of* Ely *in the County of* Cambridge, Gentleman.

Saith, That he hath known *George Glapthorne* Esquire, for about one year and a half last, all which time, he hath taken great notice of the said Master *Glapthorne* his usuall common Swearing and Cursing, (*viz.*) about a week before the time for the Election of Knights for the said Isle, which was on the twelfth of July 1654. *By God and by Gods blood*, and such like Oaths, and the Sunday at night after the said Election, he heard him curse and swear bitterly, (*viz.*) *God confound, the Devill fetch me, by Gods blood*, and such like Oaths very grievous to be heard. And he hath heard the said Master *Glapthorne* reported to be a common frequenter of women of evill fame, *viz. Elizabeth Searle* whom this deponent hath heard say that the said Master *Glapthorne* had her Maiden-head. And he further saith, he hath heard the said *Glapthorne* doth play at Cards on the Lords Dayes.

William Marshall.   *Sworn the* 27. *of* October 1654.

Bent.

William Manefty *of* Wittlefey *in the Ifle of*
Ely *Gentleman upon Oath*, faith as fol.
loweth,

That he hath known *George Glapthorne* of the fame Town and Ifle Efquire, for the fpace of twenty years laft paft; And that he hath known him to be a common fwearer, his ordinary Oathes being, *God damme me, Gods blood, by Jefus Chrift, God renounce me, by the eternall God,* with many other Oaths frequently flowing from him: This hath been his ordinary expreffions in my hearing, at feverall times in London, and in feverall Alehoufes in *Wittlefey;* as at *Dorothy Harrods, Henry Atkins, William Quickloue,* and other houfes in the fame town, and fometimes hath fworn forty of the former and the like Oaths in one hour, when he hath been gaming and at play; and likewife ftrange imprecations in his Curfings, ufing thefe words, *God confound me body and foule,* with many other fuch of the fame nature. And this I have known to be his conftant practice from the beginning of my acquaintance untill within thefe twelve moneths laft paft, fince which time I have not been much in his company; but when I have been in his Company, I have heard him fwear the former, or the like oathes. The faid Mafter *Manefty* further faith, that he hath known the faid Mafter *Glapthorne*, to be a frequenter of Women of evill fame, by their light carriage and lewd converfation, as the wife of *John Fox*, and the wife of *Symon Mee* and others in *Wittlefey*. And likewife the faid *William Manefty* going home about twelve of the clock in the night to his own houfe, being in his way, went to the houfe of one *William Martin*, being a common Alehoufe, but at that time unlicenfed, being about one year and a half fince the faid *William Manefty* did find the faid Mr. *Glapthorne* and privately heard him uncivilly familiar with the wife of the faid *William Martin*, tempting the chaftity of the wife of the faid *William Martin*, with large promifes of rewards, viz., *that he would buy her a Roll of Tobacco, Give her Husband to Brew and fell Ale, and that he* would make her Husband as rich a man as *Henry Atkins*, conditionally, that fhe would be conftant and true unto him, in her affections, and to love him with greater love then that which was due unto her Hufband; inticing of her alfo at that unfeafonable time of the night to go home with him for a Licenfe: fhe modeftly denying, fearing his incivility to her, as she told me the next morning, being taxed about it; but promised to send her Husband to him the next day. And Mr. *Manesty* further saith, that he hath heard *Elizabeth Zachary* say, that the aforesaid *George Glapthorne* had her Maiden-head.

William Manesty.

Sworn the 26 *of August* 1654.
Iohn Page.

Thomas Coney *of* Wittlesey *in the Isle of* Ely upon Oath faith, as followeth.

THat he hath known *George Glapthorne* of the same town and Isle Esquire, almost these two years, and that he hath heard him swear and curse bitterly, both at his own house and at the house of Lieutenant Colonel *Underwood* of the town aforesaid, his Oathes were, *Gods blood*, and *by Jesus Christ*, and such like execrations, his curses were, *The Devill fetch him, the Devill confound him*, & such like; & that he hath set up common Ale-houses in *Wittlesey* aforesaid which were formerly put down at the Seſſions; That is to ſay, *George Ground and Ed. Plummer*. And alſo further ſaith, he commonly heard him reported to be a man familiar with women of light and looſe converſations, keeping company with the wife of *John Fox*, and the wife of *Simon Mee*, and ſuch like in *Wittleſey* aforeſaid. And he further ſaith, that it is commonly reported that the ſaid *George Glapthorne* had the Maiden-head of *Elizabeth Zachary* of *Wittleſey* aforeſaid.

Thomas Coney.

Sworn the 26. *of Auguſt* 1654.
John Page.

Such, by the teſtimony of his contemporaries (to be received, doubtleſs, with conſiderable deductions) was George Glapthorne, whom we may fairly conjecture to have been the brother of our dramatiſt. Of oaths, of drinking, and of wenching, there is certainly a fair proportion in the plays of the latter: but what Henry Glapthorne only *wrote* from a dramatic point of view, as a repreſentation of manners, his leſs cultivated relative ſeems to have put in practice. We have abundant internal evidence that. Henry Glapthorne was a man of the moſt exquiſite refinement, and his devotion to Lucinda, who could hardly have been an imaginary perſon, ſhows that however fervent and paſſionate his love may have been, he "loved one maiden only and clave to her." After all, one cannot help having a ſort of kindneſs for the rough, burly, country brother, whoſe faults ſeem to have lain very much on the ſurface. One pictures the two together; the poet, with his keen knowledge of life and his intense enjoyment of nature, ſtrangely intermingling, looking on with a ſhrewd amuſement at the boiſterous ways of his elder brother, who alſo, perhaps, had an affectionate half-comprehenſion of the gifts and graces of the genius of the family.

In the preſent edition of Glapthorne's dramatic and poetical remains, while adhering in the main to our former facſimile principle, we have thought it beſt to introduce certain modifications ſuggeſted by the experience gained in former reprints. The original quartos of Glapthorne are printed with inaccuracy even greater than that which is common to all the plays of the period in which he wrote. That he corrected the prefs, even in the moſt perfunctory way, ſeems incredible. The verſes are run into each other in the moſt chaotic, and confused manner imaginable; verse is sometimes printed as prose, and prose as verse. Here and there one finds the absurdest mangling of words, with the substitution of words similar in form, but entirely different in meaning, and obviously suggesting their own rectification on the most casual perusal. All such errors (as far as our ability enabled us) we have silently corrected. But the antique and characteristic spelling and general integrity of the text have been retained as carefully as in our former volumes, and no merely conjectural emendations have been introduced. We have only to add that no portrait of Glapthorne, of any kind whatever, is known to be extant.

ARGALUS & PARTHENIA.
[1639.]

ARGALUS
AND
PARTHENIA.

As it hath been Acted at the Court before their MAIESTIES:

AND

At the Private-House in DRURY-LANE,

By thier MAIESTIES Servants.

The Authour HEN. GLAPTHORNE.

LONDON,
Printed by R. BISHOP for DANIEL PAKEMAN, at the Raine-bow neere the Inner Temple Gate.
1639.

The Persons.

Argalus, *beloved of* Parthenia.
Demagoras, *a Suiter to* Parthenia.
Kalander, *her uncle.*
Amphialus, *a Noble Lord.*
Philarchus, *an Arcadian Lord.*
Chrysaclea, *Mother to* Parthenia.
Parthenia.
Clitophon, *an inconstant Shepherd.*
Strephon, *a foolish swaine.*
Alexis, *another swaine.*
A servant to Demagoras.
Sapho, *a Poeticall Shepherdesse.*
Aminta.
Florida. } *Nymphes.*
Castalia.

ARGALUS

AND

PARTHENIA.

Actus 1. *Scena* 1.

DEMAGORAS, PHILARCHUS.

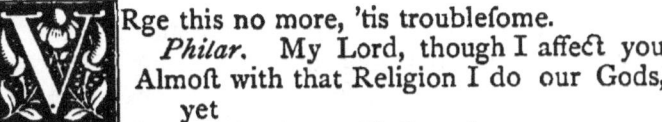Rge this no more, 'tis troublesome.
    Philar. My Lord, though I affect you
Almoſt with that Religion I do our Gods,
    yet
The conſtant motion of my will does fixe
On noble *Argalus*, and I confeſſe
His gracious merit challenges a wife,

Faire as *Parthenia*, did she staine the East,
When the bright morne hangs day upon her cheeks
In chaines of liquid pearle.
    Demagoras. I must confesse,
I have not studied the nice rules of love,
Nor can with flattering eloquence adore
A Ladies ayery shadow, court her smiles
With adoration, or with supple knees
Cringe like an humorous dancer, when the ayre
Plays with her hayre, or fret to see the Sun
Be over sawcy with her cheeks or lips:
I speake this to my glory; the big War
Has been my mistris, where in tented fields,
When I have seen a moving grove of Pikes
Advanc'd as if the splendor of their heads
Meant to obscure the Sun-beams, gore the clouds
Till they wept bloud, and heard the fiery horse
Neighing destruction to an host of men,
From their hot nostrils: there I did command
With ample Fortune; and to be repuls'd
In an effeminate Skirmish, wounds my soule
Worse than a quiver of sharp Parthian shafts
Could prejudice my body.
    Philar. I could wish
Both for your present peace, and to secure
Your future quiet, you had still confin'd
Your disposition to that war-fare; this
Is far more dangerous: He that means to win
Loves bloodlesse battails, must be strong in teares,
Marshall his Army in a Field of Sighes,
Have for his Ensigne beauty in his looks,
Under which colours ought to march kind smiles
As ablest Souldiers in the van. Smooth vowes,
And amorous oathes will batter Ladies hearts,
Sooner than slings or iron rams demolish
Resisting Citadels.
    Demag. Canst thou conceit,
That I *Demagoras*, to whose very name
Laconian Matrons have with early haste,

Argalus and Parthenia.

Payd tributary vowes, her choyſeſt mayds
Have left *Pans* Orgies to preſent ſoft Hymns
To th' honour of my merit, can decline
So much my great ſoule, as with forc'd intreats,
To beg *Parthenias* mercy; let tame fooles
Such as have hearts ſcarce fit to furniſh Doves,
Or ſpleenleſſe Lambs with courage, intercede
For female favours by ſubmiſſive prayers;
My reſolution grounded on the worth
Of my deſert, ſhall with her mothers power
Inforce *Parthenia*, were ſhe cold as ayre
In its moſt ſubtle motion, to become
In her affection fervent as the day,
That ſhe was borne in, was to gawdy light,
Or ruine her beſt comforts.

Enter Chriſaclea.

Chriſa. I am faine to be
Your moſt induſtrious advocate: my Daughter
Thinks ſhe offends in each familiar looke
Beſtowd on manhood, but I hope that Time
And Counſell may convert her to become
Loves proſelyte.
   Demag. Shee's that already Madam,
Or *Argalus* durſt not without conſent,
And patronage from her, rivall my love;
But if the boy oppoſe me in a thought,
Borrow a ſmile, or pay an amorous glance
As tribute to her eyes, were he defenc'd,
With ſome light bogge, that dances to the winds
Loud whiſtling Muſick, I would dart a frowne
Should raviſh his mortality into Ayre,
For the preſumption.
   Chriſa. 'Tis my Lord,
This rough demeanor (though it ſpeake you man)
Declares a ſpirit full of fire, which does fright
Parthenia's ſoftneſſe: Virgins loves are wone

(Like Heavens compaſſion) by ſubmiſſive prayers.
'Tis not the brave relation of a fight,
'Can move the milde breſt of a tender mayd
To ought but terrour ; ſhe will ſtart at ſight
Of ſcars though bought with honor, bleed in teares,
When wounds are mention'd ; for Lord *Argalus*
His affable and courtly carriage cals
Reſpective bluſhes into the baſhfull cheeks
Of every Virgin, that my daughters bound
By a due Juſtice, to eſteeme his worth,
With more than common curteſie, yet my will
Seconded by a Mothers kind intreats,
Shall work upon her duty to accept
You as her ſervant.

 Demag. Servant, Lady;
What mortall foole ambitious to out-vie
The Gods in honour, dare preſume to hope
That glorious title from me ? have I ſtood
(When armies timorous of a generall death,
Quaking with Panick horror, have invok'd
Divine aſſiſtance) fearleſſe, and not deem'd
Heavens power deſerving a religious prayer,
After ſo many Trophees as may clayme
Each its particular ſtar, to be eſteem'd
A ſervant to a woman.

 Philar. Nay, my good Lord.

 Demag. Perſuade the girle
T'attire like *Juno* in a dreſſe of clouds
Her beauteous head ; put off her human Earth
For Immortality, and atchieve a feat
Due to the Queen of Heaven, that with regard
The humble Senate of the petty Gods,
And Goddeſſes may tremblingly adore
The ſparkling Majeſty, yet were my will
Not ſatisfied by voluntary gift
Of her affection, my great ſoule would ſcorne it,
Worſe than the proffered ſervice of a Slave.

Enter Parthenia.

  Chry. See my Daughter,
My Lord, loofe not this opportunity,
You fhall have place, and leafure, for my pre-
   fence
Shall be no detriment to your purpofe.
                                                        Exit.
  Demag. Now Lady,
Are you in hafte, or do you flight a prefence
May challenge your obfervance ? I am come,
Confident of my merit, to informe you
You ought to yeeld me the moft ftrict regard
Your love can offer.
  Parth. Sir, I am not
(Though I affect not felfe conceited boaft)
So ignorant of my worth, but I deferve
From him who will enjoy me, a refpect
More faire and Court like.
  Demag. The blunt phrafe of war
Is my accuftom'd language, yet I can
Tell you yo'ar handfome, and direct your looks
With a becomming pofture; I muft fpeake
In the Heroick Dialect, as I ufe
To court *Bellona*, when my high defires
Ayme at a glorious victory.
  Phi. You'l fcarce
Conquer a Lady with this fterne difcourfe,
Mars did not wooe the Queen of Love in Armes,
But wrapt his batter'd limbs in Perfian filks,
Or coftly Tyrian Purples, fpeak in fmiles,
To win her tempting beauty.
  Demag. I'le bring on
Well-manag'd troops of Souldiers to the fight,
Draw big battaliaes, like a moving field
Of ftanding Corne, blown one way by the wind
Againft the frighted enemy; the Van
Shall fave the Rere a labour, and by me

Marſhald, ſhall fold bright conqueſt in the curles
Of their conducting Enſignes, while grim Death
Shall on the feather'd arrows with more haſte,
Then on his own ſhafts, fly upon the foe;
While the ſhrill Trumpet, and each piercing Fife
Shall ſing their Dirges, and the hoarſe mouth'd Drums,
Wars fatall bels, with ſurly noyſe proclayme
Their ſoddaine funerall: This brave reſolve
Vanquiſh'd my ſteele wing'd. Goddeſſe, and in-
   gag'd
Peneian *Daphne*, who did fly the Sun,
Give up to willing raviſhment, her boughes
T' inveſt my awfull front, and this ſhall proſtrat
Spight of all oppoſition, your nice ſoule
To my commanding merit.

   Par. Theſe high tearms,
Were apt to fright an enemy, or beget
Terror in flinty boſoms: Can you think
A timorous Virgin, can affect her feare,
Yeld the ſecurity of her peace and life,
To the protection of her horror. You muſt not per-
ſwade my thoughts that you who vary ſo the Scene of
love, can act it perfectly.

   Demag. Slighted in this: 'tis a contempt inhu-
mane, and deſerves my utmoſt ſcorne.

Enter Chriſaclea.

   Chri. Nay my moſt honor'd Lord, be not tranſ-
ported with a needleſſe rage, 'tis but her childiſh
folly. *Parthenia*
You have done ill to entertaine a man
Of ſuch an abſolute worth, with ſuch a meane

Exeunt Dema. and Philar

Regardleſſe value; you muſt alter this
Neglectfull temper, or my anger will

Surpaſſe my naturall love, and I ſhall chide
Your too affected nicenesse.
    Parth. Gracious Madam
The zealous duty which religious laws,
Teaches me owe my parents, would inflict
A heavy curſe for diſobedient guilt,
Upon my Innocence, ſhould I tranſgreſſe
Th' mention of your honourable will,
In what I can obey it.
    Chri. Then in this
You are reſolv'd t' uſurp the priviledge
Of your diſcretion : and not fulfill
My will in the diſpoſall of your love.
    Parth. Yes with that freedome that I would to
        Heaven
Tender my beſt obedience; but ſince love
Is by example and diſcourſe allow'd
Reaſons ſuperior, it muſt be eſteem'd
Above all duty.
    Chri. Yet there ought to be
Conſent attayn'd from thoſe whoſe power ſhu'd
        guide
Their childrens youth and actions.
    Parth. 'Tis confeſt
But not except it juſtly ſympathiſe
With their affection : you would have ſuffred
A conflict in your peace, had you been forc'd,
When your free will had yeelded up your heart,
My fathers choyſe, to' ve had it raviſh'd back,
And in deſpight of your reſolve confer'd
Upon another.
    Chri. I was not ſo childiſh
To contradict my parents, but ſubſcrib'd
To their diſcretions, as I would adviſe,
You would obey mine, and yeeld conſent
To wed *Demagoras.*
    Parth. What can your Wiſdome
Behold in him, (if with impartiall Eyes
You would ſurvay his quality) that ſhould ingage

Your inclination to inforce my love,
Befides the native fierceneffe of his looks
Apter to fright a Lady, than beget
Fancy: his courtfhips cloth'd in angry threats,
As if that Love were turn'd a Souldier,
And had unyok'd her teeme of fpleenleffe Doves,
To have her Chariot drawn by ravenous Wolves,
Tygres, or trecherous Leopards, had put off
Her wreath of harmleffe Mirtle to inveft
Her brow with Yew or Cipreffe.

   Chri. This excufe
Proceeds not from his merit, but your love
To *Argalus*, a ftranger only known
For his brifque Courtfhip, the Queen fupports
His wavering Fortune, he depends on her,
And fhould fhe faile by death, his utmoft hopes
Embrac'd a foddaine ruine.

   Parth. Argalus,
Where he more abject in his fate than your
Imagination could conceit, deferv'd
My Equalft fancy; in his youthfull looks
Sits a divinity able to inchant
Queenes to admire, nay to adore his worth,
Continued fmiles make Summer on his cheeks,
At his bright Eyes does Cupid warme his wings,
When he intends to fly at Womens hearts ;
Mufick and rich perfumes are in his breath,
Aptly refembling aromatique winds,
That fing the Phenix Exequies.

   Chrif. Can my daughter
So much decline the greatneffe of her fpirit,
Hereditary to her bloud,
To affect a perfon meerly for his fmiles,
Effeminate carriage without any proofe
Of manly valour in him,

   Parth. You miftake
His character, though he can tread in peace
An ayery meafure to the warbling Lute,
Demeane his actions with that fweet deceit

Can cofen Ladies of their foules, yet when
The glorious war does fummon him to th' field,
He does excell in feats of active armes
The ableft youth of Arcady; inftructs
Old Souldiers Martiall difcipline, that thofe
Who had beheld his fweetneffe in the Court,
Pufled in Faith, believed that conquering Mars
Had cloth'd his fierceneffe in a *Cupids* fhape,
To vanquifh fome more beautious prize than was
The blind Gods mother.
  Chri. 'Tis offenfive, Ile heare no more of this.
  Parth. Thus I'me inforc'd to prove,
Dead to obedience if I live to love.
  Chri. Your niceneffe
Muft not excufe the due refpects we beare
The Lord *Demagoras*; if the fhepherds' be prepar'd,
They fhall prefent their mirth to expell his melancholy.

        Exeunt Chrif. & Parth.

Scena 2.

Clitophon. Strephon.

Strep. Pish, you'r as fierce as an afpen leafe yo
wag every way.

Clitop. I'le tell thee honeft *Strephon*, I
No more affect a woman than the Sky
Does Birds that fore in it, they are as vaine
Inconftant as the flying fhowers of raine
In Aprill *Strephon*.

Strep. The more diffembling fellow you : why d
you proteft to every Wench you fee, you are inamor'
on her : why you fhould fee, and feeing ought to imi
tate your betters, *Clitophon*, ther's not a Laffe
That trips nimbly ore the Arcadian graffe,
When fhee does faire *Strephon* view,
Though I fly, but will purfue,
Throw her eyes out on my fhape,
Call me Pigfny, pretty Ape ;
Some there are that doe fuppofe
Loves hot fire in my nofe,
With which they fcorch'd, for pitty cry,
Blow it ou't *Strephon*, or we die ;
Others fay my head's a bell,
My hayre the ropes, that ring the knell,
My tong the clapper which though their deaths i
rings,
They fweare no Courefeu halfe fo fweetly fings ;
The hollow of my eyes, the grave,
Which with their nailes they dig : but have——
But who comes here ?

Enter Sapho, and Aminta.

Sapho. *Strephon*, you'r well met, good *Aminta*
fee,

Is he not chaſt, and faire as young Goates be,
His head like to a Cedar over-growes,
His ſtudded cheeks and rich enameld noſe.
 Strepho. I would be loath to give my face for the waſhing, Girle, now *Clitophon* doe not you imagine *Venus* girdle was my ſwathband, the maids ſo doate on my well timber'd limbs.
Here's a leg, *Sapho*, that's as neatly made,
As any that ore Shepherdeſſe is laid ;
A thigh proportionable I tak't,
I know thou longſt to feell it nak't,
A taile, ſome ſay, does hang thereby,
Which none muſt know but thee and I ;
I have a back too, though I ſay't
That ſhould not, can beare any waight,
Full limbs, with ſinews ſtrong and plump,
A luſty chine, and for my rump
'Tis ſo well made, and firmely knit,
The Nymphs are all ſtark mad for it,
Becauſe they think the reſt of my members proportionable.
 Clito. What a quick flame
Into my breſt from *Saphos* bright eyes came,
Another from *Aminta's* ; my deſire,
Erſt cold as Ice, grows active as the fire,
Deareſt *Aminta*, *Sapho* lend your eare
To my juſt vowes.
 Ami. Fond *Clitophon* forbeare
To ſweare in earneſt, I do know your heart
Was never wounded with the blind Gods dart.
 Saph. See how bright *Strephon* does intice the ayre,
To play with the ſweet belropes of his hayre.
What a ſoft murmuring the treſſes makes,
As did *Meduſa's* locks, or *Alectos* ſnakes.
 Clito. Gentleſt Virgin, white as infant ſnow,
Pleaſing as *Ladon* that does cooly flow,
Through our green meadows; truſt a loving ſwaine,
When he proteſts with truth.

Amin. There does remaine
No ſuch good property 'mongſt men on Earth,
Truth is fled to Heaven with Juſtice.

Enter Florida.

Florida the newes.
  Florid. The Lord *Demagoras* this way purſues,
And muſt have entertainment, 'tis a charge
From our great Lady, that we ſtrait inlarge
Our Paſtorall deviſes.
  Sapho. We have none
On ſuch a ſudden, leſſe ſhe will have done
Thoſe that were for *Argalus* welcome meant.
  Florid. Be preſt with ſpeed that greeting to p
    ſent——

Chriſaclea, Parthenia, Demagoras, Philarchus.

Clit. They are upon us ere we are ready for t
  action.
Chri. *Florida,* are the ſhepheards here?
Florid. Madame they are, *Caſtalia* only wants.
Chri. This Muſick ſpeaks her intrance.

Enter Caſtalia.

Pleaſe your Lordſhip,
Under this ſhadie Poplar, ſit and ſee
Our rurall paſtimes.

1. Song.

Loves a Childe, and ought to be
Wonne with ſmiles, his Deity
Is cloth'd in Panthers skinnes, which hide
Thoſe parts which kill, if but eſpide.
Hates warres, but ſuch as mildly led

By Venus *are to pleasures bed,*
There does soft imbraces fight,
Kisses combat with delight,
Amorous lookes and sighes discover
What will win a Virgin-Lover.

   Demagor. 'Tis too effeminate this; I had rather heare
The cryes of dying men than these nice straines,
Or Souldiers with loud clamours rend the aire
With shouts of victory.
   Phi. Patience my Lord, the Shepherds are proceeding to dance.

1. Dance.

   Demag. I doe not like this Morall, it includes
Something that is distastefull; a mans possest
With eminent frensie that would a minute
View these idle Morris-Dances.
   Phi. That fellow
That woo'd with such obsequiousnesse and wonne
His yeelding Mistresse, sure did represent
Effeminate *Argalus.* The other, who
With confidence attempting, was repuls'd,
Figur'd my selfe. This same was an abuse,
Such as no hospitality, nor lawes
Of true nobility can suffer. Madam
You have done well and justly. I perceive
You are as various in your giddy faith,
As your coy daughter in her choice; reserve her
For gracious *Argalus*: but if this scorne
Meet not a sudden and severe revenge,
May all my former glories be obscur'd
Though to performe it I should scale the Starres,
And snatch them like quick wilde-fire from their Spheares,
Then dart them on the earth: catch the dull clouds

And squeefe them into a deluge, and afpire
To ftartle *Jove* with terrour of my ire.
Exit. Demag.

   Chri. This is the fuddeneft paffion I have feene,
Whence had it its originall? My Lord,
Let's follow and perfwade him.
Exeunt.

The end of the firft Act.

Actus 2. Scena 1.

Argalus, Kalander, Philarchus.

YOu are too strangely timorous, your full worth
   Speakes in as loud an accent of Desert,
As the most meriting Arcadian Lord,
Who boasts his Ancestry.
  Arga. My Lord,
The faire *Parthenia* instructs all hearts.
Nobility, with Musick of her voyce;
Miriads of joyes are in her looks; her eyes
Are Natures richest Diamonds set in foyles
Of polish'd Ebony, her breath expires
Odours more sweet than issu'd from the trees
Of Balme in Paradise.
  Philar. *Demagoras*
Drunk with opinion of himselfe, declines
As much her glorious merit, as your just
Expressions honors it.
  Arga. 'T were sacriledge
Not to confesse so manifest a truth,
'T was shee when first I did salute the War
With my unable person, who inspir'd
My soule with courage active as the wind,
Gave me a manly being, and infus'd
By the divine reflection of her love,
Thoughts fiery as that passion: I do live
Only her creature. Borrow my poore heat
From the extended vertue of her flame.
  Kalan. You are too modest,
T" ascribe a greater glory to my Neece,
Than the whole stock of women ever boasted;
You'l make her proud, my Lord; 'tis an excesse
Of naturall sweetnesse in you, you must temper

With a more moderate confidence.
 Arga. Alas my Lord,
Of more sincere devotion ; every thought
My fancy offers, is a sacrifice
To the bright deity of *Parthenia,*
Whose noble freenesse, though it may afford
Me entertainment, more repleat with grace,
Than she bestowes on every Suitor, yet
My timorous hopes dare not assume that life,
As to beleeve she loves me ; pray my Lord,
You are familiar with *Parthenias* thoughts
Resolve your friends this questionable doubt ;
Whom her affectionat purity has chosen
Her loves blest favorite.
 Phi. My Lord, you know him,
He's your most intimat friend.
 Arga. My friend,
Were he my utmost enemy, and belov'd
Of faire *Parthenia,* that should be a tie
Of adoration to me : pray declare
The man must be made fortunate with the title
Of Lord of such perfection.
 Phil. He is
A noble generous and well manne'd youth,
Beares beauties ensignes in his gracious looks,
Has that supreme Divinity in his eyes
As sparkles flames, able to fire all hearts,
And the superlative vertue of his Mind,
Transcends his outward figure ; he is wise
As most mature age, Valiant in resolve,
As fame's belov'd child, Reputation,
Conjoyns the masculine graces of his soule
With lovely carriage, and discret discourse,
Has not your knowledge reach'd him yet ?
 Arga. This character
So far excelling me, undoes my hopes.
 Phi. My Lord, were 't not to secure your peace,
I'de not disclose this secret, 'tis your selfe,

'Tis *Argalus Parthenia* has receiv'd
A welcome gueſt into her open heart,
Amaſe not your quick ſenſes, 'tis a truth.
   Kalan. Your mutuall modeſties
Defer your juſt deſires, I muſt become
The moderator 'twixt your baſhfull hopes;
You do affect as timorouſly as Swans,
(Cold as the brook they ſwim in) who do bill,
With tardy modeſty, and chirring plead
Their conſtant reſolutions.

Enter Chriſaclea.

   Chriſ. Noble *Argalus*,
My honor'd brother, pray heaven our entertainment,
Be worthy your acceptance, you muſt not expect
That happy welcome here, your houſe affords
To ſuch deſerving gueſts. My Lord *Philarchus*,
Saw you the Lord *Demagoras* lately.
   Phi. Madam,
Not ſince he flung laſt night hence in a rage
From the preſentment by the Shepherds.
   Kal. Demagoras
Is of ſo haughty a diſpoſition
(Though noble otherwiſe) that I can wiſh
No alliance with him: ſiſter, I doe feare,
You are too zealous to advance the match
'Twixt him and your *Parthenia*: her's a Lord
As great by birth, and greater by the favour
Done him by th' King, but greateſt by his owne
Superlative goodneſſe, does affect her with
So true a fancie, that you much would wrong
Humanity to diſpoſe her to another,
Where ſuch a meriting Suiter does pretend
A holy intereſt in her.
   Chri. Good brother doe not
Queſtion my honour ſo much, I am loath
To give the leaſt occaſion of diſtaſte

To my Lord *Demagoras*, and fince my daughter
Cannot affect him, I conceive he will
Ceafe his unneceffary fuit, and leave her
To her owne difpofure.
 Kala. I wifh it.
My Lords, and fifter, honour me to transferre
Your companies to my Caftle ; it doth ftand
Opprefs'd with folitude, and mournes the lacke
Of noble hofpitality, like a widow
Depriv'd of a lov'd husband. I doe long
To fee Dame *Ceres* crown'd with wreathes of wheat,
Kiffe plumpe cheek'd *Bacchus* there in daily feafts,
To view my table furnifh'd with fuch guefts
As would efteem 't no trouble to adorne it
A yeare or two together, and there finde
No entertainment like a bounteous minde.
Exeunt.

Scena secunda.

Enter Parthenia with a Lute, & Exit.

Enter Demagoras.

This way she went, I followed her thorow the grove of Cypresse to this Bower, she cannot be farre off. *Exit.*

     Song.   *Parthenia within.*

Parth. O *Argalus!*

Enter Demagoras.

It was her voyce, *Parthenia's* voyce, she nam'd
Her minion *Argalus*: that sound (though cloth'd
In the inchanting accents of her breath)
Was harsh as Screech-owles, or the Whiflers notes,
And shall be fatall to her as the straines
The Syrens (dancing on the peacefull Seas)
Bestow on wretched Mariners. Come forth,

        Drags out Parth.

Imploy your airie numbers on your owne
Proud beauties Epitaph.
 Parth. What meanes my Lord,
This rude intrusion on my retir'd thoughts?
How dare you hand me thus? Uncivill man
Forbeare this boldnesse.

Demag. Perſwade me to't.
When you can ſing the world into a ſleepe,
Or tame wilde lightning with a teare; you'd beſt
Try if the paſſing ſweetneſſe of your tunes
Can (like the voyce of Magick) charme my rage
To pity, or bring *Argalus* to your reſcue;
Would he were here, and arm'd with ſulphurous clouds,
Like *Jove* imbracing *Semele* in fire,
This hand ſhould ſnatch thee from his circular flames
To my revenge, inforce him to behold,
Helpleſſe, the preſent ruines of thy beauty.
   Parthe. Your threats cannot affright me; I defenc'd
With mine owne innocence, feare not your malice,
Should it invade my life; your foule intent
Will (like an arrow ſhot upright) deſcend
On your owne head. But pray declare my Lord
Why you thus riot on my guiltleſſe ſelfe.
If 'cauſe I cannot love you, I will die
That cauſes Martyr.
   Demag. Die! your Fates reſerve you
Not to ſo brave a period as death
From my great hand: I'le ſtick on thee a ſhame
Worſe than the poore deprivall of thy life,
Such as will kill thee daily with conceit
Of thy unequall'd miſery.
   Parth. Perhaps
He does intend my raviſhment. My Lord,
Miſchiefe I ſee in your diſtracted looks
Pretended to my purity: Oh doe not
Murder mine honour; I'le reſigne my breath
With freedome to your fury. Surely Sir
A virgins gore (ſooner than blood of kids)
Will mollifie your heart of Adamant
To a ſoft fleſhie ſubſtance.
   Demag. Doe not prate,
Nor with loud clamours fill the wood, nor queſtion

What my intent is. Though you had not lov'd
   me,
You need not in contempt have throwne your
   heart
On that effeminate *Argalus*; that wrong
Fills my vaſt ſoule with horrour, and invites
My active thoughts to a ſevere revenge,
Since he whom I can name, but in contempt,
Uſurps my lawfull priviledge ; otherwiſe
The injury with patience had been borne,
Revenges cauſe is an immediate ſcorne.   *Exeunt.*

Enter Strephon, Clitophon, Sapho, Aminta.

   Clito.   Gentle *Aminta* heare me.
   Amint.   Have you done ?
Winding Meander firſt ſhall ſtraitly runne,
Roſes in winter flouriſh, and our flocks
Weare golden fleeces in ſtead of woolly locks,
Ere *Clitophon's* falſe heart doe ſerious prove,
And entertaine the perfectneſſe of love.
   Streph.   'Tis her love to me makes her ſlight
Clitophon thus. This 'tis to be a handſome man :
I ſhall doat ſhortly (ſeeing my lovely Phyſnomie in
ſome cleare ſpring, the Shepherds looking-glaſſe) on
my owne ſhadow, and like *Narciſſus* leap into the
waves to embrace it.
Which is ſhe among the Swains
On whom the gentle *Strephon* dains
To caſt a ſheeps-eye, nod or wink,
But does her ſelfe immortall think ?
Who indeed has ſuch a face,
So full of a bewitching grace.
My head loves pillow, where he does reſt
As ſafe as Magpie in her neſt.
My forehead ſweetly is beſpred
With Violets, and Tulips blew and red :
The amber Couſlip, and the corall Roſe,

Pretious complexion of my sweeter nose.
My eyes are elements from which fall showers
That make my cheeks a spring of severall flowers.
So is my head a nose-gay growing on (
  stalke,
My body is the garden, though it walk;
And ther's no woman but may well,
To th' worst part about it smell.
My armes are Dragons that defend all these:
Now view in me living *Hesperides*.

   Sapho. Who looks on *Strephon* that will
  suppose
The blushing Piony growing in his nose?
The yellow Primrose that in woods had wont
To flourish, springs up in his amber front.

   Streph. I had a face of brasse indeed should I d(
this for truth: shee'l praise me shortly into the star(
and then I shall (for a new Planet) be set
Shepherds Kalender. What a gull's this *Clitoph*
how long might he live ere he be in such favour w
the Shepherdesses.
Why when on him they will not gaze,
On me they stare with much amaze;
And when on him, as on a Clowne,
With lowring lookes they scowle and frowne,
Let gentle *Strephon* but vouchsafe
To let them looke on him, they laugh.

   Clitoph. Oh you are pleasant *Strephon.* Sa,
  say,
Are you as cruell as *Aminta*? Day
Loves not the Sunne-shine dearlier than my flame
Is equally devoted to your name:
To yours *Aminta* joyntly, Oh you two,
Are clearer, sweeter than the morning dew
Falling in May on Lillies, fairer farre
Than *Venus* Swannes, or spotlesse Ermins are.
Which first vouchsafes me answer? There d
  flie
Immediate comfort from *Aminta's* eye:

Sapho ſpeakes joy in ſmiles: but Virgins, here
Comes beauties abſtract, who has no peere.

Enter Florida.

Grace me, deare *Florida*, with one bleſt looke.
   Florid. Away diſſembler; Fiſhes ſcorne the
    hooke
They ſee laid bare before them: but prepare,
The other Shepherds hither comming are,
Attending on my Lady and her gueſts.
This muſicke does invite us to *Pans* feaſt.

Enter Kalander, Argalus, Philarchus, Ca-
ſtalia ſinging.

Great Pan *to thee we doe confine*
This fleece of Wooll. This bowle of Wine
To father Bacchus. *Ceres deare*
This garland of the wheaten eare
Accept. Silvanus *we preſent*
Theſe fruits to thee, thy bounty ſent.
And you maids, from whoſe each eye
Winged ſhafts of love doe flie,
Doe not ſhame to let your feet
In a countrey meaſure meet
With theſe yauths, whoſe active parts
Will play the theeves, and ſteale your hearts.
                          Dance.

   Kaland. Shepherds, we owe our gratitude to your
thankes.
   Sapho. Lords, and Ladies, thankes to all
That grac'd our harmleſſe feſtivall.

                           Exeunt Shepherds.

   Kalan. I doe admire we wanted my faire Neece

At thefe folemnities : me thought the fports
Shew'd dull without her ; noble *Argalus*
My beft wifhes wait upon you.

Exit. Kala

  Arga. Your honours Creature : I much won
    where
Parthenia has beftow'd her felfe.
  Phi. Shee cannot .
Be abfent long, fee here fhe comes ;

Enter Parthenia.

Madam, you were expected here, the Shepherds
Did in their Paftorall prefentments move
Dully without your prefence. Why thus vail'd,
Extend your glorious beauty, and ecclipfe
The emulous day with brightneffe : Heavens prot
    me,
What ftrange delufion's this?
  Arg. Surely a mift
Shades our amazed opticks, or has fome
Black Devill taken her habituall forme
To mocke our erring fancies ; 'tis her face
Vail'd in a robe of darkneffe, yet her eyes
Shoot their accuftomed brightneffe through
    clouds,
To tell the admiring gazers, two fuch lights
Cannot indure privation : Horror friend !
What fhould portend this ominous fight? Deare Mad
Have you devis'd this embleme of difguife,
That when difperc'd 't may give more per
    luftre
To your moft exquifite figure.
  Parth. Oh my Lord,
Looke not on fuch a monfter, left my fight
Infect your fpotleffe purity. I am

(Stop your innocent eares, left the harfh found
Pierce them with horror) poyfon'd.
   Philar. What ignoble villaine,
Madam, has fpoil'd natures moft glorious frame,
Demolifh'd fuch a beauty as the moft
Cunning Painters with their skill fhall never imitate?
   Arga. Let her name
Guefle at his appellation that has ventur'd
This irreligious blemifh to white truth;
And were his heart wrapt in a marble rock,
Fenc'd with a Mine of Adamant, this hand
Should from the ftony casket dig it out,
And with his vile blood poyfon all the world.
   Parthe. Deare Sir, the employment of this fruitlefle rage
Cannot attach him for this mifchiefe. 'Twas
Demagoras, who mad with the conceit
That for your fake I did neglect his love,
Surpris'd my guiltlefle perfon in the wood,
And with a juyce (more poyfonous than the foame
Of angry Dragons) fprinkled my cleare face,
By th' powerfull venome ftraight ore befpred with this
Contagious leprofie, and then he fled.
   Arga. Whither? What place can be fo ftrong to guard
So mercilefle a Tyger? Should he mix
His converfation with unfetled aires,
Breake (like a cunning Pioner) through the earth,
And hide himfelfe i' th Center, fome quick wind,
Or hideous earthquake, would inforce him thence
To his deferved punifhment. Oh friend!
Me thinks this object fhould affright the light
Into a fad concealment, force the clouds
To drop upon the earth in floods of teares,
And drowne it everlaftingly.

Philar. Poore Lady.
Parth. Doe not Lords
Urge violent rage to difcompofe your peace, I w
    (like
The pleafing aire) wrap in that cloud, my head,
That has infected it, and feeke out death:
Nor doe I grieve for my vaine beauties loffe,
Since fhivering ficknefle, or the hand of age
Would have perform'd that office which l
    poyfon
Ufurp'd upon its luftre: this onely wounds
My fraile refolve, fince I beleeve that you,
Lord *Argalus*, affected me, that I
Should be fo wretched, as to be depriv'd
Of that indifferent forme, for which I might
Have merited your favour.
    Arga. Gracious foule!
Inforce my immortality from my breft,
Which like a flame (inclos'd 'twixt walls of braffe
Strives to afcend to heaven, and fetch from thence
Thy ravifh'd beauty: 'twas thy excellent minde
That I admir'd; no noble foule can fix
Onely on flefhly glory; and fince that
Remaines intire, immoveable as faith,
I fhould undoe my honour, in revolt
From facred truth, fhould I renounce thy love:
I'le yet imbrace thy Nuptialls with a heat
Holy as altars incenfe; for thy face!
A thoufand virgins with immaculate teares
Shall weep upon it, bathe it in their bloods,
Till (from the different colours) the frefh Rofe
And glorious Lillie, in that fnowy field,
Regaine their ancient feats, and re-create thee
The abfolute Queene of beauty.
    Par. Oh my Lord,
Your fancie wanders in diftracted paths
Of vanquifh'd reafon; fince infortunate I,
Muft like a piece of Alablafter fpoyl'd

By an unskilfull Carver, needs become
A moſt imperfect ſtatue.   Since I cannot
Boaſt any thing that's meriting your love,
Strive to forget *Parthenia*, who will ſeeke
Some deſert, where poore mortall never trod,
To ſpend the wretched remnant of her life in.
Farewell my Lord, hereafter wiſh to meet,
As I doe, in one tombe, one winding ſheet.

The end of the ſecond Act.

Actus 3. Scena I.

Enter Demagoras and servant.

A Re all our forces muster'd.
    Serv. They are my Lord.
  Demag. Let them be
All in a readinesse. I meane this night
T' attempt *Kalanders* Castle ; my great soule
Is not yet satisfied by my revenge
Upon *Parthenia's* beauty : the contempt
(Cast on me by refusall of my match)
Cannot be wash'd off, but in streames of bloud.
  Sera. But my Lord, thinke on *Kalanders* stren
  Demag. I know my owne.
And 'twere a sin 'gainst my undaunted courage
To doubt its large sufficiencie has not power
To vanquish any enemy. Let hosts,
Conjoyne to hosts, affront me ; yet this arme
Has an innated vertue, that shall force
Victory from their multitudes, as due
Onely to my deservings. Let the Captaines
Prepare our forces, while in this grove I meditate
The sweetnesse of my just revenge.
  Arga. Pray Sir to whom belong yon forces.
  Serv. To Lord *Demagoras*, there is the Gener
                                            Exit Ser

  Arg. You'r happily encountred, Doe you k
me ?
  Demag. Though such things as you are,
Fit onely for effeminacie and sport,
Doe seldome meet my knowledge, you are,
If I mistake not, *Argalus* ; I sent you

A glorious prefent lately, your *Parthenia*
Drefs'd in new robes of beauty, fuch as might
Intice your wanton appetite to love.
    Arga. Villaine, to glory in thy moft detefted act,
Shewes that thy Fiend-like nature has forgot
All lawes of noble manhood; but I finne
To interchange a word with fuch a Monfter;
Yet before thou doft fall by me, as, if heaven have not
Loft all its care for innocence, thou muft doe,
I'le force thee heare the blackneffe of thy mifchiefes.
What devill cloth'd in human fhape, except
Thy barbarous felfe, would have atchiev'd the wrack
Of fo much matchleffe beauty.
    Demag. 'Twas too meane,
Too light a facrifice for my revenge,
Had her whole Sex beene there, attired in all
The glory of their beauty, and you Sir prefent,
My anger had invaded them, and fpight
Of your defence, converted their choice formes
To the fame loathfome leprofie.
    Arga. Peace Monfter.
Each fyllable thou uttereft does infect
The aire with killing peftilence; it was
Heavens never-fleeping Juftice that directed
My erring perfon hither to revenge
Parthenia's murder'd beauty on thy life.
Nay ftare not on me Sir, were you defenc'd
With heaps of men as numerous as your finnes,
This fword fhould force a paffage, and dig out
Thy heart from that black cabinet of thy breft,
And caft it a prey to Vultures.
    Demag. You'r very confident
Young gallant of your fortune, prithee goe
Poore boy and fight a combat in the court
With fome foft Miftreffe, dance, or touch a Lute:

Thou art a thing so abject thou 'rt not worthy
The anger of *Demagoras*; arme, be gone,
Lest I doe frowne thy soule away: My sword
Will be an uselesse instrument 'gainst such
A childish enemie.
   Arga. Glorious Devill,
My furies growne to that unequall height
'Twill not admit more conference; thy crimes
Are now ripe for my punishment: though Fiends
Guard your black brest, I'le peirce it.
   Demag. So valiant?
I shall chastise your fury.

Fight, Demag. falls.

   Arg. Parthenia,
Thou art in part reveng'd, and if mine owne
Death doe succeed his, I shall goe in peace
To my eternity.
   Demag. Sure great *Mars*
Has put on armes against me in this shape,
For 'tis impossible mortality could
Atcheiv *Demagoras* conquest. Farewell light,
'Tis fit the world should weare eternall night.

Dies.

   Arg. I hate to triumph
O're his loath'd carcase, which should be a prey
To Wolves and Harpyes: O *Parthenia!*
Here lies the Fatall Cause of all our mischiefes;
And sure no soule will at his death repine:
Revenge, when just, 's not humane, but Divine.

Ent. Serv.

  Serv. Where have you left my Lord?
  Arg. There lies your Lord.

Exit A

  Serv. Dead?

Curst Fate, that so much greatnesse
Should suffer this great overthrow, and fall
From such a height to a sad funerall !
Exit.

Amphialus and Philarchus.

Amphi. 'Tis such a cruelty, as no report,
Though it discourse of rapes, and timelesse deaths,
Has ever equall'd.
   Phi. The successe will speake
The wonder more prodigious. The poore Lady
(Still lovely in her sorrow) after this sad rape
Of her rare beauty, privately stole thence,
And with that strictnesse has obscur'd her selfe,
That though inquest (though many indeavour'd
In her desir'd search) can attain the least
Discovery of her present being.
   Amph. How beares *Argalus* this sad disaster ?
   Philar. As a man
Whose noble courage, 'bove the crosse of Fate,
Seemes patient at his misery.
   Amph. He and I
Are both made up of sorrow, our full griefes
Might (like two swelling Oceans when they meet
In a contracted channell) aptly combat
For rough priority. *Philoclea*
My glorious Cousin, will by no intreats,
No services, yet be induc'd to love ;
That I was forc'd, against the naturall zeale
I beare the King my Uncle, to transgresse
(Such is the power of my fancy) the strictnesse
Of my obedience, captivating her
By force, to whom by a most free consent
My soule before was prisoner.
   Phi. I could wish,
Noble *Amphialus*, that your desires
Might both atchieve forgivenesse, and successe:
I'm none of those strict Statesmen, though I love

My King, that hate your vertues for this fact,
Becaufe I know the greatneffe of your fpirit
Attempted it not for inveterate hate,
Or for ambition, but to gaine her love.

    Amphi. *Philocleas* love, upon whofe meane thought
The Art of Memorie's grounded, and infpires
Each organ of our meditating fenfe,
With their perfections merit.

    Phi. But my Lord:
How brooks the king the bold detention
Of his faire daughters? Sure he will invert
Some fudden forces on you, and compell
Their back-deliverie.

    Amp. He fhall firft inforce
Mortality into nothing. I did fend,
To avoid effufion of more humane bloud,
This faire defiance, that he fhould elect
A Champion daring fingly to oppofe
Me in a combat, and if Fate decreed
My fall by him, fecurity for the freedome
Of his imprifon'd daughters.

    Phi. Did his Grace
Accept the noble offer?

    Amp. With a freedome
Fitting a King, but who the perfon is
That hopes to gaine a Trophee by my death,
Fame has not yet divulg'd. This urgent bufineffe
Hinders my vifit of my Lord *Argalus*;
Prefent my true hearts fervice to him, tell him I
Doe inwardly diffolve into a dew
Of bleeding paffion for his loffe, and would
To re-inveft bleft quiet in his heart,
Act o're the Scene of dangers I have pafs'd
Since I knew earlieft manhood, fo your Lordfhip
Will pleafe to pardon my rude hafte, I muft,
As to my friends, to my owne affaires be juft.

                                            Exeunt.

Enter Clitophon, Strephon, Alexis.

Clito. Perſwade me not to this, there is no woman
Worthy my love, they are all too falſly common
To every Suiter.
    Alex. Why *Clitophon* ſay you ſo, who are bleſt
With her ſociety whom I love beſt ?
Yet in her preſence I'm forbid to move
My ſuit, nay dare not name the name of love.
    Stre. 'Tis your own flat foolery *Alexis*; you ſhould
with garbe and geſture paſtorall, with as much ſcorne
as you would o'returne your enemy at football, con-
temne the force of woman, Why ?
Women are ſhadows, fly away
When follow'd, or deſir'd to ſtay;
But if you ſlight them, they will ſue,
Follow, intreat, nay flie to you:
But if ſtiffe and ſtrong you ſtand,
You may tread them at command.
But lie downe, the pretty Elves
Will ſtraight fall under you of themſelves.
Like my Spaniell, beaten, they
Will lick your lips, and with you play.
This is the reaſon why
They love me ſo doggedly;
You might by my example edifie,
And live in peace *Alexis*.
    Alex. Why *Strephon*, you uſurpe without a cauſe
The priviledge of their love; your carriage drawes
Their laughter, not affection; you appeare
To them for ſport, not for your perſon deare.
    Streph. Ther's your foolery ſtill, thou haſt com-
merc'd it ſeemes with none but thine owne ſheepe,
and art farre ſillier than they: your woman is the
greateſt diſſembler in the world, and where they toy
and jeere, they moſt affect:
Finally women are ſlippery, as at their tayles are
    Eeles,

Their mindes as light as are their heeles.
And every one's for what fhe feeles:
And fo with my opinion, farewell.

   Clito. Stay honeft *Strephon*, I did late compofe verfes in hatred of them.

   Stre. They are not profe, pray read them.

   Clito. Who would truft a woman, when
They'r the onely curfe of men?
Syrens fing but to intice,
They men to a fools paradife:
Hyæna's fpeak, 'tis to betray
To certaine ruine, fo doe they;
Crocodiles fhed teares of flaughter,
Women weepe when they meane laughter.
Inconftant, cruell, falfe, unkinde.
Are attributes that fuit their minde.

   Stre. Now, as I am true Arcadian, thou would'ft be whipt for this; *Cupid* fhall cite thee into his Court for this by fome of his villanous Apparators, where his wide confcienc'd Proctors, and their Clerks, fhall with their pen and inkhornes beat thy braines out: if thou fcap'ft that, Ladies fhall beat thee to death with their Monkies, you jack-a-napes; chambermaids fhall worry thee to death with kiffes, than which there can be no greater tyranny; then, the very Cooke, and Milkmaids, fhall in fcolding profe, bafte thee into a jelly, or charme thee into May-butter; you fhall anfwer this, I'le peach, I'le play the Informer.

   Clito. I'le not recant it, nor deny this truth,
Alexis you fhall heare it juftified.   *Exeunt.*

   Enter Kalander, Argalus, and Philarchus.

   Kalan. Where met you Lord *Amphialus*?
   Phi. In the grove,
'Twixt Mantinea and his Caftle, while
Our fervants led our horfes down the hill,
We did exchange fome accents in difcourfe.

The noble youth, as hopefull of fucceſſe
In his defigne, as brave in his refolve ;
But the great rumour'd warfare 'twixt the King
And him's converted to a fingle fight
Betwixt *Amphialus* and what champion
The King will venter to ingage in fuch
A caufe of weighty confequence.
 Kalan. I'm glad :
Arcadia long bleft in a happy peace
Shall by the letting of fo few veines bloud
Continue in her quiet; it was fear'd
This fad domeftick quarrell would have coft
More lives than might with juftice have beene fpar'd ;
But 'tis not yet divulg'd by fame whofe valour
Will be imploy'd i'th combat.
 Phi. His knowledge
Has not yet attain'd the notice of 't : My Lord,
He does prefent his beft refpects to you,
Deplores your forrows with a brothers griefe, intreats
  you
Have fo much mercy on your glorious youth,
As not to fpend its blooming pride in fighes.
 Arg. My Lord, I thank him, and rejoyce his
  Fate
Has forted him fo honourable a triall
Of his undoubted valour : for my griefes,
They doe increafe on me, like a difeafe,
Spreading through all my faculties, which fhakes
My foule into an agony of death,
And will, I hope, ere long, diffolve this flefh
Into forgetfulneffe.
 Kalan. Nay good my Lord,
Renounce this paffionate temper, wee'l depart
Hence to my Caftle, expell our cares with feafts,
Hunt the wild bore that will with mafculine rage
Refift the hunters, till he foame to death,
View fwift hounds running hotly in purfuit
Of the chac'd game, and from the neighb'ring hills
Force Ecchoes to their fhrilneffe.

Arg. Alas my Lord:
The fole conceit of faire *Parthenia's* loffe
Would from a heart of marble force falt teares
Cold as the dew the ftone diftills, invite
An unremorfefull Crocodile to fhed
Drops as fincere as does the timorous Hart
When he o'reheares the feath'red arrow fing
His funerall Dirge.
 Kala. See *Alexis* accompanied with a ftranger
 Lady.

Enter Alexis and Parthenia.

 Alex. Sir, this Lady, newly arriv'd from *Corinth,*
 has
Some bufineffe fhe will difclofe to none but you.
              Exit.
 Parth. My vow's abfolv'd.
 Arga. Angels, or if there be a power has charge
Of humane frailty, fhrowd me with their wings;
The fight of this divinity will ftrike
More than my Eyes, my Reafon, and inforce me
Here to die gazing.
 Phi. Bleffe me! 'tis fure *Parthenia.*
 Kala. My vertuous Neece recover'd.
 Arg. 'Tis her face.
I have examin'd with induftrious eyes
Each line, each lovely circle that adornes
This beft perfect piece of nature, and all fpeakes
Parthenia's figure.
 Parth. My honour'd Lords.
 Arg. 'Tis her voyce!
The fame well-founding mufick did inchant
With its melodious harmony my heart.
Let me adore the miracle.
 Parth. My Lords:
Doe not diftract with a deceiv-ing joy
Your noble foules, I will not feeke to fold
Your thoughts in doubtfull errour; you miftake,

I'm not *Parthenia*.
 Arg. What delusion playes with our faculties?
 Parth. My Lord, afford me patient hearing, my discourse
Containes much consequence, you never lov'd
Parthenia dearlier than my selfe: we wore
The very figure of each others mind,
As well as body, and I should transgresse
Th' integrity of our inviolate truths;
Not to fullfill each scruple of her will
With ceremonious duty, she being dead.
 Arga. O my just feares!
 Phi. Deare Lady, is she dead?
 Par. Dead, cold in her dark urne,
As was her Icy chastity; she did arrive
Some few dayes since at Corinth, where resolv'd
T' obscure her self to all but mee, kind heaven
Pitying her sad disaster, by mild death,
Translated her to the immortall blisse
Prepar'd for innocent lovers.
 Arga. Sure I am
Insensible of misery, or my brest
Would burst with fulnesse of my griefes; deare Lady
Informe me where *Parthenia* is intomb'd,
That like some humble pilgrime, I may visit
The holy place with a religious zeale,
And bathe her virgin ashes in my teares,
Weepe o're her grave till from my drops arise
Some crystall pyramid to tell the world:
Parthenias monument.
 Par. You interrupt,
What my sad heart, as an unwelcome load,
Desires to be disburdend of: before
Her dying breath, she did injoyne me by
All our friendships rites, when I had laid
Her corps in earth: straict to repaire (with notice
Of her expiring) hither.

Phi. Deere my Lord,
Be not so much distemper'd.
    Parth. Tell, quoth she,
My noble mother that I dy in peace,
Even with *Demagoras*; commend me to my love,
My dearest *Argalus*; informe him that
His very name flies with my soule to heaven,
There to remaine for ever; and ingage him
T' accept of you as my last guift, you are
So like *Parthenia* that, hee'll love you for
My memory: So with a constant truth
To my dead friend I'm come, my Lord, to offer
What she bequeath'd, her legacy of my love,
To your acceptance.
    Arga. Madam, I must rest
For your kind wish your servant; but in me
Parthenia only must have room to live,
While I have vitall motion. Had she impos'd
What charge (but this) soever, I'de endevour
It's strict performance: but I am resolv'd
As she enjoy'd my first, my latest love
Shall on her memory waite till we do meet
I'th happy shades together.
    Part. Sure my Lord,
This is contempt of my desert, I must not
Be thus repuls'd: to satisfie your feares,
I am your true *Parthenia*.
    Argalus. *Parthenia*.
    Part. Yes, and by the Queen of Corinth cur'd
whose skill and care clens'd my fowle leprosie.
    Arga. *Parthenia*, 'twas well your wisdom by degrees
Diffus'd this comfort; had you showr'd it all a once,
T'would like a torrent have o'reborne the banks
Of my amaz'd mortality.
    Kal. Come, discourse
Your story at your leisure, *Argalus*

Take your *Parthenia*, treachery nor hate
Cannot undo the firme decree of Fate. *Exeunt.*

Enter Sapho. Aminta. Strephon. Clitophon.

Strep. Ile try your impudence, have you the face
To deny your libell *Clitophon* ?
 Clit. Good *Strephon* urge me not, I ſhall not want
Audacity to expreſſe them to recant.
My juſt opinion were injuſt, and fit
To ſtaine my reſolution, and my wit.
 Amin. *Clitophon*, how dare
You arm'd with boldneſſe greater than diſpaire
Venture abuſe to woman, or defile
That name with ſcandall, to whoſe meaneſt ſmile,
You have done worſhip ?
 Sapho. Prais'd with flatt'ring art,
Each look, each lineament, as the beſt part
Of Natur's choyfeſt workmanſhip: but men
Are more inconſtant than light whirlewinds; truſt
The ſea with feathers, or March winds with duſt
Rather; and let their words, oaths, teares, vowes paſſe,
As words in water writ, or ſlipery glaſſe.
 Clit. This is more jugling. O! with theſe h' as found
A paſſage through my Eyes, to give a wound
To my poore Heart: it is their looks beget
This ſoddaine alteration, which as yet
Does but with infant feathers ſtrive to fly
To heaven, tels Juſtice of the injury
I have done ſacred womanhood: hence
Thou ſcrowle detracting ſpotleſſe innocence.
Aminta deare forgive me, *Sapho* ſee
How my teares diſtill.

Stre. If they were every one as big as a Turnip,
fhould not ferve to feed my anger: well wenches,
you doe pardon him, may your maidenheads be
burden to you, till you bee forefcore at leaft, the
may you turne Witches, and fome Goblin get them
or elfe perifh in your Virginity, and leade Apes i
Hell for't: Nay if you do forgive him, I will have yo
arraign'd of treafon againft *Venus,* and *Cupid* fhall b
your blind Judge, and condemne you for the fact
to loofe your heads; your maidenheads I mean(
and have a man of fourefcore and ten for you
Executioner.

Sapho. Deare *Strephon,* do not frown, it doe
    difgrace
The fallow color of thy wither'd face.

Stre. You would faine cog your felfe into m
favour again; but till you bee converted fror
this *Clitophon,* you fhall not kiffe the worft pa
about me.

Saph. O fay not fo,
Thou art more fweet than Yewe or Mifcletoe.

Alex. O *Clitophon, Aminta,* every voyce
Be fill'd with admiration, fing, rejoyce,
Till th' earth dance like our young Lambs, ti
    trees
Grow active at the mufick; all degrees,
Of greefe are banifh'd: all our flocks fhall play
For joy: *Parthenia,* O *Parthenia.*

Clito. What of *Parthenia*?

Alex. Is return'd, her right
Beauty new fhining like the Queen of night,
Appearing frefher after fhe did fhroud
Her gawdy forehead in a pitchy cloud:
Loves triumphs in her eyes; audacious I,
That durft name love, and faire *Aminta* by:
Be dumb for ever.

Sapho. Stay *Alexis,*
She fhall now revoke that loving tyranny,

Since our *Parthenia's* return'd, I'le turne
My Elegiack ſtrains away, and burn
In high love raptures.
   Alex. She muſt ſtrait be wed
To Lord *Ar-galus*, the bridall bed
Is in preparing.
   Sapho. At a verſe of mine,
Hymen ſhall light his Nuptiall flaming pine,
I will enchant them to embraces free,
With a devoted Epithalamy;
Till I ſing day from *Tethis* armes, and fire
With ayry raptures the whole morning quire,
Till the ſmall birds their Silvan notes diſplay
And ſing with us, joy to *Parthenia*.
Dance & Exeunt.

The end of the third Act.

Actus 4. Scena I.

Argalus. Parthenia. Kalander.
Philarchus.

Kalan. Sit my moſt honour'd Coſen, you are Lord
Both of this houſe and feaſt; the honeſt Shep-
  heards
Were taken too much o' th ſoddaine to provide
A fitting entertainment; but they've ſtriv'd
With their moſt early haſte, t' expreſſe their duty:
Sapho inſpir'd with her Poetique fury,
Will ſpeake your Epithalamy;
They do intend to dance too, I ſee;
This Muſicke declares their purpoſe.

Muſick.

Enter Shepheards and Shepheardeſſes.

Sap. The joyes of health and what the ſpring
Of youth, ſtrength, happineſſe, can bring
Wait upon this noble paire;
Lady, may you ſtill be faire,
As earlieſt light, may you enjoy
Beauty, which age cannot deſtroy,
May you be fruitfull as the day,
Never ſigh but when you pray,
Know no griefe, but what may be
To temper your felicity.
And you my Lord, may trueſt fame
Still attend on your great name,

Live both of you espous'd to peace,
And with your yeares let love increase,
Goe late to Heaven, but comming thither,
Shine there two glorious stars together.

Song and Dance.

Kalen. Does these presentments please you? our dull wits
Are not so fortunate, in rich conceits
As your quick Cyprian intellects.

Exeunt Sheepherds.

Arga. You vouchsafe
Too much to grace them, but *Parthenia*
The King as conscious of my meane desert
To make me seeme more worthy of thy love,
Has by imposing a command, confer'd
An honor greater on my sprightly hopes,
Then the addition of estate or bloud
Before enrich'd me with possession of.

Part. Let me participate your happinesse,
My dearest Lord, what is it?

Argal. An honor which like the Eldest child of
Fame treads on the neck of glory.

Kalan. Come, my Lord, let's leave these happy lovers to themselves.

Part. What may it portend tell me, and Ile rejoyce
As much to heare it, as when I recover'd my poyson'd beauty.

Arga. Thou shalt know 't,
And with lowd acclamations sound my fate,
For most compleatly happy: by the King
I am elected instantly to meet
In single opposition, honors type
The brav'st of Soldiers and the best of men,
The noble Lord *Amphialus*.

Par. Bleſſe me divinity ! can you conceive my Lord
That act an honor, upon which the loſſe
Of the unvalued treaſure of your life
Has ſtrict dependence? ſure my Lord, the King
Cannot be ſuch a Tyrant to employ
You in your infant age of peacefull love,
To ſuch a cruell warfare.

Arga. Now I ſee,
Parthenia loves not *Argalus,* if ſhe wiſh him
Turne recreant to his valour ; what account
Unleſſe of Coward, ſhall I give the King?
Should I refuſe this honorable taſke ;
Which but to meet I'de ſcale ſtar-neighboring rocks,
Travell through defarts, ſcarcely known to beaſts,
And combat all that durſt oppoſe my paſſage,
To this brave enterpriſe.

Par. My deareſt Lord,
This reſolution does oppreſſe my ſoule,
With torments worſe than death ; there's not a word
Which you have utter'd, but like mandraks grones,
Or howles of wolves affrights me : Can there be
Such a contempt of my regardleſſe love
Be got ſo ſoon? Can you forſake my bed,
Before I ſcarce conceive my ſelfe a wife,
Or you a husband? Oh *Argalus,* I thought
We ſhould have liv'd, and taught the erring world
Affections primitive pureneſſe ; grown like Palmes
(That do with amorous mixture twine their boughes
Into a league-union) and ſo floriſh,
Old in each others armes ; when now if thou
Proceed to triall in this bloudy taske,
My feares do with prophetike motion tell me,
We are undone eternally.

Arga. Have you
So ſlight an eſtimation of my worth,
In managing bright armes, that you can feare

My perfons fuffrance, O *Parthenia*?
Thou wouldſt deprive me of that fame, which
  time,
Should he decline his reſtleſſe courſe away,
Shall never equall, from my youth-full head:
Thou wouldſt detaine a chaplet of ſuch bayes,
As not Peneian *Daphne* firſt transform'd
Could boaſt the like for freſhneſſe: dry my love,
Thoſe ſacred eyes drowned in chriſtall ſtreames,
Or if thou wilt, Ile kiſſe away thy teares,
In ſtead of heavenly Nectar.
  Part. This but ads
To my misfortune, Sir, I am your wife,
And never yet requeſted any grant:
Unleſſe your love deny me now my firſt
And only ſuit, leave my good Lord to tempt
Your deſtiny: *Amphialus* is ſo good
In his kind love to women; that I doubt not
To find ſome meanes without your honors breach,
To put this fatall combat off.
  Arga. No *Parthenia*,
'Tis but in vaine to tempt me with your prayers,
Could he ſpit thunder would afright the Gods,
Or wore at each lock of his haire a flaſh
Of piercing lightning, yet I ſhould attempt
To ſnatch the fiery chaplet from his head,
And as a garland of victorious bayes,
Wreathe it about theſe temples.
  Par. Well my Lord,
Since no perſwaſion will re-claime your will,
Goe, and be happy in your diſaſtrous task;
My maids and I will pray each houre to heaven
A thouſand vowes for your ſucceſſe; I give
You my free licence; O that deathfull word
Comes from the Organs of my troubled ſoule,
As a conſtant does from a timorous maid,
To an inforcing raviſher.
  Arga. Why now,
Thou art my beſt *Parthenia*, doubt not love,

But I will bring white victory to crown
Thy glorious front; give me but one kind look,
'T will fill me with heroick force: let's in,
And feareleſſe take a happy parting kiſſe,
Suſpicion hinders loves immediate bliſſe.

Exeunt.

Enter Clitophon, Strephon, Alexis, Sapho, Aminta, Florida.

 Clit. Sweet *Sapho*, will you ſtill perſiſt, and kill
Whom you might ſave?
 Sapho. 'Tis your owne various will
Inforces my contempt; but here's no place
T' afford our loves an anſwer: the kinde graſſe,
That decks the plaines, will ſmile when we do ſit
On its green tapistry, and aptly fit
Our wilde affections: Shepherdeſſes, let
Our woolly charge within our folds be ſet,
Leſt the hoarſe Wolfe to fate his ravenous thirſt
With blood of Lambes, doe through our weak flocks
  burſt;
After let's meet upon the neighbouring plaine,
And there determine of our loves: I'le ſtraine
A little on your patience to rehearſe,
On the late Nuptials, this enſuing verſe.
 Amint. Doe my deare *Sapho*.
 Flor. Shepherds, attend her Layes.
 Amint. They get us credit, and our *Sapho*
  Bayes.
 Sapho. The holy Prieſt had joyn'd their hands, and
  now
Night grew propitious to their Bridall vow,
Majeſtick *Juno*, and young *Hymen* flies
To light their Pines at faire *Parthenia's* eyes;
The little Graces amourouſly did skip,
With the ſmall *Cupids*, from each lip to lip;
Venus her ſelfe was preſent, and untide

Her virgine Love; when loe, on either fide
Stood as her handmaids, Chaftity and Truth,
With that immaculate guider of her youth
Rofe-colour'd Modefty: Thefe did undreffe
The beauteous maid, who now in readineffe,
The Nuptiall tapers waving 'bout her head,
Made poore her garments, and enrich'd her bed;
While the frefh Bridegroome, like the lufty Spring,
Did to the holy bride-bed with him bring
Attending mafculine vertues; down he lay'd
His fnowy limbs by a far whiter mayd,
Their kiffes linke their minds, as they embrace
A quire of Angels flew about the place,
Singing all bliffe unto this paire; for ever
May they in love and union ftill perfever.
   Amin. 'Tis almoft fung for the nuptialls,
Why was't not fung with mufick?
   Saph. *Caftalia's* voyce would have beene tir'd
     with it.
Come, let's depart,
Love though obfcur'd ftill flames about the heart.
Exeunt.

Enter Amphialus, Argalus, Philarchus.

   Amp. I could have wifh'd the King
Had deftin'd any to this fatall task
But noble *Argalus*; in him there refts
Such a commanding fulneffe of true worth,
That as't will be a glory to o'recome,
'Twill be a griefe equall to think 'gainft whom
The prefent fury of my arme muft be
Unwillingly directed.
   Arg. Famous *Amphialus*,
'Tis fo much honour to be held your friend,
'Twere indifcretion in me to admit
A thought of being your enemy: we two

Should meet, my Lord, to revell, not to fight:
But fince th' injuſtice of our Fates does force
This ſad contention; deare *Amphialus*,
Think that two brothers may with hot reſolve
Strive to atchieve one crowne, yet ſtill be friends.
The lawrell deſtin'd for my head will wither
If it be ſnatch'd from thine.

   Amph.   More famous *Argalus*,
Under whoſe hand the great *Demagoras* fell.
Theſe attributes of curteſie doe ſpeake
Your noble natures freeneſſe; you and I
Should rather exerciſe our able armes
In one anothers quarrell, than imploy them
Upon our ſelves.   Deare *Argalus*, our fates
Are too injuſt t' ingage our ſwords againſt
Our bodies; for in harming thee, I offer
Wounds to my ſelfe; we two retaine ſo much
Affinity, by friendſhip, we muſt needs be
One individual ſubſtance.

   Phi.   Good my Lords,
Since there's that ſympathie of love and nature
'Twixt your two ſoules, diſſolve it not; the blow
That ſhall divide your hearts will be more impious
In ſep'rating that union, than in cutting
Your twiſts of life aſunder.

   Arga.   *Philarchus*, you are ſo noble,
Our wills deſir'd you an indifferent Judge
In our unwilling difference, ſince you are
An equall friend to both.

   Amph.   *Philarchus*,
We two are fortunes ſcorne that we ſhould be
Such friends in ſoule, yet by our deeds be thought
Severeſt enemies.   Deare *Argalus*,
Let not thy lenity regard my life,
Which is ſo worthleſſe, 'tis a weight I wiſh
Rather to loſe than keepe: but guard thy owne,
Preſerve that precious bloud, which I ſhall grieve
To ſee diffus'd on earth, nay rather weepe
Than ſhed a drop of it.

Arg. How much, my Lord, you vanquish him with curtesie
Whom your arme means to conquer? But *Amphialus*,
Since we are mutuall friends, and yet must seeme
Mutually enemies, to testifie
'Tis by our fate, not malice, we are foes,
I'le make thee my full Executour; bestow
A gift upon thee of that pricelesse worth
Posterity shall never boast its parallell.
When I am ashes, if there be a wretch
(For some there are that dare blaspheme the Gods)
Does injure my *Parthenia*; prithee friend,
Let be thy Care to punish that contempt
'Gainst vertuous purity: and as the last
And most supreme inducement of my love,
If by thy hand I perish, let my heart
Be sent to my *Parthenia*.
   Amph. The same justice
I beg of thee, my *Argalus*, to have mine
Convay'd to my *Philoclea*; and if fame
(As it may chance) traduce me after death,
Noblest *Argalus*, justifie thy friend,
Thy poore *Amphialus*; and defend the deare
Authour of my misfortune, sweet *Philoclea*; otherwise
Posterity inform'd by bad report,
May black her precious memory; and say
A worthlesse man fell by thy sword.
Let us embrace, my *Argalus*, and take
A true, though sad, farewell; and once
Let us employ our hands against our hearts.
   Arg. Kill our selves mutually; for who first does fall,
Leads but the way to th' others funerall.
                                                              Fight.

Enter Parthenia.

Parth. Eternall darkneſſe feaze me: O my Lord,
You are reported to be thrall to love;
For her ſake you affect moſt, doe not make
A breach in ebbing nature; More! This bloud
Clothing the graſſe in purple, does convert
My heart to Alablaſter. O *Argalus*!
  Arg. O *Parthenia*! Never till now unwelcome have I liv'd
To ſuch an abject lowneſſe, that my life
Muſt (like a malefactors) be by prayers
Redeem'd from death. Let us renew the fight.
Ha! Me thinks I tread on ſlippery glaſſe, my unſupporting feet
Dance meaſures on light waves, and I am ſinking
Into the watery boſomes, there to reſt for all eternity.
  Amph. I have ſeene
So dying tapers, as it were, to light
Their owne ſad funerall; expiring, dart
(Being but ſtirr'd) their moſt illuſtrious beames,
And ſo extinguiſh.
  Parth. Angels, if ye have charity, afford
Some Surgery from heaven. Now I ſee the cauſe
Why my ſad heart (fill'd with propheticke feare)
Sought to have ſtopt your journey: and why I
Compell'd by power of overruling Fate
Follow'd you hither. Oh *Argalus*!
  Arga. *Parthenia*, I doe feele
A marble ſweat about my heart, which does
Congeale the remnant of my bloud to Ice;
My Lord, I doe forgive you, friend, farewell.
Parthenia, ſhowre on my pale lips a kiſſe,
'Twill waft my ſoule to its eternall bliſſe.
Parthenia, O *Parthenia*.   *Dies.*
  Phi. So cracks the cordage of his heart, as Cables

That guide the heavie Anchors, cut by blasts
Of some big tempest. My Lord, your wounds are
    many,
And dangerous, 'tis fit you doe withdraw
And have 'm cur'd.
　　Amph.　I am carelesse growne, my life
Is now more odious to me than the light
Of day to Furies ; Madam, I am past
The thought of griefe for this sad fact, and am
Griefes individuall substance : pray forgive me,
Heaven knowes it was not malice that betray'd
Your Lords lov'd life ; but a necessitous force
To save my owne. Joy comfort you : thus Fate
Forces us act what we most truly hate.

　　　　　　　　　　　　　　　　Exit.

　　Phi.　Deare Madam, calme your passion, and re-
    solve
To arme your soule with patience.
　　Parth.　Patience Sir ?
Doubt not so much my temper, I am calme.
You see o'th sudden as untroubled seas.
I could stand silent here an age to view
This goodly ruine. Noblest *Argalus*,
If thou hadst died degenerate from thy selfe,
I should have flow'd with pity, till my teares
Had drown'd thy blasted memory ; but since
Thou perish'd nobly, let thy soule expect
A joy, not sorrow from me : the greene oake
Lawrell, and lovely mirtle shall still flourish
About thy sepulchre, which shall be cut
Out of a Mine of Diamonds ; yet the brightnesse
Proceeding from thy ashes shall out-shine
The stones unvalew'd substance.
　　Phi.　Sure she is growne insensible of her griefe
Or fallen into some wilde distraction.
　　Parth.　You mistake ;
'Tis not a fury leads me to this strange

Demeanour; but conceit that I should sinne
Against my *Argalus*. Should I lament
His overthrow? No Blest soule,
Augment th' illustrious number of the starres,
Outshine the *Ledan* brothers: Ile not diminish
Thy glory by a teare, untill my brest
Does like the pious Pellican's, break forth
In purple fountains for thy losse, and then,
It shall diffuse for every drop thou shed'st
A Crimson river, then to thee Ile come:
To die for love 's a glorious martyrdome.

              Exit.

The end of the fourth Act.

Actus 5.   Scena 1.

Enter Strephon, Clitophon, Alexis.

Clito. 'Tis certaine my *Alexis*; have not I
    (Who in their presence for love dayly die)
A cause to blame my destiny, and be
Oppres'd with a continuall melancholy?
    Alex. You are your owne Oppressour.
    Clito. O wretched fate!
I in their presence doat on every one,
Yet in their absence am content with none.
    Stre. Yet I am in a farre worse case
Than any of you both alas.
This villaine *Cupid* play'd the knave,
Or at my birth his mother gave
Some of her beauty to my naturall parts,
Which doe allure even stony hearts,
That I am weary of so many
Good parts, and would lend some to any.
I *Clitophon*, even every limb
About thee can with beauty trim,
And never mifs'd: I dare be sworne
There's not an inch about me worne,
Which has not, all the Maids can tell,
Waiting on it of love an Ell.
    Alex. O far more happy *Strephon*.
    Stre. I doe mocke me *Alexis*, I will surrender
you that happinesse with all my heart:
Were there but only two or three,
Or foure or five did doate on mee,

I grant you then 'twere very well,
The handfome then fhould beare the bell;
But there's not in this face a wrinckle,
Nor on my pretious nofe a pimple,
Nor a haire upon my chin,
(But thofe you fee are very thin)
Nor any fquint comes from mine eye,
But that fome wench for it does fry
In loves hot furnace: Though ne're fo coy,
Each Laffe would my good parts enjoy.

   Clito. Why does not *Strephon* then,
Make ufe of time, and chufe the richeft Jemme
Out of this Mine of beauty, and enrich
Himfelfe by marriage?

   Streph. My fingers itch at thee to heare thee talk
fo foolifhly: Would'ft have me make an Anatomy of
my felfe?
Or doft fuppofe
That unto one I'le wed my nofe,
And to another all the reft
Of this fweet face? A pretty jeft.
Should I pretend my felfe to match,
The wenches then would play at catch
That catch may; each get a limbe,
Or rather with themfelves in rage,
They cruell civill warre would wage,
And with thofe terrible weapons, their nailes,
Which them in battell never failes;
And farre more terrible tongues, in fpight
They'd fighting fcold, and fcolding fight.

   Enter Sapho, Aminta, Florida.

   Clito. Still deareft *Sapho,* cruell Tygers may
By prayers and teares be mov'd, though cruell they
Delight in murder; you doe feeme to take
Your naturall fierceneffe from them, there cannot be

So much sterne rigour in humanity,
As to contemne a suppliant, and prove
To him most cruell, who does truliest love.
    Saph. You are too fickle *Clitophon*, you see
Leaves in green Autumne scatter'd from each tree
By the rude winds; you are more light than they,
More fading than the flowrey dresse which May
Attires the prickly thornes in; lighter far
Than frothy bubbles, or dispers'd smoakes are.
Yet I should love you, did not *Strephons* eye
Dart flames might fire a marble heart; they fly,
With nimble wings about me; *Strephon* see
She who refuses him, will yeeld to thee.
    Ser. Would you could perswade me to't my nimble
toung'd *Melpomene.* I must not bee injust to wrong
my friend *Clitophon*, my friend's my friend, sweet
Sapho: and you are a woman, of which gender
(thanks be to Heaven and my good parts) I have
indifferent choyse, a hundred or so. If you *Aminta*,
or you *Florida* love me, the best comfort or course
you can take
Is to run mad for my deare sake.
And hang your selves, for you'l so prove
True lovers hang'd in chains of love.
    Amin. A cruell resolution: *Sapho*, well,
We must resolve not to lead apes in Hell.
And we have vow'd never to match but where
Strephon vouchsafes to give us; for you two,
Unlesse he please, our wils can nothing do.
    Stre. Come hither *Clitophon*, you love this witty rogue, this *Sapho*.
    Clit. Deare as my own eyes.
    Stre. That's deare enough; and you *Alexis* love *Aminta*.
    Alex. I dare not name that word, yet ther's in me
A most severe and lasting constancy,
To faire *Aminta*.

Clit. O gentle *Strephon*, let kind pitty move
Thy honeſt heart, not to deprive our love
Of its true comfort.
    Stre. I ſhall be ſure now to be famous for ſome thing,
Your hands, your hands, my pretty payre of turtles.
    Amin. Will you forſake us *Strephon* ?
    Saph. Will you give me away ?
Whoſe heart deſires to live only by your affection.
    Stre. I cannot helpe it, leſſe I ſhould diſtribute my ſelfe amongſt you ; I'me very glad the matter is depos'd into my handling ; theſe wenches are in good hope now that I will have one of them my ſelfe, and that makes them refer themſelves to mee : here *Clitophon*, take *Sapho*, and you *Alexis* the beautifull *Aminta* : But bee ſure to confeſſe you have but my reverſions. You'l give mee leave to kiſſe your wives, or ſo, when you are married, Ile not goe an inch further, as I am a true Arcadian ; and ſo ſhake hands, and Heavens give you joy. Now *Clitophon* you're excellent at that ſport, ſhall's not have a friſque or ſo at your Wedding, ha ?
    Clito. We'r all your ſervants.

Dance.

    Saph. Now *Strephon* wee have ſuffered you to play the foole all this while,
Receive our true opinions of you.
    Stre. I, come, let's hear't.
    Sap. Thou haſt a face
So full of vileneſſe, it does diſgrace
Deformity it ſelfe ; ther's not a woman,
Were ſhe to filthy proſtitution common,
That could affect thee.
    Flori. Ceaſe to torment him *Sapho*, the pretty elfe
Begins to ſee the beauty of it ſelfe :

We muſt attend our Lady.
   Sap.   *Strephon* go,
And hang thy ſelfe, or elſe reſolve to ſhew
Thy ſelfe no more, but like an Owle by night,
Or keep thy ill-favourd countenance to affright
Wolves from our ſheep: Come lovers, now 'tis time
To celebrate our joyes, which then renew
When proofe has ſeal'd our fancies pure and true.

Exeunt.

   Stre. Now doe I perceive my ſelfe an errant aſſe, and could hang my ſelfe in earneſt, were I ſure but to dy in jeſt for't: theſe wenches are ſhee-furies, and I hope in time to ſee them grow ſo abominably ugly, that they may hate them: for to ſay truth,
Theſe women are mere Weather-cocks,
And change their minds more than their ſmocks;
Have hearts as hard as ſtony rocks,
And toungs that lie worſe than falſe clocks,
By which they catch men like Jacks in a box:
And ſo with my curſes I leave them.   *Exit.*

Enter Philarchus. Amphialus.

   Phil. 'Twould be the ſafeſt way my Lord, and which
Would beſt ſuit with your honour; be a means
To gaine faire *Philoclea*.
   Amphi. That bleſt name
Charmes me to adoration: O my Lord,
Philoclea's love is like a mine of wealth,
Guarded by watchfull Dragons; there attend
Legions of feares, and unrelenting thoughts,
On the unvalued treaſure.

Phi. I could wiſh
You would expreſſe a more indulgent care
Towards your ſelfe: you ſee the angry King
Griev'd for his daughters, and *Zelmanes* loſſe,
Attempts what ever may invade your life;
I ſhall endevour your reconcilement with him; but my Lord,
Farewell, I know you wait ſome oppoſite; I wiſh
Your actions crown'd with a deſerv'd ſucceſſe.

Exit Phi.

Amphialus. This honeſt Lord engages my ob-
ſervance: how my fate
Plays the ſly tyrant with me, and involves
My thoughts in killing paſſions: flames meet flames
With equall reſolution, and contend,
Like *Cadmus* earth-borne brothers to deſtroy
Each other by their fury; feare kils hope,
But a new riſing from the former urne,
Takes vengeance on the murd'rer: wretched I
Live as to live were every houre to die.

*Enter Sapho. Aminta. Florida in mourning,
Parthenia after.*

A moſt ſad apparition ſuiting well
The inward horror of my mind! this Knight
Sure ſhould not be my enemy, he fights
Under my very colours; Noble youth,
If what your outward figure ſpeake, does chal-
enge
Relation to your mind; I ſee no cauſe
We ſhould indanger our mortalities
In this infortunate quarrell: there appeares
So great an outward ſympathy, it tels
My ſoul wee ſhould not combat.

Parth. Teach your feares

This fruitleffe hope : I come not hither arm'd
With refolution big as Fate, to part,
O'recome with aeyry treaties ; fooner thinke
To charme the Genius of the world to peace,
When earthquakes have affrighted it, than with
Well-worded eloquence, to decline the height
Of my wak'd wrath.
   Amph. Sir, you promife
An Early conqueft o're me, but there refts
In mee a manly pitty, would not ftaine
My conquering hands in your too innocent bloud ;
I would not have your vertue, gentle youth,
Be like a toward Cedar overwhelm'd
By an outragious tempeft blafted ere
It come to full growth : if for honors Caufe,
And to atcheive fame, you attempt my life,
Let me defire you to employ your force
On fome leffe fortunate Warrier. I am loath
To triumph in the guiltleffe fpoiles of your
Yet blooming honor.
   Par. Read thy friends this dialect of cowardife :
Know, to incenfe thee more, I'me one that hate
Thy deare *Philoclea*, with fo dire a fpight,
That I pronounce her one, who lives upon
The fpoile of innocent vertue, that has caus'd
Guiltleffe effufion of more Noble bloud,
Than ever fill'd hers or your bafer veines.
   Amph. Then I fee,
You come to raile, and muft chaftife the wrong
You do inflict on her, whofe fpotleffe foule
Is fo much ignorant of the leaft guilt,
It underftands it not : recant this wrong
Opinion of her purity, and leave off
To wake an anger that had rather fleepe,
Than rife to hurt you.
   Part. I fee then I muft adde
New truths to affright your cowardife : Your miftris
Is the decay of more fame-worthy foules,
Than fhe has hayrs or vaine bewitching looks

T' inthrall your wanton paſſion : on your heart,
My ſword ſhall write this for a ſerious truth,
And underneath it, that unworthy lie
You have pronounc'd, in juſtifying her free
From my juſt affirmation.
   Amp. Fiends could never have ſo incens'd me,
                    Fight, Her Helmet fals off.
Bleſſe me ! ſure ſome Angel's entred
Into armes againſt my unworthy ſelfe ;
Thoſe golden locks, ſurely are *Pallas* head-tyre, or the Queen
Of Love has maſqued her ſelfe in *Mars* his ſhape,
So to betray my luckleſſe arme to ſlaughter
Of the worlds exquiſite beauty.
   Par. Now my joy
Exceeds the greateſt trophees : *Argalus*,
Me thinks I ſee him riding in a chariot drawn by Doves,
Cut the bright firmament, and there attend
My wiſh'd aſcention.
   Amph. Some mountaine that
Has ſtood the longeſt rage of time, unlooſe
Its ſtony roots, fall on me, that I never
May be on earth remembred ; deereſt Lady
Looke up, and let me ſhowre a floud of teares
Into your wounds : diſtraction ſeaze me ; may I
Like ſome black prodigy contemn'd by light
Never be more diſtinguiſh'd.
   Part. Nay my Lord,
Do not let paſſion diſcompoſe your thoughts.
You've done an office for me, that blots out
All my conceit of hatred : pray, forgive me,
I injur'd your *Philoclea* ; arm'd for death,
I came to have it from that hand which ſlue
My *Argalus* ; weepe not girles,
I do not need your moyſt religious teares
To uſher me to Heaven : Looke how an hoſt
Of Sainted lovers on their turtles wings,
Conducted by my *Argalus*, approach

To waft me to Elifium; take my breath
That flies to thee on the pale wings of death,
Argalus, O *Argalus.*
           Dies.

 Amph. Can I retaine mortality, and behold
This impious act of my dire fate? this piece
Of new demolifh'd Nature, were it plac'd
For its own Ivory figure on a Tombe
Of pureft Alabafter, would be thought
One with the ftones white fubftance: Maids, convay
Your Ladies body hence, while I depart
To find a grief out, that may breake my heart.
           Exit.

 Amin. Haplefle Lady,
Let us refolve not to outlive her, but
Like conftant fervants, waite upon in death
Our murd'red Miftris.
 Sapho. Our poore lives cannot
Redeeme her loffe, nor pacify her ghoft,
For her late flaughter. I have compos'd
An Elegy on her death, and beauty: heare it.

  Happy Arabians, when your Phœnix dies
  In a fweet pile of fragrant fpiceries,
  Out of the afhes of the Myrrhe-burn'd mother,
  That you may ftill have one, fprings up another.
  Vnhappy we, fince 'tis your Phœnix nature;
  Why could not ours, our only matchleffe Creature,
  Injoy that right? why from Parthenia's *urne*
  Should not Parthenia *glorioufly returne?*
  O, there's a reafon: 'tis 'caufe Natures ftore
  All fpent on her, is now become too poore
  To frame her equall: fo that on her Herfe
  My trembling hand fhall hang this funerall verfe.

  True loue, and beauty, none can boaft to have,
  They both are buried in Parthenia's *grave,*

Who was loves, glories, beauties, vertues pride,
With her love, glory, vertue, beauty dyde.

Now girles,
Strow flowers upon the body, while our teares
Imbalme her memory; and what ever eares
Shall heare this ſtory, may with Juſtice ſay,

None lov'd like *Argalus* and *Parthenia*.

FINIS.

THE HOLLANDER.

[1640.]

THE HOLLANDER.

A Comedy written 1635.

The Author
HENRY GLAPTHORNE.

And now Printed as it was then Acted at the Cock-pit in *Drury lane*, by their Majesties Servants, with good allowance.

And at the Court before both their Majesties.

LONDON:
Printed by *I. Okes*, for *A. Wilson*, and are to be sold at her shop at Grayes-Inne Gate in Holborne. 1640.

The Perſons in the Play.

Artleſſe, a Doctor of Phyſicke.
Vrinal, his man.
Mixum, his Apothecary.
Free-wit, a yong Gentleman, and a Sutor to the Lady *Know-worth*.
Sir *Martin Yellow*, a jealous Knight.
Popingay, his Nephew.
Fortreſſe, a Knight of the Twibill.
Sconce, a Gallant naturaliz'd Dutchman.
Captayne Picke.
Lady *Yellow*.
Miſtriſſe *Know-worth*, her ſiſter.
Miſtreſſe *Mixum*.
Dalinea, the Doctors daughter.
Lovering, a Chamber-maid diſguiſed

The *Scene* London.

To the great hope of growing nobleneſſe, my Honourable friend, Sir *Thomas Fiſher*, Knight, &c.

Sir,

The knowledge of your ſtill increaſing *virtue* has begot in all men love, in me admiration, and deſires to ſerve it: as cunning Painters expreſſe more ſignificant Art in modell, then extended figures, I have made election of this little of-ſpring of my braine, to ſhow you the largeſt skill of my many indearments to you; and as an Ambaſſadour from the reſt of my faculties, to informe you how much devotion the whole province of my Soule payes to your worth and goodnes. Had I bin endow'd with ſuch bleſſings (noble young man) I ſhould have preſented you a wel mand *Hawke*, or an excellent

The Epistle.

Courser, gifts (becaufe more agreeable to your Difpofition) more fit to have bin tendred you: But I am confident you know that a Booke (as it is my beft inheritance) is the moft magnificent facrifice my zeale can offer; this Play therefore accept, beft Sir, from him who is nothing more ambitious then of the title of your

true fervant and

honourer,

Hen: Glapthorne.

The Hollander.

Actus primus. Scena prima.

Doctor and his Wife.

Doctor.

How doe thefe new Guefts like us?
   Mrs. Very well:
That fortnight they've beene here, I have obferv'd
From them not the leaft relifh of diftafte;
The Lady and her fifter are fo good
Themfelves, their innocence cannot miftruft
Ill in another, fpecially in us,
Who doe affume that formall gravity

Might dafh prying eyes : But is the fifter
Cur'd of her Ague perfectly?

Doct. The Spring
Does not produce an Ague but for Phyficke,
She's cur'd, and onely does expect her fifter,
The Lady *Yellow*, otherwife I feare
We fhould not have her company.

Mris. Green-fickneffe take her,
I thought it had beene that, and then my Art
Would have beene requifite. I fhould have found
Some lufty youth that would have given her phy-
ficke,
More powerfull to expell that lafie humour
Than all your Cordialls : Heaven, I can but thinke
How in this feven yeares, fince we came to towne,
The Tide is turnd with us : when thou wert an
Inne-
Keeping Apothecary in the Country,
The furniture of our fhop was Gally-pots,
Fild with Conferve of Rofes, empty Boxes,
And *Aqua vitæ* glaffes : and now thou art
My moft admir'd Doctor, walk'ft in Sattin,
And in plufh, my heart.

Doct. Applaud my wit that has effected it.

Mris. You will grant I hope
An equall fhare to me ? Was it not I
That firft advis'd you to fet up a Schoole
For Female vaulters, and within pretence
Of giving Phyficke, give them an over-plus
To their difeafe. How much this has conduc'd
To our advancement, forgetfulneffe it felfe
Cannot deny.

Doct. Nor will I, my deare affociate, I have
now
Atchiev'd a wealth fufficient to procure
My felfe a licenfe, though the murmuring Doctors
That doe not bite-backe it, though they watch
All opportunities that may undoe
My eftimation : we muft therefore arme

Our felves with circumfpective care : be fure
Thofe vertuous gentlewomen, who are now
Domefticke guefts, have no caufe to fufpect
A mifdemeanour here, nor that our daughter,
A virgine could as morning ayre or Ice,
So timerous of fociety, that fhee feemes
Neglectfull of mankind, be expos'd to every common
    eye,
Frequents our houfe, we muft be politicke, wife, or our
    ftate,
Will foone embrace a ruine.

Enter Vrinall.

Vrin.   Are you the Doctor *Artleffe* pray fir ?
Doct.   My name is *Artleffe.*
Vrin.   Sir, I am fent from Mr. *Mixum,* your Apothecary, to give attendance on you.
Doct.   Your name is *Vrinall*, I take it ?
Vrin.   You take my name by the right end fir, my father was a brother of mafter *Mixum's* function : marry my mother told me a Doctor got me, for profeffions fake I hope you'l ufe me kindly.
Doct.   Doubt not good *Vrinall*, if thou beeft not crack't, canft thou hold water.
Mift.   Well, that is, bee fecret, infooth husband, the young man will be very good at a dead lift, to ferve our patients turnes, he has a promifing countenance.
Vrin.   A good fubfidy face miftris, but mafter *Mixum* has certified me, that hither come Ladies and gentlewomen, City wives and country wives, and the better fort of faylors wives : Nay wives of all forts, but Oyfter wives, fome to have the falling ficknelle cur'd, others the inflammation of the blood, the Confumption of the body and lungs; if I doe not to any man or woman adminifter a glifter,

vomit, potion, *Iulip*, *Cordiall*, or what phyficke your worfhip fhall thinke fit, with dexterity, fay I am no found *Vrinall*, and beat me to pieces.

Doɛt. I believe thee, but did *Tom Mixum* give you nought in charge to fay to me?

Vrin. O yes fir, hee bad mee tell you hee had a fat Goofe in the pens, only for your pulling : a yunker of a thoufand pound *per annum*.

Doɛt. Sayft fo, what is he, knoweft thou?

Vrin. I faw him fir, he was a proper man: but I thinke has not much more wit then my felfe, he feemes of a good eafie difpofition, and may I believe, be led by the nofe as quietly as the tameft Beare in the garden : he has not wit enough to be a knave, nor manhood enough to be an honeft man : this is my opinion of him fir, when you fee him you'l underftand him better.

Enter Popingaie, Sir Martine Yellow as his man.

Pop. With licences, is not this houfe a receiptacle for finners?

Doɛt. Now you are in't perhaps it is, what meane you?

Pop. Pifh, feeme not to obfcure, is it not in plaine termes, a houfe of eafe.

Doɛt. There is one in the garden fir.

Pop. Where one may do his bufineffe without fear of Marfhall, conftable, or any one of that moft awfull tribe.

Vrin. Surely this gentleman comes to take a purge, hee talkes fo cleanely.

Pop. Shall I have anfwer fir? I come as hot from fea, as a Hollander from herring fifhing, I have an appetite, the moft infatiate citizen who frequents your manfion cannot tame ; had fhe beene fed with amber poffets, eaten fparrowes egges, or her accuftom'd bevendy, been the juice of Clare or Sparagus.

Doct. What abuse may this be?
Perhaps your most officious pander monsieur
That for a shilling will betray his sister
To prostitution, did mistake, begone,
Or shall I fetch a gentleman will whip
Your hot blood out of you.
   Vrin. Shall I runne for the Beadles mistris?
   Mist. No goe to the next Justice for a warrant, and make haste, be sure Ile have the knave smoak'd for abusing my house.
   Pop. This must not fright me, doe you not keepe a pimping roaring varlet, noted as much as pig, have you not constant she souldiers in your citadell, none such, had Hollands Leager, Lambeth Marsh is held a Nunry to your Colledge.
   Vrin. And the three Squirrels in the towne, I warrant a very sanctuary to it.
   Pop. Come here's gold, be not so bashful, Mistris pray receive it, I know you are open handed.
   Mist. Art. Now I defie thee for a Rascall: *Vrinall* why run you not to the Justice, his man would have taken your money ere this time.
   Pop. Yet least I should mistake you, though I am by all truth confident this is the house: pray resolve me; has the Lady *Yellow* a chamber here?
   Vrin. Yes sir, she lies in the yellow chamber, and has done this two months.
   Pop. I did believe it.
   Vrin. Nay you may believe mee if you will: I know neither Lady *Yellow*, nor yellow chamber, I have not beene here above half an houre.
   Doct. *Tom Mixum*, sure sent this fellow hither, he's so unmannerly, silence *Vrinall*, what if that Lady have a chamber here sir?
   Sir Mart. Now he comes to the purpose.
   Pop. Nay speake directly suppositions: include a doubtfull fence, if she have not, I shall repent the error of my language and crave your mercy.

Doct. Impudence I thinke, beyond my own refts in this youth, I muft finde out his meaning: tis perchance fome one fent from her jealous husband, whom fhe told me, in difcontent was travel'd, prithee wife goe in, and tell the Lady *Yellow*, here is one wifhes the knowledge of her.

Mrs. Art. Hang him young whifling, he know a Lady, pity of his life firft.

Doct. Doe as I bid you: *Vrinall* attend your miftris in.

Vrin. Yes, I will attend her in and in too, to do her any fervice.

Exeunt Vrinall, and Miftris.

Doct. Sir, the uncivill language you have given me,
Might juftly ftirre a paffionate man to rage;
But it no more ftirs me then the light wind,
If you've relation to the Lady *Yellow*:
She's one whofe vertues merit that refpect,
Twould be a ftaine to manners not to ufe
The meaneft of her friends with due regard:
Pray fir what is fhe to you?

Pop. As any woman elfe is for my money, onely I muft confeffe, I have an itch, a tickling thought to her before the reft of common proftitutes: I know fhe'l lodge in none but vitious houfes, which inforces me thinke yours is fo.

Doct. Tis a mifconceit,
Ime forry for her fake whom I efteem
So chaft, the pure untainted Doves may envy
Her unftain'd whiteneffe) fhould be caft upon
My innocent houfe, expect Ile fend her to you,
Shee'l fhape you a juft anfwer, would fhe were
As they fufpect her.

Ex. Doct.

Sir Mar. This Doctor is difhoneft, fpeakes untruth,
My jealoufie is juft, that any man

Should fo undoe his reafon; in beliefe
Of womens goodneffe, as on their loofe foules,
To venture his creation ; nay transforme
His effence by them : for a cuckold is
Natures huge prodigy, the very abftract
Of all, that is wonderfull : contempt and fhame,
Are accidents as proper to his brow,
As haire and whiteneffe.

Enter Lady Yellow.

Pop. Is this fhe fir ?
Sir Mar. I nephew that's the monfter.
Pop. If *Africke* did produce no other monfters there would be more cuckolds in it then Lyons, but to my bufineffe, Madam the old tradition of this houfe invites your knowledge to conceive for what I fent to fpeake with you.
Lady. As yet indeed it does not.
Pop. Truely it does, I hope I fhall obtaine
The virgine glories of this daies encounter,
Come fhalls kiffe, and then retire into your chamber.
Lady. My chamber, fure your manners lies in your berd, what doe you take me for ?
Pop. An excellent creature ; one whofe meaneft fmile
Would tempt a votary earneft at his prayers,
Before the image of his tutelar Saint ;
To vary his fix'd brow : yet I muft tell you,
You are a factreffe of the Divells, one
Who fell damnation pleafingly as Afps
Infufe their itching venom : a ftanding poole,
On whofe falt wombe the too lafcivious fun
Begets of Frogs and Toads a numerous off-fpring,
Compar'd with you is empty of corruption.

Lady. Ist so, have at him, a strange complement
    to win a Lady,
Sir by your first discourse I had imagin'd
You came to spend part of this cheerefull morne
In amorous dalliance with me, I am apt
For entertainement of it, as a bride
Long time contracted to some exquisite man
Is on her wedding night, but your quicke change.
Did not my glasse assure me no great blemish
Dwels in my cheekes, would urge me to mistrust
An imperfection in them: they are my owne sir,
I doe not weare (though its common among Ladies)
My face ith' day-time only, and at night
Put off the painted visor, this haire beleive it,
Was never shop-ware, you may venture on me,
Let but your creature keepe the doore, my chamber
Is empty for you.
    Sir Mar. Impudent strumpet.
    Pop. Can you be a woman,
And utter this, the hot desire of quailes,
To yours is modest appetite, you carry
A stone about you, not to warme your blood
Oppress'd with chilly cold, but to enflame it
Beyond all sensuall heat, which you would extin-
    guish,
(Had you a soule about you) with your teares,
Or weepe with the continuance that tall Pines
Diffuse their gummy drops in summer, and
Faster then trembling Isicles, or snow,
At their own dissolution.
    Cady. This is stranger yet sir, I see you come to con-
    vert mee
Prompted with a zeale would choake ten precisians
    earnest in
Their hot house of convention, alasse poore youth
    thy want
Of practice in the sweet delights of love,
Undoes thy judgement, can there be a joy

Equall to this to have a fprightfull Lady,
Whofe every lineament fpeakes captivity
To the beholder, clafpe with the fame ftrictneffe
That curling billows doe embrace a wracke,
Her lovers necke, kiffe clofe and foft, as moffe
Does fome oregrowne Oake ; but I fee tis vaine,
To prate to thee whofe ignorance may plead
Excufe for thy fond herefie ; goe depart,
Turne Eunuch and referve thy voyce, perhaps
T'will purchafe thee a petty Cannons place
In fome blinde chantry.

Enter Doctor and Dalinea.

Doct. Ile cut off their difcourfe, if fhee be right ile have my benefit out of her : *Dalinea* attend her Ladyfhip, Madam I feare you take cold here, your Sifter, Miftris *Know-worth* expects you too within ; Gentlewoman you cannot complaine you have been us'd uncivilly ; pray now depart, tis time.

Lady. They may returne to the wife man my husband, from whom I'm fure they come, and tell him my difpofition, ha, ha, ha.

Exeunt Lady, and Dalinea.

Sir Mart. Flames rife on flames fucceffively, the fpheare
Has no fuch fire as I doe harbour here.

Pop. What divine creature fhould the other be, well mafter Doctor, we fhall be even with you.

Exe. Sir Mart. Pop.

Doct. I, doe you pleafure fir, the fmall Riveret
Does in its cold waves, feeme to drench the fun
(When like a riotous drunkard) his hot rayes
Suckes up the pearly waters, if this Lady

Weare in her breft, the burning fpots of luft,
They fhall encreafe, and like the Starres, light her foule
To th' firmament of pleafure.   The bufineffe firrha ?

Enter Vrinall and Sconce.

Vrin.   The bufineffe firha, he's gotten into th' Lordly phrafe
Already, Sir the gentleman I fpeake off ?

Doct.   Is this he ? would you have ought with me fir ?

Scon.   *A mon Dieu*, this is the Doctor : *Foutra* I would faine fpeake to him, Sir I fhould bee happy to initiate my knowledge in your acquaintance Mafter *Mixum* an Apothecary, at whofe fhop I ufe to eate Eringo Roots, did recommend me to you.

Doct.   Honeft *Tom Mixum*, you are welcome; what's your defigne with me ?

Scon.   Fame does divulge you to be a man experienc'd in the Arts.

Vrin.   Of coufenage and lying excellently.

Scon.   Which does concerne our bodily health.

Doct.   And you perhaps labor of fome difeafe,
And come to feeke for remedy, I can
As *Gallen* or *Hipocrates*, read a lecture,
On maladies, their caufes and effects,
Tell by the countenance of a man, the ill oppreffes him,
You by that *Linea curva* ith' altitude of your horofcope,
Should be fubject to *Calentures*.

Scon.   Neen up mine feale min here : ick neet, infection vanifh I never was fubject to difeafe, but the gentile itch which I obtaind in the Low Countries.

Vrin. Twas in hot fervice certainely.

Doct. With licence fir, let me defire your character, I long to know you, Symptomes of worth declare you in my opinion noble.

Scon. I fhall explaine my felfe by land fhape a far off, my father was a Dutch man.

Vrin. Which makes him looke fo like a fmoak'd weftphalia ham, or dry Dutch pudding.

Scon. And one in the confpiracy with *Barnevet*, at whofe hanging he fled ore hither.

Vrin. And the gentle noofe had knit up him, and a hundred of his country men, our land would not be peftred fo with butterboxes.

Scon. Thinking to have purchas'd a monopoly for Tobacco: but that the Vintners tooke in fnuffe, and inform'd the gallants, who had like to have fmoak'd him for't.

Doct. An admirable project.

Scon. Afterwards he undertooke to have drayn'd the Fens, and there was drown'd, and at the ducking time at Crowland drawne up in a net for a widgin.

Doct. Pray fir what tribe was he of?

Scon. He was no Jew Sir, yet he would take pawnes, and their forfeits too, and has left me fuch as you fee, I am a proper man: a trifling patrimony, a thoufand pounds per annum.

Vrin. I admire no man begs him for a foole, and gets it from him.

Doct. May I requeft your name?

Sco. My name is *Sconce* fir, Mafter *Ieremy Sconce*, I am a gentleman of a good family, and can derive my pedigree from *Duke Alvas* time, my anceftors kept the inquifition out of *Amfterdam*.

Vrin. And brought all Sects in thither.

Scon. And tooke their furname from Kickin pot, the ftrongeft Sconce in the *Netherlands*.

Vrin. An excellent derivation for a Dutch-man, Kickin-pot.

Scon. I had a good ſtrong coſen taken in by th' enemy, laſt ſummer, Skinks Sconce Mr. Doctor, my cozen german once remov'd by a ſtratagem of hay boats a fire on them.

Doct. That ſhould have beene before they came there Maſter *Sconce*.

Scon. But tis thought our nation had recover'd it ere this, but that the villanous Dunkerkers at ſea met with the Herrinbuſſes and made ſtocke-fiſh of them.

Urin. They beat them ſoundly then it ſeemes.

Doct. Have you no brothers Mr. *Sconce?*

Scon. Not any that I know of, as I am gentleman, nor was there any of my name till of late, that gallants have begot me nameſakes in every Taverne.

Doct. But the buſineſſe you have with me is unrelated yet, and I have haſte, pray what may it concerne?

Scon. A houſehold matter Mr. Doctor; I would be loath to be accounted troubleſome, I ſhould be none of your vulgar gueſts though : *Mixum* has inform'd me you have faire lodgings in your houſe, convenient for eaſe and pleaſure, might I be ſo much engag'd to your goodneſſe, as to affoord me a hanſome one for my mony, it ſhould be an endearement conſpicuouſly trenching upon my gratitude, and render me your oblig'd ſervant everlaſtingly.

Vrin. As long as his money laſts, that is.

Doct. If that be all, for *Tom Mixums* ſake, were chambers ſcarcer, you ſhould not be denyed. *Vrinall* bring the gentleman into the dining roome, Ile goe acquaint my wife with it.

Exit Doct.

Scon. *Vrinall,* art thou ſtil'd *Vrinall?*

Vrin. It is my right and title to be term'd ſo.

Scon. Come hither my ſweet Raſcall, canſt keepe councell, there's gold for thee, thou ſhalt have a new caſe ſirrha, wilt thou be true to me?

Vrin. I will fteale nothing from you Mr. *Sconce.*

Scon. Thou lookft not like a man of theft, I mean in a defigne.

Vrin. Tis not to convey gold over, in hollow anchors, to pay your Countrimen fouldiers; if it be, Ile heare no more of it.

Scon. Pifh, not that neither. *Mixum* thou knowft him, doft not?

Vrin. Twas he preferd me hither.

Scon. I did imagin't; my fine *Vrinall* reports thy Mr. to have the rareft falve.

Vrin. The weapon falve I warrant.

Scon. Which would, if I were defperately hurt, cure mee without a Surgeons helpe.

Vrin. So I have heard indeed.

Scon. Now *Vrinall*, it is our Countrie Cuftome onely to Stick or Snee. But couldft thou but procure this pretious falve, I would confront the gliftering fteele, out-face the fharpeft weapon.

Vrin. My Mafter is very cautious in parting with it.

Enter Freewit.

Free. Save you gentlemen, belong you to this houfe?

Vrin. No fir, this houfe belongs to us.

Free. Miftris *Know-worth*, the Lady *Yellowes* fifter, fhe is not ftirring?

Vrin. Tis a lye fir, fhe is.

Free. Your wit is very fcurvy Sir: if you ferve a Creature here to carry meffages; pray deliver one to her.

Vrin. I may chufe whether I will or no though.

Scon. Nay, and he fhall chufe fir.

Free. Prethee good friend let him; ile doe't my felfe.

Vrin. Nay, that you fhall not neither: what ftand I here for? But fir, 'tis not the fafhion of this liberall age, to imploy a man of merit in a meffage without confideration: your Lawyers Clark will not acquaint his Mafter with a Clyents caufe, untill his fift be be foundly greas'd: Why may not I then ufe the priviledge of my office? Sir, wee Doctors men take *aurum palpabile* for Reftorative: you are not unfurnifhed fir.

Free. O thou wouldft have money; there's for thee, prethee Intreat her prefence.

Vrin. Inftantly, inftantly, noble fir. Mr. *Sconce* pray bear this worthy gentleman company.

Exit Vrinall.

Free. Why fhould fhe lodge here? all fimilitude
Explaines this houfe for vicious, and this Doctor
For an impoftor: Though fhe have bin ficke,
She might have found to remedy her difeafe,
Another, and more fam'd Phyfitian
Than this: She ftayes perhaps to beare
Her fifter company. Whatfoere's the caufe,
Who dare deprave her innocence, or caft
A thought of blemifh on her vertues? Light
Diffus'd through aire (although fome thicke-brow'd
 fogge,
Or fickly vapour doe invade ayres fweetneffe)
Suffers no loath'd corruption. Thornes may gore
With envious pricking, the difcoloured leaves
Of the chafte wood-binde, but can never blaft
Their unftain'd frefhneffe.

Scon. Now in the name of madneffe what ailes this man? Sir are you jealous of your wife before you have her?

Free. What if I be fir.

Scon. She may chance Cuckold you after you have her for it.

Free. Good Coxecombe hold thy pratling.

Scon. Coxcombe? how Coxcombe to a naturallis'd Dutchman? Death fir, fhall I blow you downe with my Can; or fhew you Twibill.

Free. How Sir?

Scon. Nay, bee not angry man, I meant no harme, tis but a complementall falutation, I purchas'd of the Mr. of the Order oth' valiant Knights of the Twibill.

Free. A new Order of Knight-hood that, may I know the inftitution.

Enter Miftris Know-worth, Martha, as Mr. Lovering leads her.

Know. Servant welcome: *Lovering* intreat That gentleman to withdraw with Mr. Doctors man.

Love. Sir, my Miftris begs your abfence.

Scon. Beggars are no chufers my friend: fhe fhall Undergoe no contradiction: but Madam, tis the fafhion, As I tak't, to falute at meeting, and kiffe at parting.

Kiffes her.

Vrin. You had beft kiffe her double Mr. *Sconce.*

Scon. Lady, ferviture voftre & a vous affi Monfieur trefnoble.

Vrin. He lookes like a fquirrill indeed: this way fir.

Exeunt Lovring, Sconce, Vrinall.

Free. I hope you grow to perfect health, The Native beauty that once fild your cheeks,

Like to the budding Rofe puts forth agen,
After cold winters violence: and your lips
On whofe foft touch had it bin poffible,
Death would have dy'd himfelfe, begin to fhew
Like untouch'd Cherries, pale with Morning dew,
Which once fhak't off, the purple fruit afpires
With amorous blufhes to intice the fmall
Linnet and wanton Sparrow from their Layes,
To doate on its pure tincture, till they eate
What they admir'd.

   Know. ——O you are pleafant fervant; did you know
How neare I am to death, and for your fake,
Your humour foone would alter.

   Free. Truely, faire one,
It is a fweetneffe in you, I could wifh
Were temper'd with leffe paffion: (Your much care
Of my unworthy felfe;) tis but a fortnight,
Since laft my eyes enricht their needy fight,
By the reflection of thefe ftarres, and had
The leaft ill feas'd me, you had bin the firft
Whofe eares would have receiv'd it; harmes are apteft
To be reported where they are leaft welcome.

   Know. They are indeed, and one of yours is come
To kill my knowledge; fuch a one, as had
You worne a common heart, no ftrong difeafe
Could have difpatched fooner.

   Free. ——I feele
No inclination in my faculties
Tending to fickneffe: I have never yet
By nightly furfets forc'd my youthfull blood
To a diftemper.

   Know. Would your youthfull blood
Has ne're forc'd you one. Perfidious man,
Had I atchiev'd the patience of a Saint
(Seclude my love to thee) I fhould in rage

Title thee worthleſſe : nay, a name above
That hatefull appellation : did you never
Injure a Creature of your mothers one *Martha* ?
    Free. Ha : how meane you Lady ?
    Know. In the blacke act of Sinne, when you deſign'd
Her honour, as a carcaſſe to the Grave,
Where ever ſince your deed of ill was acted,
'T has ſlept loſt and forgotten.
    Free. By juſt truth.
    Know. Invoke your falſehood, if you dare erect
On the blacke number of your heedleſſe oathes
A monument to perjury.   White truth,
Flies from the ranckorous poyſon of your breath,
As from a ſtifling dampe.   Can you deny.
Without a bluſh what I have urg'd ?
    Free. My reſolution ſtaggers a tall Oake,
Whoſe weighty top has diſcompos'd his roots)
When whirlewinds doe aſſault it, ſits unmov'd,
Ballanc'd with me, to recollect the ſtrength
Of impudence, and deeply contradict
Her mightieſt affirmation, were to wage
A feeble warre with truth.   Say I did Miſtris ;
Twas ere a thought reciprocall enjoynd me
A ſerious duty to you and your mercy,
In which you doe approach as neare heavens good-
    neſſe,
As heaven does bleſt eternity, wil't pardon
That witleſſe error in me.
    Know. Truth I ſhall not :
The harmleſſe Mirtle firſt ſhall live in froſts,
And the pale Couſlips flouriſh, ere warme ſhowres
With quickning moyſture raiſes them to tell
The early Violets they are not alone
The Springs prime Virgins : my peculiar wrong
I freely pardon : but if you reſpect
Your conſcience, ſeeke that injur'd woman, and
Reſtore by ſacred marriage the ſad loſſe
Of her deprived fame.   Doe it *Free-wit*, heaven

Will smile at thy integrity; my teares
Shall strive to wash your crime away.

Ex. Mrs. Know.

Free. She weeps: so choice flowers, when extracting fire,
Inforces their soft leaves to a mild warmnesse,
Doe through the Lymbecke temperately distill
Their odoriferous teares. But tis most just
To lose a chaste love, when distain'd with lust.

Exit.

Explicit Actus primus.

Actus secundus. Scena prima.

Sconce, Vrinall, with a boxe of weapon salve.

Scon. BUt are you certaine *Vrinall* this oyntment is Orthodoxall; may I without errour in my faith believe this fame the weapon falve Authenticall?

Vrin. Yes, and infallibly the creame of weapon falves, the fimples which doe concurre to th' compofition of it, fpeake it moft fublime ftuffe; tis the rich Antidote that fcorns the fteele, and bids the Iron be in peace with men, or ruft: *Aurelius Bombaftus Paracelfus*, was the firft inventer of this admirable Unguent.

Scon. He was my Country-man, and held an Errant Conjurer.

Vrin. The Devill he was as foone: an excellent Naturallift, & that was all upon my knowledge, Mr. *Sconce*; and tis thought my Mr. comes very neare him in the fecrets concerning bodies Phyficall, as Herbes, Roots, Plants vegetable and radicall, out of whofe quinteffence, mixt with fome hidden caufes, he does extract this famous weapon falve, of which you now are Mr.

Scon. There's a Welch Doctor ith' City reported skilfull in compounding it.

Vrin. He? a meere Digon a whee; his falve, why it is Cafe-baby to my Mafters: I dare be fworne tis nothing but Methegling boyld to jelly, the blades of Leeks, mixt with a Welch Goats blood; then ftampt, and ſtraind through a peece of *Britiſh* Freeſe, or one of the old laps of *Merlins* Jerkin.

Scon. Probable *Vrinall.* That Welch Doctor I doe not like: I did attempt him for the weapon ſalve, and like a *Turke* hee anſwer'd me, that *Hollanders* were *Jewes.*

Vrin. They are a rebellious nation that's certaine.

Scon. And that the ſalve was onely made for Chriſtians; there is a City Captaine too; I know not how you ſtile him.

Vrin. Not *Iohn a Stiles*, the Knight of the poſt is it?

Scon. No, no, a very honeſt gentleman; but he's reported to have atchiev'd the ſalve in *Lapland* among the witches, and to be very liberall in imparting it to his friends, an Aldermans daughter *Vrinall* may, and they ſay a witty gentlewoman.

Vrin. Is't poſſible, Mr. *Sconce?* they have few ſonnes of that condition.

Scon. Had a deſperate hole made in her by a gentleman, with his But-ſhaft, as in her Country garden he was ſhooting at Penny pricke; was, when none elſe could doe it, cur'd by this Captaine.

Vrin. By this light a trifle, a meere trifle, the very ſcraping of our Galley-pots performes more monſtrous wonders: there was a Puritane Mr. *Sconce*, who, cauſe he ſaw a Surpliſſe in the Church, would needs hang himſelfe in the Bell-ropes.

Scon. Why did not the Sexton ring him by the eares for it?

Vrin. Him my Mr. feeing, did for experience ſake anoynt the nooſe wherein his necke had bin, and it recovered him.

Scon. Is't poſſible he ſhould ſo eaſily eſcape a hanging! but on good *Vrinall.*

Vrin. Nay ſir Ile tell you a greater miracle: You heard of the great training laſt Summer maſter *Sconce*?

Scon. O when the whole City went in Armes to take in *Iſlington*; marry I heard the Ale-wives curſe the report of their Muskets, it made their Pies and Cuſtards quake ith' Oven, and ſo come out dow-back't, which almoſt broke the poore Harlots.

Vrin. I then Mr. *Sconce* there was at leaſt three-ſcore blown up with a basket of powder, thirty of their lives my Maſter ſav'd.

Scon. Rarer, and rarer yet: But how good *Vrinall*?

Vrin. He dreſs'd the ſmoake of the powder as it flew up Sir, and it heald them perfectly.

Scon. O that any body would blow me up, to ſee how I could cure my ſelfe. Still on good *Vrinall*.

Vrin. Nay there are thouſands of this kinde: but now I thinke on it ſince, it did commit a villanous miſchiefe.

Scan. Could it ever doe a miſchiefe *Vrinall*?

Vrin. Yes, yes, it has done a moſt notorious one, ſufficient to exauctorate its power, and almoſt anni-hilate the vertue of it.

Scon. What was't good *Vrinall*?

Vrin. I could e'ne weepe to tell you ſir: tis ſuppos'd twill never recover the favour of gentle-men and City wits, they are quite out of conceite with it.

Scon. But why ſhould they be ſo *Vrinall*?

Vrin. I ſcarce dare anſwer Sir, for feare you hate it likewiſe. Twas ſuch another miſchiefe.

Scon. Prethee what? nay on my gentility *Vrinall*.

Vrinall. Why ſir, it cur'd two Serjeants, and their yeomen.

Scon. How? two Serjeants.

Vrin. Who otherwiſe had drunke Mace-Ale with the Devill.

Scon. A Capitall crime that fame, to cure two Serjeants.

Enter Doctor, his wife: Mixum, his wife.

Doctor. Tom *Mixum* I thanke thee for the man
Thou fentft me; tis a moft ferviceable knave;
I've fet him to pull yon bird of Paradice, yon parcell
Dutch: thou fentft him hither too.

Mix. I knew he was for your purpofe, Mr.
Doctor: this is the gentleman I told you had one
thoufand pound *per annum*, and would be a match
for Mr. Doctors daughter.

Scon. There was a touch for him indeed *Vrinall.*

Doct. It will, indeed, now I confider on't, I had
rather fhee fhould marry a wealthy gull, than a witty
Beggar; Wife and Mr. *Mixum*, will you difcourfe a
little with the gentleman, found his intent and prone-
neffe to a match, and as you finde him ufe him; Mr.
Sconce I fhould be glad to wait on you, did not urgent
affaires withdraw me.

Scon. Mr. Doctor I faw you not before: I am
forry fir, you will be gone fo foone, I fhould have
chang'd fome fillables with you.

Doct. Another time fweet Mr. *Sconce.*

Tom Mixum, Vrinall, Exeunt with Doctor.

Mrs. Mix. A very good fortune Mrs. *Artleffe* for
your daughter, and not to be neglected: fhall I fpeak
to him, or will you forfooth?

Mr. Art. Perhaps hee'l fpeake to us: fee kind
gentleman.

Scon. Lady, my manners does command mee
leave you: you would perchance be private by your
felves, or peradventure *Vrinall* were more behoofefull
for your company: then I adiew Víroes.

Mrs. Mix. Pray ftay fir, we have fome bufineffe
with you, (let me alone to trye him Mrs. *Artleffe*)

befides wee had rather be private with a gentleman, then by our felves: they fay you Dutch-men are the kindeft men, and love a woman heartily, you kiffe fo finely too.

Scon. You fhall feel that prefently [*kiffes her*] there was a touch for you: Nay Mrs. *Artleffe* you fhall not blame my manners, I have a lip, a piece for you [*kiffes her*] and there was a touch for you Lady.

Mrs. Mix. So pleafe you fir, I have another touch for you too [*kiffes him*] Muft trie his difpofition Mrs. *Artleffe.*

Scon. A very ftrong touch that fame; fhe will beleaguer me I thinke, and her Cannon fhot will bee kiffes, they almoft blow mee over. Surely the Minikin is enamoured on me.

Mrs. Art. Motion it to him Mrs. *Mixum.*

Mrs. Mix. Pray give me leave to feele his minde firft, Miftris *Artleffe*: Tis pitty fir, you are fo long unmarried; you are an exceeding handfome Gentleman.

Scon. Yes, yes, I know that well enough, I might ferve for a gentleman Ufher, were my legges fmall enough: there are Ladies would confume halfe the revenews of their Lords, on fuch a man of Chine and pith as I am.

Mift. Mix. Fie mafter *Sconce*, thinke not of Ladies fir, they are fo imperious, a man muft ferve them as they doe command, at every turne and toy comes in their head; they'l puffe and fret elfe, like their taffata petticoats with often brufhing up; I will proteft to you, you had better fet your mind upon fome honeft country Gentlewoman, or Citizens Daughter, Mafter Doctor has a hanfome girle (though I fay it before her mothers face) only fhe wants the audacity, which a man would put into her; would you were married to her: Sir, fhe may doe worfe, I dare affure you.

Mift. Ari. Yes, indeed may you mafter *Sconce*, have you not feene her yet? tis a pretty puling baggage, fo it is, marry ere I would make her a Lady, fhee fhould be a new Exchange wench, your Citizens wives they are the goodeſt creatures, live the fineſt lives.

Miſt. Mix. Very right, miſtris *Artleſſe*, good foules, did you but know fir, what tender hearts they have, how kind they will be to a gentleman that comes to deale for their commodities, they will ufe him and it were their owne husbands.

Scon. Ile lay my life this musk-melon has a minde to ufe mee fo : I care not much to give her a touch, or fo, fhe's of the right fife, but Miſtris *Artleſſe* fhould I have your good will, if I could love your daughter.

Miſt. Art. Certainely fir, were you of Engliſh blood, I fhould like you better.

Miſt. Mix. Fie Miſtris *Artleſſe*, when I was a maid, I had a defire to be a kinne to all nations : I have tried fome Engliſh men, and they are like my husband, meere meacocks verily : and cannot lawfully beget a childe once in feaven yeares.

Scon. A touch, by this light, that's the reafon there are fo many baſtards in the city.

Mi. Mix. Your Spaniard as a neighbour of mine, told me who had liv'd among, is too haſty, he will not give a woman time to fay her prayers after fhe is bed : your French is with a woman as with an enemy, foone beaten off, but miſtris *Artleſſe*, if you will marry your daughter to the moſt compleat man, let him be Dutch : they are the rareſt men at multiplication, they will doe it fo readily.

Scon. They be indeed very good Arithmeticians.

Enter Lady Yellow, Miſtris Knoworth.

Miſt. Art. Here comes the Ladies : Miſtris *Mixum* we'l depart, they muſt not know our conference.

Miſt. Mix. Adiew kinde maſter *Sconce*.

Exe. Mrs. Art. Mrs. Mixum.

Scon. Adiew min vroen, I have a peſtilent mind to this talking harlotry, I will to her, but if I ſhould obtain the Neapolitan beneach, a creeke ith' backe, or ſo, from her, 'twould be but a ſcurvy touch, that for me, I ſhould be forc'd to ſwim ith tub for it, or be hang'd by the armes, and ſmoak'd like a bloat herring, I had forgot my pretious ſalve, ſhould I be ſerv'd ſo, 'twere but dreſſing the weapon that hurt mee (which I can have at any time) and be ſound agen, ha other donſella's: Madams, they are creatures of Pluſh, and Sattin, Ile accoſt them.

Know. This is the gentleman I told you of, I wonder what his quality may be, our Landlord the Doctor is a much fam'd man, and ſurely very honeſt.

Scon. It ſhall be ſo, my Engliſh is not compleate enough to hold diſcourſe with Ladies of regard, my naturall Dutch too is a Clowniſh ſpeech, and only fit to court a leagurer in: no your French ſhall doe it, and thanke my memory, I am perfect in it, tis your moſt accompliſh'd language, there's ſcarce a gallant but does woe his miſtris in the moode, but if they ſhould not underſtand me: well I will experce me it.

Sconce cringes to the Ladies.

Lady. He meanes to ſpeake ſurely in cringes.

Scon. Madame tres puiſſant en le command, de touts ceurs de ceſt monde, ie que Jui Jemond & invite en tant de lieux que ie ne ſcay ou aller pour abrir mon ſayn : a vn bewtie digne de mon acceptance.

Lady. Heyday, what's this, how ſhould he know Who can ſpeake French.

Know. He ſuppoſes it, prithee anſwer him ſiſter.

*Scon. Suiuant voſtre treſchier virtue, Ie fui ſi liberal
Que ie abadonne renie & renounce a tout mis biens*

H 2

De mon vid mon Engin mon alayne mon fang & mon
Penfir (pour ie ne faurioye, que dire) proueior mon
Ceur mon affection tout a voftre plaifeur.
  Lady. *Aprochés ie ne vou's morderay pas.*
  Scon. *Si ie ne vous fay tratement t' el que*
A vous appartient, ie efpere que voftre
Noblez te contera de mon bon intention.

Enter Sir Martine, Popingay, and Vrinall.

  Vrin. There is the Lady you enquire for.
  Sir Mart. Thank thee my friend, there's for
Thy paines, depart.

Exit Vrinall.

Nephew ftand cleare, obferve.
  Scon. *Sil y' a chofe en mon petit povoir en quoy ie vous puiffe*
Servir & aider commandes moy librement.
  Lady. *Vous Efte fort & liberal de fuparoll monfieur.*
  Sir Mar. At it fo clofe, fo now he wrings her hand,
And fhe fmiles on him: and her fifter laughs
At the lafcivious pofture, that I could
Command a flafh of lightning, or ufurpe
A minute the prerogative of death
That I might force a ruine on them, fuddaine
As water falls from mountaines, yet fo wretched,
They might defpaire and damne themfelves, what fay they?
  Pop. They fpeake French, I underftand them not.

Scon. kiffes the Lady.

  Mart. O that's the ages bawd to luftfull contracts,

Hell feife them, may their lips, like twins
In mifchiefe grow together, that their foule breath
May have no vent, leaft like fome poifonous fogge,
It doe infect the aire.
Kiffes her hand.

Scon. Per dona mi Madam apré's le's leures le maine.
Sir Mart. Againe, why ftrait,
If I ftand ftill, they'l to the very act,
I fhall behold my felfe transform'd to beaft,
And like an innocent lambe, when the keene knife's
Prepar'd to flit his wefand never bleat
But in calme filence perifh; villaine divell
Hadft thou as many lives as thou haft fins,
This fhould invade them all with fwift rage
Of fire or whirlewinds.

Runs at Sconce, hurts him in the arme, Sconce difarmes him.

Lady. Heavens bleffe yee
Innocent gentleman: fifter my husband.
Know. I feare he has mifchiev'd him.
Scon. You thinke you have hurt me wonderfully I warrant.
Pop. Good fir be more your felfe.
Laughs.

Scon. Give me thy hand, tis but a touch ith arme man, thou art a valiant fellow, I warrant thee a twibiller, run a tilt at a man before his weapon is drawne, your Lady would not have don't Ime fure, but tis no matter, thou haft done me a curtefie, or otherwife I fhould not take't fo patiently, (I fhall by this meanes experience my precious weapon falve) hold, thou wilt fight no more, there's a twibill for thee, thy fword Ile keepe till wee next meet, *Ladies beso los doights de voſtre blanch mains*, adiew comrade remember I am beholding to thee.

Ex. Sconce.

Pop. He's gone, but has left his hanger behinde him.

Lady. Siſter prithee ſpeak to him, he has put me in ſuch a fright, I cannot.

Pop. Sir be not ſo extreamely paſſionate,
Diſcourſe your grievance mildely, heare her anſwer,
Then cenſure juſtly of her.

Know. Brother I admire
A perſon of your breeding ſhould tranſgreſſe,
Civility ſo highly, to attempt
Upon a gentleman, who to my knowledge
Injur'd you no way.

Sir Mart. He is your champion, and you his Ladies.

Know. How ſir?

Sir Mart. His proſtitutes I might have ſaid O creature,
Who art ſo bad, the preſent age will queſtion
The truth of hiſtory, which do's but mention
A vertuous woman, with what impudence
Canſt thou behold me, and a ſhivering cold,
Strong as the hand of winter, caſts on brookes,
Not freeſe thy ſpirits up, congeale thy blood
To an ere'laſting lethargy. The ſtarres
Like ſtraglers, wander by ſucceſſive courſe,
To various feats yet conſtantly reviſit
The place they mov'd from: the Phœnix whoſe ſweet-neſſe
Becomes her ſepulcher, aſcends agen
Veſted in younger feathers from her pile
Of ſpicy aſhes, but mans honor loſt
Is irrecoverable, the force of fate
Cannot revive it.

Lady. Sir tis paſt my thoughts,
What ſhould incenſe you to this jealous rage

'Gainſt me your loyall wife, when no one blemiſh
Lyes on my ſoule that can give teſtimony
Unto my conſcience that I have not ever
Truely and chaſtely lov'd you.
  Sir Mart. Yes juſt ſo the greene
Willow and ſhady Poplar love the brooke,
Upon whoſe bankes they're planted, yet infect
By frequent dropping of their witherd boughes,
Its wholeſome waters ; that thou ſhouldſt be faire
And on the white leaves of thy face beare writ
The character of fouleneſſe, ſwallow up
In thy abyſſe of ſin, thy native pureneſſe,
As the high ſeas that doe with flattering curles
Intice the ſpotleſſe ſtreames to mixe their waves
With the inſatiate billowes, that intombe the innocent
    rivers.
  Lady. O me unfortunate woman.
  Pop. Good uncle ſpeake more kindly to her, alaſſe
ſhe weepes.
  Sir Mar. I ſee it nephew,
So violent raine weepes ore the purple heads
Of ſmiling Violets, till its brakiſh drops
Inſinuate among the tender leaves,
And with its waight oppreſſe them : theſe are
    teares,
Such as diſtill from henbane full of poiſon,
And craft as ſhe they come from : tell me woman,
Who haſt not ſhame enough left in thy cheekes
To cauſe a bluſh, darſt thou uſurpe the name
Of good or vertuous, when theſe eares can wit-
    neſſe
Thou didſt ſollicit yeſterday this youth,
To ſate the ravenous heate of thy deſire,
With all the eloquence well worded luſt
Could borrow to adorne its painted fowleneſſe.
  Lady. Was it you indeed ? I'm glad I know't
    deare ſir,
Had I the chaſteſt temper, that fraile fleſh
Could ever boaſt of, your ſtrange uſage of me,

Would undermine it: to forfake my bed,
Before my blood fcarce relifh'd the delights
Attending on young nuptialls, fo that I
Expect no anger from you if I feeke
That from the charity of other men,
Which your neglect (though you in duty owe it)
Will not allow me.
 Know. Well faid fifter.
 Sir Mar. Life fheel tell me ftraight
She will retaine before my face fome flave,
Some ftrong back'd monfter to performe her hot
Defires with able activeneffe, the flow
Motion of Snayles that carry on their heads
Their fhelly habitations to the pace
Of my dull rage, is fwift as érring flames,
Which had it not been leaden wing'd; as fleepe,
Ere this had feis'd the monfter.
 Lady. Ha, ha, ha, the man is fure diftracted, ha, ha, ha.
 Pop. Heyday, here's laughing and crying both with a winde,
As boyes doe, a juglar's but an affe to a right woman.
 Lady. Good fir will you walke? the gentleman hee's in a terrible fweat, fhould he ftand ftill, he may chance catch an Ague.
 Know. A Cardus poffet were very foveraigne for him, I perceive his fit is comming.
 Lady. How doe your husband, fweet heart, what not fpeake? I thought your jealoufie ere this had driven you into France, but now I'fee you feare to bee fea-ficke, you have found mee out it feemes; I hope ere long you will provide Goffips for the child I goe with, marke you ducke.
 Sir Mar. If I ftay, my rage
Will hurry me to mifchiefe, better leave her
To certaine ruine, then betray my felfe
To danger of it, when ftrong tides meete tides
In a contracted chanell, they their force,

Refigne to th' wearing of the troubled waves
A frothier livery, then when Oceans
Encounter with full liberty, the windes
Imprifond in the Cavernes of the earth,
Breake out in hideous earthquakes, paffions fo
Encreafe by oppofition of all fcornes,
Tis moſt opprobrious to be arm'd with hornes.

Ex. Sir Mar.

 Lady. He leaves you here fir as his fpie, do's he not?
Pray wait upon your mafter, I fuppofe he is fo.
 Pop. Pardon me Madam, he is my uncle.
 Lady. Which of his fifters fonnes are you?
 Pop. The Lady *Popingaies.*
 Lady. My cofen *Harry Popingay*; I cry your mercy fir : your good mother knowes, and grieves Ime fure, to fee her brother wrong me as he does : fhould I tell her how you dealt with mee too, fhe would chide you foundly.
 Pop. Your goodneffe Madam will forgive it on my fubmiffion and forrow for it.
 Know. Weel beg it for you fir.
 Lady. Sifter he has it, were it poffible
To worke a reclamation on this man,
From his fond jealoufie, I would not wifh
A change to be an Empreffe.

Enter Dalinea.

 Dal. Madam, my mother does entreat your Ladyfhips company in your chamber, Mrs. *Mixum* has brought the conferves my father did appoint her.
 Pop. Tis the fame face, or elfe fome Angel does Affume this fhape to mocke mortality,
With the true forme of beauty.

Lady. Nephew pray fee us oftner, and ufe all meanes to gaine your diftracted uncle from his frenfie, fifter fhall's walke; *Dalinea* be it your care to fee my Nephew forth.

Exe. Lady and Knoworth.

Dal. I fhall Madam.
Pop. Life fhe fpeakes too
A tempting language, fuch was our firft mothers voyce,
While fhe was innocent, moft perfect woman.
Dal. Would you have ought with me fir?
Pop. Yes bright vertue.
Dal. That title relifhes flattery for ought you know:
I may be vicious.
Pop. Goodneffe deludes it felfe then,
I cannot flatter Lady, you miftake me:
What I fhall fpeake, comes from an innocence
Yet undefild by falfhood.
Dal. Speake quickly, if it concerne me, otherwife I muft
Entreat a licence to depart.
Pope. You cannot
Affoord example of fuch cruelty
To following Lovers, to deprive my fight
So foone of yours, for whofe leaft view, the darke
Cimmerian, blinded with continuall fleepe,
Would rowfe his heavy eyelids.
Dal. Nay, and you
Begin to run a complement out of breath,
You'l drive me hence indeed: (believe me fir)
Had I not lik'd you well, my modefty
Would fcarce have fuffered the leaft enterchange
Of words (but fince it has done) pray be briefe,
What tends your conference to?
Pop. I love you Lady
With the religious fancy, that one Saint

Affects another; such a heate as mine
Was that, with which the first who ere knew love,
Had their soules warm'd (essentiall) not as now
The common garbe is to adore a lip,
Or any other lineament, but for
The abstract of perfection, which do's glory
In being deriv'd from one so good as you are,
Am I become your captive.
 Dal. This to me,
Sounds as the empty whistling of the ayre
Does in some hollow vault, unspotted truth
Informes my ignorance, there's not a person
In all the multitude of men loves chastly.
 Pop. Be so charitable
As to believe I can, who never yet
Knew flame was vicious, my desires retaine
Their maiden purity, no other object
Did ere attract my soules unblinded eyes,
But your faire selfe.
 Dal. Then I believe you sir,
No man will be so worthlesse to dissemble
With me, who cannot thinke but all the world
Intends the same reality that I doe:
Yet tis an errour, which perswasion scarce
Shall free me from: that every woman ought
To love a man with that indifferent heate
She fancies other women, without sence
Of difference twixt the Sexes.
 Pop. Soule of sweetnesse,
How equally an Angels intellect
Informes her sacred Reason: to love chastly,
Could not have bin defin'd with juster strictnesse,
Had we produc'd the constancy of Swans,
Or never changing Turtles, as our patternes,
(T'had but describ'd chaste love) the Palme that prospers,
(Not but by's fellow) and the Vine that weaves
Of her owne leaves a thinne, yet glorious mantle

For her naked lover. Doe but embleme what
Her truth has utt'red: but refolve me faire one,
Could you affect fo?
   Dalin. If that were all
Requifite to love, I could; but there's obedience
A Nuptiall wreath brings with it, which I feare
My frailty would fcarce keepe, and to become
Perfidious to a vow were fuch a finne
As I fhould quake to thinke of.
   Pop. You alledge
Vaine difficulties: I perceive your looks
Would be propitious to me, did your will,
Afham'd perhaps to fuffer fuddaine conqueft,
Not play the Tyrant with them, and call backe
The crimfon Nectar from your well-form'd Cheeke
To guard your heart from yielding: come, let's kiffe,
The modeft heate proceeding from my lips
Will thaw your foule to foftneffe.
   Dal. Away, we may not;
If true——chafte love had refted in difcourfe,
I could have beene its votary, but a thought
Of any thing beyond it, is to me
Dangerous as fickneffe: farewell fir.

                                      Ex. Dal.

   Pop. Sure fome white Cherubim,
Comming to teach the irreligious earth
The ancient truth; in its fwift flight to heaven,
Pronounc'd that happy farewell to the foules
Its muficke had converted. I've not loft
In my firft tryall, like fome ventrous man,
Who findes the Indies, though he get fmall wealth,
Yet he fets forth agen, in hopes at laft
To lade his winged veffell: Ile returne,
That fire's not out, which does in Afhes burne.
                                            Exit.

        Explicit Actus fecundus.

Actus Tertius, Scena Prima.

Sconce folus, dreffing his weapon.

Scon. SO, now it workes : the operation I believe is not on the fuddaine, and my wound rancles as faft as if hee had runne his Rapier through a Head of Garlicke, or wafh'd it in Aqua fortis ; and this weapon falve, fo much extold by th' Twiball Knights, commended by *Mixum*, deified by *Vrinall*, and adored by my believing felfe, procures no more miraculous effect, than if it were *unguentum album*. Well, I am confident yet, there's no defect ith' *unguent* ; my blood, my blood is fure anathemated ; carries fome curs'd impediment about it, that difannuls the vertue and incomparable force of the divine falve. This Dutch blood of mine, guilty of Bacon greafe, and potted Butter——Soft, who are thefe ? my Cozen *Fortreffe*, Generall of the Twiball Knights ; and his affiftant *Pirke*, with Mr. *Mixum* ; twere a detriment to valour to complaine before them.

Enter Mixum, Fortreffe, and Pirke.

Mix. Yonder's your Cofen talking to himfelfe : pray Gentlemen draw neare. Mr. *Sconce* I brought thefe friends to vifit you.

Scon. Thanks good Mr. *Mixum*, Cofen *Fortreffe*, and my Diminutive Captaine *Pirke*; give your hands, you are welcome, very welcome.

For. Health to the Weather-cocke of my Kin, the noble Signeur *Ieremias Sconce*.

Pirke. Propitious, and auſpicious be thy ſtarres, man of renowne and merit : ha thy arme in ſling my *Palmerin* : Confuſion Captaine *Fortreſſe*, he weares a wound about him.

Scon. No, no, a touch, a meere touch, a Flea-bite, Captain *Pirke*.

Mix. Is't not recover'd by the ſalve Mr. *Sconce* ?

Scon. Yes, as good as whole ; the weapon ſalve will remedy it.

Fort. Yes, paſt all chance it will : twill mundifie and purge your body Coſen : I uſe to combate three or foure at once, every ſpring, purpoſely to be let blood a little : it does me good all the yeare. after.

Scon. I am very glad of it. But tell me Coſen *Fortreſſe*, how fares it with the reſidue of the blades, the valiant Twiball Knights, the famous brethren, doe they walke in Coat gelt, or all a mode in *Dunkirke* Cloaks ?

Mix. Thoſe faſhioned Cloaks I never heard of before : I mervaile my Tayler gets not a patterne of them ; Pray ſir, what is a *Dunkirke* Cloake ?

Pirke. Not know a *Dunkirk* upper garment, a leaguer Cloak ; behold my *Io*, this Cane, this ſtaffe of office ; this wee ſtile the Millitarie Caſter.

Mix. Twill hardly keepe a ſhoure of raine out that.

Scon. Are they confin'd to Chamber ſtill, for want of Boots, or Linnen ? I love to heare of their proſperities.

Fort. Why Coſen they are well, but in the accuſtom'd garbe, the frugall brimme, and petty feather : they expect moſt carefully thy admittance into our Order.

Scon. 'T ſhall be done after my wedding Coſen. I have got, doſt heare ſirrah *Pirke* a girle of mettall, the

The Hollander.

Doctors daughter Bully, *Fortreffe*: Flesh of Milke and Roses Blade.

For. But Cosen, tis necessary, you inrole your selfe into the Family before you wed: our order, like the Knights of *Malta*, does admit no persons espoused: but with this difference, if they receive the Order Batchellours, they may then marry and yet retaine the title.

Scon. Say you so Cosen?

For. Certaine truth my *Io*: we met upon our grand Exchange last night, our place of trade and consultation, and there concluded some decrees, necessary for supporting our Commonwealth.

Pir. How perdition Captaine? how durst you meet without me? or conceite that decree valuable, which the voyce of Captaine *Pirke* has not assented to. Refuse me sir, the brethren of the Blades shall rue their bold confrontment: vengeance doe you take mee for a boy, or some *Pigwiggin*? consult without me?

Scon. Patience, good Captaine *Pirke*, I would faine heare them.

Pirke. He reads his necke-verse, reads them in my presence: Death rob me of the priviledge of my place and dignity Captaine, confound you, I could shew you *Twibill* for it.

Mix. What does this *Tom Thumbe* meane troe?

For. Why sirrah Dandiprat, you might have given attendance.

Pirke. What without a summons, you can send *Iacke Shirke* your Beadle, to congregate the meaner branches of the Brotherhood, not a Picke-pocket I warrant you, but had notice of it: and must I be forgotten? by my man-hood tis base.

Scon. You have given the Captaine too bold a touch Senior *Pirke*; thou art just like the Mouse to the Elephant, borne to vexe him: but prethee for my sake let him read them.

Pirke. Your sake prevailes, or otherwise——

For. Attend then Cofen *Sconce*; our Orders Ile affure you are fuch, as the moft envious Juftice, nor their Goofe-quill Clarks, that fmell at new Bridewell, and Finsbury fhall not exclaime on.. *Imprimis*, it is generally decreed.

Pirk. How, generally without me ? Fire of *Styx* this is infufferable.

Scon. Good Captaine *Pirke*, on cofen *Fortreffe*.

Fort. That no knight of the Twibill; as Whiskin or allye gentleman fhall prefume to lead or convey any of the fifters of the order, *viz.* Striker, Cockatrice, or Gynimeg through the watch after twelve, unleffe he fee them afleepe, or be in fee with the Conftable, under the penalty of being fent to the houfe of Correction.

Pirk. Renounce me fir, this order Ile not figne to, it favors of cowardife, feare to convey a fifter through the watch, tis againft Our noble inftitution.

Fort. Next it is enacted, that none of the groomes of our wardrobe fhall offer to deprive any man of cloake, coate, or hat, unleffe it be in the darke, as they feare to anfwer it at the next affifes, and be burn'd in the hand for it.

Scon. Twould be a hot touch for them cofen *Fortreffe*.

Fort. Next it is decreed, that the receivers of our rents and cuftomes, to wit divers Rookes, and Saint Nicholas Clearkes fhall certainely ufe no more flights to get more then they can clearely come off with, under penalty of being carried up Holborne in a cart, and at Tiburne executed, which may tend to the diffolution of our whole fraternity.

Scon. But have you concluded nothing for the fifters, I long to heare them ?

Fort. O yes cofen, we have confinde them to a certaine price, a ftipend reafonable, fo that they fhall not need to dive into pockets.

Scon. They will doe that if you would hang them cofen.

Pirk. I doe difclaime that order, Captaine *Fortreffe* your wifedome fhould have well confiderd at what charge they are, for coach or hand litter, fpecially thofe of the gentile garbe, next their ufhers muft be maintaind, paint payd for, cloaths provided and the matron fatisfied, thefe things confiderd, could you bee fo cruell as to confine them to a price by valour fir, I am afham'd on't.

Fort. Tis mended by the next order, they are prefcrib'd from wearing Plufh and Sattin, unleffe in peticoats.

Scon. You will not have them like the Jewes at Rome weare party coloured garments, to be knowne from Chriftians?

Fort. By no meanes fir, we would have every one take notice of them, but Marfhalls men, Beadles, and Conftables, and therefore have ordain'd that they fhall weare Beaver Hats, Poak'd Ruffes, Grogram Gownes, or at the beft wrought Taffata, Foxe Skinne Muffes, Moehaire peticoates, Bodkins and Crofcloaths edg'd with gold lace.

Mix. This is the habit of our Rotterdamians.

Fort. The only fhape to hide a ftriker in : ever while you live, your city is moft fecure from officers, and moft notorious to gentlemen, they will take up your city ware at any rate. Befides while they flanted it in plufh, 'twas an abufe to gentlewomen and Ladies, we have er'd in queftioning them for females of our tribe, and had our pates broake for it.

Scon. But cofen is this edict generally confirm'd by all the fociety of the Twibillers Knights and Ladies.

Fort. Tis univerfall cofen, only for Captaine *Pirkes* name, wee left a blanke, there's the decree fir, read it if you pleafe.

Pirk. Twas the fafeft courfe to leave a blanke for me, or I had Blank'd your whole decree! I had by magnanimity.

Scon. Imprimis, I Captaine Furibundo Fortreffe.

Mix. A fearefull name that fame.

Scon. Knight great mafter of the order of Twi-bill: Lord of no Cloke, Vifcount Ratan, cane and one fpur.

Mix, You are but an ill cocke of the game it feemes.

Scon. Count Freefe, gray Felt, and mony-lacke, Duke of Turnbull, Bloomesbury, and Rotten Row, Lord paramont of all Garden-Alleyes, Gun Ally, and Rofemary Lane.

Mix. He has more titles then the great Turke. Proceed fir.

Scon. Chief commander of all Twibills, dangerfeild and whiskins, who will quarell in Tavernes with a man, and not fight in the field with a moufe. And of the refidue of the fraternities of huffes, divers dammes and decoyes, fole fultan and grand figneur, have to the premiffes fet my mighty hand, together with hands of our trufty and our couragious affiftants (this blanke's for you Captaine *Pirke.*) *Holofernes Make-fhift, Rofiran Knock-downe,* and twenty fix more of our principall companions of the order.

Fort. Nay there are others too, bury not their appellations in oblivion, they merit memory.

Scon. To which at our command alfo are fubfign'd our moft illuftrious and remarkable fifters (they are flit nos'd perhaps) (there was a touch for them cofen *Fortreffe*) *Donna Iefabella Garreta,* mother of the maids of Lambeth Marfh, with her confpicuous confort, at the three skipping Conies in the towne, (a touch that) you meane the three Squirrels, you are cunning cofen *Fortreffe,* together with our moft induftrious fervant *Pythagoras* Pigge.

Pirk. I gave him that name from his tranfmigration into caft fuites, who has put his petie toes to it, and finally the woman that fings ballads, has her name trunled at the taile of it.

Mix. I mervaile mafter Doctor has not fet his hand to this.

Scon.   Seald with the feale at armes of our order, *viz.* Three Rooks volant in a field fanguine, two broken jugs the fupporters, and a Twibill for the creft, and given the fecond day of this prefent month, at our manfion royall, or place of meeting in the long gravield walkes in our ufuall fields.

Enter Doctor, Vrinall, Freewit, Sir Martine.

Sir Mar.   Well Mafter Doctor you'l remember me,
And have an eye unto my nephew, I truft
Her with you.   Farewell fir.
Exit Sir Mart.

Doct.   Doubt it not good fir *Martine*.
Fort.   Captaine *Pirke* pray retire unto the brothers of our Society: entreat them to prepare againe to morrow, for my cofen *Sconces* enfeafement.
Pirk.   Upon compulfion fir, I fhould refufe, marry on faire entreaty I doe flye, good and high fates looke on you.
Ex. Pirk.

Doct.   Sonne *Sconce* (I'm bold to call you fo) how do's your arme?
Scon.   Indifferent fir, but yet I have not found that rare effect ith' weapon falve you fpoake of, *Vrinall* I feare fince it cur'd the two ferjeants and their yeomen, the vertue has beene much extenuated.
Doct.   Twas your ill dreffing the weapon: give me your fword fonne, this is of the right falve the welfh Doctor makes, this fhall fave my credit.

Annoints the weapon.

Now *Vrinall* take this weapon, lap it warme in linnen cloaths, and locke it in my fonne, your anguifh fonne will foone be mitigated.
Scon.   I have a touch of it already fir.

Free. I have feene experience of this weapon falve, and by its moſt myſterious working knowne fome men hurt, paſt the helpe of furgery recover'd.

Mix. Marke you that maſter *Sconce*, the gentleman may be believ'd.

Free. Yet I cannot
With my laborious induſtry invent
A reafon why it ſhould doe this, and therefore
Tranſcending naturall caufes, I conclude
The uſe unlawfull.

Scon. He is unlawfully begotten fir, dares tearme it fo, there was a touch for him cofen *Fortreſſe*; I cald him ſonne of a whore, and he would take no notice of it.

Doct. But pray fir, why ſhould it be unlawfull?

Free. Caufe Confcience and religion difallow
In the recovery of our impair'd healths,
The affiſtance of a medicine made by charmes,
Or fubtle fpells of witchcraft.

Scon. His mother was a witch, faies this maide, fo there was another touch for him cofen *Fortreſſe*, fon of a witch, but he underſtands not that neither.

Doct. Conceive you this to be compounded fo?

Free. Ile prove it maſter Doctor.

Scon. The proofe of a pudding is the eating, in your teeth fir, a pudding in his teeth: you know what I meane cofen *Fortreſſe*, another touch for him, but al's one, he has wit in's anger, and wil not underſtand me.

Fort. If he durſt blunder for it Cofen *Sconce*.

Free. Yet to avoide a tedious argument,
Since our contention's only for difcourfe,
And to inſtruct my knowledge, pray tell me,
Affirme you not that this fame falve will cure
At any diſtance (as if the perfon hurt

Should be at Yorke) the weapon, dres'd at London,
On which his blood is.

Doct. All this is granted 'twill.

Scon. Nay we'l grant you more fir (that it will not) and yet prove it, and you ſhall prove your ſelfe a (ſo you ſhall.) There had been another touch for him coſen *Fortreſſe,* but I fear'd hee would have underſtood me now, ere you ſhall prove it.

Fort. Silence coſen *Sconce,* let's heare the whiffler if he cannot verifie his words, ſink me my Jo, he ſhall taſte arme of dangerfield.

Free. Out of your words ſir Ile prove it Diabolicall, no cauſe
Naturall; begets the moſt contemn'd effect,
Without a paſſage through the meanes, the fire
Cannot produce another fire untill
It be apply'd to ſubject apt to take
Its flaming forme, nor can a naturall cauſe,
Worke at incompetent ſpace: how then can this
Neither conſign'd to th' matter upon which
Its operation is to cauſe effect;
Nay at ſo farre a diſtance, worke ſo great
And admirable a cure beyond the reach
And law of nature; yet by you maintain'd,
A naturall lawfull agent, what dull fence can credit it.

Scon. Very authenticke this, well if the divell have tane the paines to be my ſurgion, my arme I feare will be poſſeſt, I feele an evill ſpirit in it already.

Fors. Reſpect the Doctors anſwer.

Doct. Sir, you ſpeake reaſon, I muſt confeſſe, but every cauſe
Workes not the ſame way; we diſtinguiſh thus:
Some by a Phyſicall and reall touch
Produce: So Carvers hewing the rough Marble,
Frame a well poliſh'd ſtatue: but there is
A virtuall contact too; which other cauſes
Imploy in acting their more rare effects,

So the bright Sun does in the folid earth,
By the infufive vertue of his raies,
Convert the fordid fubftance of the mold
To Mines of mettall, and the piercing ayre
By cold reflexion fo ingenders Ice ;
And yet you cannot fay the chilly hand
Of ayre, or quickning fingers of the Sunne,
Really touch the water or the earth.
The Load-ftone fo by operative force,
Caufes the Iron which has felt his touch,
To attract another Iron ; nay, the Needle
Of the fhip guiding compaffe, to refpect
The cold Pole Articke ; juft fo the falve workes,
Certain hidden caufes convay its powerfull
Vertue to the wound from the annointed
Weapon, and reduce it to welcome foundneffe.

 Scon.   The falve is legitimate agen, Cofen *Fortreffe*, O rare Doctor.

 Mix.   Nay, you fhall heare him tickle the gentle-men I warrant you.

 Free.   This, Mr. Doctor, is
A weake evafion, and your purities
Have fmall affinity ; the glorious Sunne
As tis a generall inftrument of heaven,
In all its great productions, and the Ayre
An Elementall agent, naturally
Ingender Mettalls in the earth, and Ice
On the felfe frifling waters : The Load-ftone
As tis a fimple body, may afford
That vertue to the fteele by fecret power
Of all-commanding nature. But that this,
This weapon falve, a compound, fhould affect
More than the pureft bodies can, by wayes
More wonderfull than they doe, as apply'd
Unto a fword a body voyd of life,
Yet it muft give life, or at leaft preferve it.

 Scon.   Pifh, he talkes like an Apothecary to the Doctor.

 Doct.   You miftake, it does not,

Tis the blood flicking to the fword atchieves
The cure: there is a reall fimpathy
Twixt it, and that which has the juyce of life,
Moyftens the body wounded.

Fort. Rare *Paracelfian,* thy Annalls fhall be cut in Brafle by Pen of fteele.

Free. You may as well
Report a reall fimpathy betweene
The nimble foule in its fwift flight to heaven,
And the cold carkaffe it has lately left,
As a loath'd habitation; blood, when like
The fap of Trees, which weepes upon the Axe
Whofe cruell edge does from the aged Trunke
Diflever the green Branches from the Veines,
Ravifh'd, forgoes his Native heate, and has
No more relation to the reft, than fome
Defertleffe fervant, whom his Lord cafts off,
Has to his vertuous fellowes.

Enter Miftris Know-worth.

Know. Mr. *Free-wit* return'd agen, and in difcourfe
With Mr. Doctor: Ile not difturbe your conference.

Doct. So pleafe your Ladyfhip we had even done.
I am glad fhe's come to refcue me.

Scon. There was a touch for him Cofen *Fortreffe, victus, victa, victum,* he lookes like a Schoole-boy vanquifh'd at capping verfes: harke you fir, repent your errour, and in time you may bee fav'd; you fee the vertue of the falve the Doctor had drefs'd his Speaking weapon with it. It hurt you, and it has cured you Beware you fall not into a relapfe: there was another touch for him Cofen *Fortreffe.* Doctor give your hand (father I fhould have faid) fome fam'd Hiftorian, fome *Gallo-Belgicus* fhal Chronicle thee and thy falve, there was a touch for him Cofen *Fortreffe*. Come you fhall fee my Miftris.

Exeunt Sconce, Fortreffe, Mixum, and Doctor.

 Know. Mr. *Freewit* have you yet found the in-jur'd
Woman out, I motion'd at laft parting?
 Free. Truely Miftris, had fhe bin worthy the feek-ing, your
Command fhould not have beene protracted, but
'Twere a ftaine to my owne honour to be inqui-fitive
After a proftitute, and a blot to your
Difcretion, fhould nice judgments know you enjoyn'd me
So manifeft a folly.
 Know. 'Twas a greater, to be the author of her fhame,
Whom now you flight fo infinitely.
 Free. Could I flight her more,
'Twere a due juftice which I owe my felfe,
(In hazarding the forfeit of your love)
Undone by her, but your moft ferious thoughts
Will fure convert your foule from the intent
Of my moft certaine ruine, which your laft
Difcourfe perhaps, for triall of my faith,
Seem'd to invert upon me.
 Know. You miftake;
Needleffe are fecond trialls, when a firft
Proves you perfidious ; doubtleffe you confirm'd
Your love to her, with the fame fad protefts
You've done to me (yet left her) for her fake,
And in revenge of womans innocence, martyr'd by you,
I here to heaven pronounce a fure disjunction
Of our loves and vowes for ever.
 Free. O referve that breath,

Which ought like facred incenfe to be fpent
Onely on heaven, or in delivering notes
May charme the world to peace, when raging
    warres
Or Earth quakes have affrighted it. Confum't
On no fuch ufe, horrid and ominous,
As if it threatned thunder to the earth,
Or would infect the genius of the ayre
With Mifts contagious (as if compos'd
Of Viper fteame) O and you were wont
To be fo good, that vertue would have figh'd
At the unwelcome fpectacle) if you
Had appeared woman in a paffion,
(Though of the flighteft confequence) O do not
Renounce that Saint-like temper, it will be
A change hereafter burthenous to your foule,
As finne to one, who all his life time bleft
With peace of Confcience, at his dying minute,
Falls into mortall enmity with heaven,
And perifhes eternally.
 Know. Thefe words
Have not the effectuall Oratory you firft had,
When I was confident, as day of light,
Your youth had beene as deftitute of vice
As of deformity. So a fweet ftreame,
Whofe bubling harmony allur'd the Birds
To court its moving muficke, when it mixes
With impure waters, with the noyfe affrights
The eares, before delighted in it.
 Free. This is too fevere a Juftice, and extends
To cruelty, had fome intemperate rage
Purpled my hand in murther (though the guilt
Would have beene written in a larger Text
In Confcience blacke booke ; yet the punifhment
Had not bin halfe fo hideous. I fhould for that
Have fuffered bnt a temporary paine
At worft ; and my truely repentant foule
Perhaps have had free entrance to the place
Confign'd to penitents, when now, like fome

Manacled Captive, or difeafed wretch,
On whom each minute does beget a death;
I like a flow fire by my owne foft ftames,
With Tortoyfe fpeed extinguifh.

    Know. Sir, your words
Are fuperficiall, as a fhadow which
The morning Sunne produces and blacke night
Renders forgotten: and no more excite
Beliefe in me: that what you utter's truth,
Then Mandrakes groanes doe a conceite of death
In perfons refolute, while I have yet
A fpecious memory left, that once my heart
Tendred you dearly; I would counfell you
Firft to indeavour to finde out that maid,
(If that fucceed not) not to thinke of me,
As one affianc'd to you by a neerer
Intereft then other women are that never
Had converfation with you.

    Free. Had **a** froft,
Sharpe as a tedious winters Northerne blafts,
Congeal'd your mercy, my unfained teares
Should with moyft warmth diffolve it, miftris you
Approach fo neare the attributes of heaven,
That had you liv'd ith' fuperftitious age,
More pretious gums had fum'd upon your altars,
Then on all female deities. O forgive me,
A rigorous tyrants breath will fcarce pronounce
For one and the firft crime, fo ftrict a fentence:
You fhall not goe yet if you will recall it,
Lovers will bleffe your piety, and fubfcribe
To your fuperlative goodneffe.

    Know. Pray defift, affoord me liberty to retire, I
cannot alter my refolution.

    Free. Yet reclaime it;
Some divells fpleene has lately fraught your breft,
And banifh'd thence milde pitty, boiftrous winds,
Force fo the gentle and untroubled feas,
To fwallow up fome fhips, its naturall calme-
    neffe

Would have tranſported ſafely with their wealth
To their deſired harbors) were my thoughts,
Not fix'd with that religion upon you
That are my prayers (when I repent) on heaven,
I ſhould not thus tranſcend the lawes and ſtrength
Of manhood, and like ſome diſtreſſed babe
Left by its parent to the deſolate woodes,
Or ayres cold charity, ſo long implore
A new and holier union twixt our ſoules,
Then ere had link'd them: which when you have tied,
Time ſhall depend like ſummer on your brow,
And your whole life be one continued youth,
(Such were the ſprings in paradiſe) and when
You paſſe to be a ſharer in heavens bliſſe,
Virgins and innocent lovers ſpotleſſe teares,
Hardned to pearle by the ſtrong heat of ſighes
Shall be your monument.
    Know. I ſhall relent
Spight of my ſetled will if he continue
Theſe moving ſupplications: Sir becauſe
You ſhall not blame my cruelty, or judge
Tis for regard of any thing but my honour,
I doe forſake you, if ere to morrow night
You finde that woman, get her to renounce
Freely her title to you, I agen
On promiſe of your future loyalty
Will ſtand the triall of your wavering faith,
Perhaps be yours agen: you have
Receiv'd my utmoſt meaning.
                                Exit. Know.

    Free. How I adore
This conſtancy of worth in her, though
It make againſt my ſelfe, well I muſt to my taske,
That labour's richeſt that moſt paines doth ask.

              Explicit Actus tertius.

Actus Quartus. Scena prima.

Enter Doctor and Lady Yellow.

Doct. 'TIS a ſtrange humour Madam, and con-
demnes
Your judgement of much indiſcretion,
Did I not know it lawfull; nay no way
But that for the recovery of your health,
I ſhould not urge it thus, you are lately falne
Into a deſperate melancholy, and your blood
Can no way purge ſo well as by
Performance of what I have declar'd.
    Lady. Truth ſir I weigh not at ſo high a rate, my life
That to prolong it to an irkeſome age,
I ſhould deſtroy my honour, neither doe I
Finde any ſuch ſtrange fickneſſe raining on me
As you have urg'd; pray as you love me ſir,
Unleſſe you meane to drive me from
The houſe, repeate this argument no more.

Enter Sir Martine and Vrinall.

    Vrin. Why looke you ſir, my maſter has
Perſwaded her as much as lay in him, and
He has a tounge able to coſen the divell: but twill
not doe,
She is too honeſt believe it, for your nephew Sir *Mar-
tine,* ſhee

Has kept her chamber ever since she came,
None but my selfe has seene her.
   Sir Mar. It shall be so, the holy law of heaven
Made us one individuall, the strickt league
Twixt man and wife, ought to confine both soules
To a most constant union, injur'd woman.
   Lady. My husband and on the suddaine, speake you to me sir.
   Vrin. His mouth opend Ime sure, sir the Dutch Gentleman.
   Doct. O my sonne *Sconce*, come hither *Vrinall*.
   Lady. This acknowledgement cannot
Be serious from him, good Sir *Martine*
Has your wilde fancy not impos'd enough,
Temptations on my fraylty that you come after
So many strange indignities, againe to delude me.
   Sir Mar. Tis misery of customary sinners when they meane
A reall truth, then their precedent ills,
Deprive it credit, Madam not that night,
That sacred night which spred its starry wings,
(Like Curtaines shadowing the Altar) ore
Our Hymeneall couch ; could witnesse more
Sincerity of indissolving love 'twixt us,
Then does this minute if your soule,
(Which is so passive it may justly challenge
A Martyrs temper) can dispense with pas'd
Absurd distastes, and like a Saint for humane
Condition is too vengefull freely pardon
What I amisse have acted.
   Lady. As you are my husband sir, and consequently my head.
   Vrin. How many Ladies in towne are of that minde.
   Lady. And ought to be the guider of my youth,
I will not stand on that nice terme of honour,

With you whom duty ties me to obſerve
With more then ſuperficiall care, t' injoyne
A penance for your folly ; the light ſmoake
Findes not a ſurer buriall in the ayre
(To whoſe embraces with ambitious haſte
On azure wings it ſoar'd) then has your guilt,
In this forgiving boſome, this pure kiſſe ſeales the agreement.

 Sir Mar. She offred firſt too, and methought ſhe kis'd
As ſhe would eate my lips, the ravenous touch

Sir Mar. ſtarts.

Of her hot fleſh has ſeard me up like graſſe
In ſummer time, and her fowle breath like blaſts
Of Southerne windes, has quickned my dead fire
Of jealouſie, nay rais'd it to a greater
Heate then my former.

 Lady. What ayle you fir on a ſuddaine ?

 Sir Mar. Viper, toad, out of my preſence, ere my juſt wak'd
Rage, get to its height, whence like a Falcon towring
At full pitch ore the trembling fowle, it will ſeaſe on thee.

 Doct. Madam tis beſt to leave him, I feare he's abſolutly franticke ; *Vrinall* looke to him, leaſt he act ſome violence on himſelfe, pleaſe your Ladiſhip withdraw.

 Lady. Soft patience guard my heart : wheres no offence,
One ſafely may rely on innocence.

Exit Lady and Doctor.

 Vrin. Why ſir *Martine*, how doe you ſir ? not ſpeak ? now by my life, he lookes like a ſtaggerell newly come to his Hornes, flings his head juſt in that manner they do not touch the feeling, yet Sir *Martine* : in time they may be three and foure at top, and ſerve to hang hats and cloakes on in the beſt knights hall in towne.

Sir Mar. O *Vrinall*.

Vrin. O *Vrinall*, what a pittifull noate was there, that very found has almoſt crack'd me to pieces : Sir *Martine*, good Sir *Martine* what ayles you? or rather what ayles your wife, that you hum and haw ſo after kiſſing her, her breath is ſavory, I dare bee ſworne ſhee has neither eaten Onions nor drunke Aquavitæ.

Sir Mar. O no, ſhe is like a too ripe, ſo extreamely ſweet,
Shee poiſons like the hony which ſmall Bees
Sucke from the Aconite, the Panther ſo
Breaths odors pretious as the Sarmaticke gums
Of Eaſterne groves, but the delicious ſent
Not taken in at diſtance choakes the ſenſe
With the too muskie ſavour.

Vrin. You ſhould have kis'd her as the Court faſhion is, upon the cheeke, but pray ſir, why are you ſo jealous : yet cannot prove your Lady has a trick with her toe, or turnes oftner than an honeſt woman (if ſhee do) had not you better like an old Stag, caſt the cogniſance of your order into the hedge, then like a wanton Pricket, runne full Butte at every one you meet, as who ſhould ſay ; take notice of my horns. I am aſhamed of it ſo I am.

S. Mar. Do'ſt not believe I am? a hideous cuckold.

Vrin. And muſt you needs cry Cuckow therefore. There are knights in towne who know their Ladies to be Hens oth' game, and live by tredding, yet like mettle Cockes they never hang the Gills for't, they are ſure faire Gameſters uſe to pay the boxe well : eſpecially at In, and In, (the Innes of Court Butlers would have had but a bad Chriſtmas of it elſe) and what care they, ſo they can purchaſe pluſh, though their wives pay ith' hole for it.

Sir Mar. Can there be such monsters?

Vrin. Monsters, they are men Sir *Martine*, such as you are: onely they are velvet browd a little: but heare me Sir, if a man would venture faire offer to give a certain knowledge of your wifes honesty.

Sir Mar. Doe that, and be my genius *Vrinall*.

Vrin. You would have an evill Angell of me, Ile tell you sir; my master intends privately this night to wed his daughter to the Dutch younker *Sconce*, the house will be at quiet, and your Lady left alone in her chamber, her sister Mistris *Knoworth*, being to goe to Church with them.

Sir Mar. What of this?

Vrin. Soft and faire Sir *Martine*, I will ith' evening steale you into the Ladies chamber when she's in bed, come to her, and in the darke, (thats the only time to deale with a woman) (and as another man) trie what you can doe with her: if she consent (the worst) you doe but cuckold your selfe, if hold out, being a woman alone, in bed, and in the dark having a man standing by her, you may then conclude her an honest wife, and your jealousie foolish, as your vexation needlesse, you thinke I have no wit now I warrant.

Sir Mar. According as my soule could wish.

Vrin. Why law you then, who's the foole now? Sir *Martine* come in the evening, I will not faile you.

Sir Mar. Nor I hopes of triall, fare you well,
A jealous man has in his heart his hell.

Ex. Sir Mar.

Vrin. Well knight, if I doe not fit your jealous head, let me bee sung in ballads for an erranter coxcombe then your selfe.

Enter Miſtris Artleſſe, Miſtis Mixum, and Dalinea.

Miſt. Art. Well ſaid minx, you will not have him but you had beſt conſider and doe as I and your father would have you: or you ſhall trudge for it, you ſhall be his wife.

Miſt. Mix. Nay in ſadneſſe Miſtris *Dal.* you are too blame, the gentleman is an honeſt gentleman, I and a kinde man I warrant him to a woman; your mother and I have made triall of him, and finde him of a very good diſpoſition, come chicke you ſhall have him.

Mrs. Art. Nay let her chuſe and bee hangd, proud baggage who will refuſe a gentleman of my owne chuſing, but Ile ſend him to you and ſee if thou darſt deny him, for thy life, come Miſtris *Mixum.*

Exeunt Miſtris Artleſſe and Miſtris Mixum.

Dal. Was ever innocent virgin thus betrayd
By cruelty of parents, who for wealth
Have ſold my youth to ſlavery, the cold
Aſhes of injurd maids ſurround my heart,
Or ſome divine dew, ſtead of blood repleniſh
My ſwelling veins, circle my thought with Ice,
Thou power of chaſtity, that like the freſh
Primroſe uncropt, by any hand, I may
Returne my ſelfe as pure and white
To earth, as when I came from't.

Vrin. How doe you Miſtris *Dal.* alaſſe poore gentlewoman, would they have thee coverd with a Friſland horſe, a Dutch Stallion: now ſhame upon their ſoules that wiſh it, he's neighing here already.

Enter Sconce.

Scon. Vrinall, my cofen *Fortreffe* and the reſt oth' Knights will be here preſently; pray you prepare the muſicke and the wine, I would not faile in the moſt diminute ceremony.

Vrin. Of a moſt abſolute coxcombe, I ſhall provide them ſir.

Exit Vrinall.

Dal. Now begins my horror,
The fatall Bell ſhould it proclaime my death,
Were ſpheare-like muſicke to his night-crowes voyce;
Yet I muſt heare it and retaine my ſenſe,
Continue ſubject to a daily noyſe
From the ill boding monſter.

Scon. Lady or Madamoſell, Vfroe or Seniora what you pleaſe, or in what language to be entituled the Miſtris of my thoughts, the complemental garbe is cuſtomary, and though I have learn'd by converſation with the Twibill Knights to kiſſe my hand, believe me I had rather beſtow my lips on yours; our naturall Dutch contracting is the beſt, without deceit or ſhadow, there we only goe to th' taverne and be ungue browd, then drunke together. Ther's all our ceremony, and tis lawfull marriage too.

Dal. Would you would ſir, better conſider with your ſelfe and match where your own cuſtomes are obſerv'd, my feare my quality will never ſuite the liking of your Dutch manners.

Scon. Manners Lady, you miſtake I've none at all; ere we will diſagree about manners, Ile be as clowniſh as an Upland Bore, foutra, tell a Dutch man of manners ?

Dal. Yet ſir have ſo much charity.

Scon. We deteſt that worſe then the former, tis Papiſticall, and was with that religion baniſh'd our reform'd Commonwealth: but to our buſineſſe, pretty foule, I fhall give thee touch mon and get a burger of thee.

Dal. Gentle fir, there ought to be in manhood a divine
Pitty, believe me as I tender truth,
I cannot fet the fmalleft of my thoughts
On your ill welcome love, therefore I befeech you
Not to proceed in my unfortunate match
Which will be fatall to us both, for goodneffe
Have fo much mercy on me.

Scon. An excellent touch that, as if there could be mercy in a Dutch-man, and to a woman? if there had beene any, the Nuns at Tilmont had not beene us'd fo horribly laft fummer: why fhould you fay you cannot love me? tis a falfe touch Ime certaine of it, I fhall know anone, till when receive your lips in pledge that no fuch words fhall iffue forth of them, adiew Lady, anone we muft to the old touch of Matrimony.

Ex. Sco.

Dal. The hand of death
Shall give me firft a bride to fome darke grave,
Where I will mixe with wormes before the Prieft
Knit fo unjuft an union, the kinde graffe
Will fure be greene ftill on my Sepulchre,
And fpotleffe Virgins annually dance
A fairy ring about it.

Enter Vrinall and Popingay in difguifed cloathes.

Vrin. Now if you doe not catch a Roach in her troubled waters, I fhall conclude you a gudgion: fpeake to her, a woman has ever a hole open to receive a mans tale, believe it you fhall have my my affiftance, and if I doe not fecond you confidently, may my tongue be cramped, my wit breech'd; and the machina of my invention ruind perpetually.

 Pop. Fairest creature.

 Dal. Had you said wretched'st, Mistris you had given me
My proper attribute.

 Pop. Can there be on earth,
A savagenesse so great as will conspire
To afflict so rich a goodnesse? yet by your eyes
Adorn'd by those cleare pearles which doe transforme
Even sorrow to a lovelinesse beyond
Indifferent beauty, I conceive some fiend
Rested in humane shape (for man would never
Have dar'd so vile a sacrilege) in hope
By your pure teares, t'extinguish his owne flames
Caus'd this distemper in you.

 Vrin. Pish you are long to speed, be
Short and quick, that pleases Ladies.

 Pop. I had a younger brother, though not fully blest
In your sweet knowledge, yet once his tounge
Was his hearts bold embassador, and deliver'd
A true narration of his zealous love,
Which is in him so permanent, that when
His eares receive a notice that your faith
Is plighted to another, twill be Juice
Of balefull hemlocke to his braine, convert it
Either to suddaine madnesse or a sleep,
Cold and erelasting.

 Dal. I remember once
A nephew of Sir *Martines* did sollicit
That which he term'd my love, but I conceiv'd
His meaning rather was to cause discourse,
Then that his strict intention had resolved
His promises performance.

 Vrin. Did I not tell you she would come about?

Pop.   Truſt me Lady,
The ſolitary Nightingale who ſings
To her loſt honour a harmonious ditty,
Loves not the thorne ſo dearely, to whoſe pricks
She ſets her featherd boſome, as Ime ſure
My brother tenders you, the gawdy light
May ſooner be obſcur'd by wandring ſmoake :
Nay the eternall eſſence of the ſoule
Become corporeall and reviſite earth,
After its flight to paradiſe, ere he
Deſcend to variation of his love,
Could you affect him.
   Dal.   Had your brother been
Of the ſame diſpoſition and ſoft ſweetneſſe
That I perceive in you (though this be our
Firſt enterview) there could not have beene molded
(Had I beene borne to entertaine loves heat)
A man that would ſo fitly ſympathize
With my condition, nor whom I ſhould fancy
With more intire perfection.
   Vrin.   Strike home, and ſure the iron's hot
   already.
   Pop.   Behold him Lady,
Whoſe every motion does as from the ſpheare,
Receive a lively influence from your lookes ;
The modeſt ſilence of the temperate Even,
When zephire ſoftly murmures to the flowers
A wholeſome farewell undiſturb'd by ſtormes,
May ſooner reſt in one continued night,
Then can my ſoule in quiet without juſt
Aſſurance of your love, which if you grant,
Times native Belman, the ſhrill Organd Cocke
Shall ceaſe to carroll Mattens to the morne,
The earely Larke that whiſpers to the Sun
A conſtant Augury of a beauteous day,
Shall loſe his light plumes in the checkerd Clouds,
Ere I my reſolute chaſtity, nor can you
Invent evaſions to decline my ſuite,
Since on its grant relyes the only hopes

Of your redemption from the barbarous armes,
Of him you were efpous'd to.

Dal. This furprize,
And your ftrong vowes would batter a refolve,
Downe in a breft that could be flexible
To eafy love, but fince I cannot frame
My confcience to a warrantable zeale
Toward any man, Ile rather fixe my hate
(For that muft of neceffity accrue
To him that weds me) on a perfon worthy
Contempt, then on your felfe, whofe worth do's chal-
 lenge
A noble and reciprocall regard
For your affection, bleffings on ye fir,
Thinke not amiffe of me.

Exit Dalinea.

Vrin. Now the curfe of a tedious virginity light on ye, you will not be tupped by a Dutch Ram, a Haufen Kender, a Weftfally Bore-pig, now the iniquity of a fwagbellied Hollands Burgers get thee with childe of a dropfie, if thou marrieft him, why how now Mafter *Popingay*, ftroken with a Plannet ? tis a female Star, as changeable as the Moone, goe to your chamber, I heare company approaching, this Dutch Butter-Firkin fhall bee melted to greafe ere he fhall have her truft to it.

Pop. Paffion on paffion fall when hopes are
 fpent,
The beft of comforts is a forc'd content.

Exit.

Vrin. So here comes my blades, now plot but
 hit,
And *Vrinall* fhall be ftil'd the Lord of wit.

Exit.

Enter Sconce, Fortreffe, and Knights.

Scon. Cofen *Fortreffe* welcome, welcome Captaine

Pirke, valiant brothers, nay gentlemen, then your accoutrements be of the vulgar cut, be not daunted, tis hereditary to Low Country fouldiers to weare off reckonings, the time ſhall come the little worme ſhall weave, and ſilken tribute pay to men of ſervice, give me your hands gentlemen, I ſhall be one of you anone, but Coſen *Fortreſſe*, what baſhfull youth is that that dares not thruſt his noſe out of his coate, for feare the winde ſhould blow it to his face, ha?

Fort. Tis flat enough already, this my Jo, nay ſhow thy Phiſnomy, h'is our quondam truſty attendant, but now Knight of the Twibill, Pithagoras Pig.

Scon. Is this the famous off-ſpring of great hog? we ſhould be kindred certainely, my Anceſtors were Bores, give me thy fore-foot ſirrah, and tell me coz, why doſt not wander 'into a new skin? this begins to crackle vilely.

Pirk. O tis for want of baſting ſir.

Fort. No my Jo, hee caſts his skin but once a yeare, like the poore ſnake: well, he has done our Order ſpeciall ſervice; but coz, where are the preparations the vancarriors coz, to the ſolemnity of your inſtalment? renounce me, if you vilifie the inſtitution by diſregard of properties, this hand ſhall never croſſe the Twibill ore thy head, nor give thee thy avant chevalier, while thou art mortall my Jo, I ſay I ſhall not.

Pirk. No matter ſir *Sconce*, by the head of valor, my ſelfe ſhall dub thee.

Font. Who you King *Twadle*? Muſhrome you dub him?

Pirk. Yes, I *Gog, Magog*, I dub him *Gargantua*.

Ent. Vrin.

Scon. Nay good coſen *Fortreſſe*, Captaine *Pirke*, this *Vrinall* I could e'ne fill him to the brim with curfes, but here's my agent; come where are the mufitioners *Vrinall*?

Vrin. They will bee loud enough by and by, I warrant you.

Fort. This is legitimate blood of the Spanifh grape my Jo.

Scon. Lufty facke credit me coz, twill give the touch, *Vrinall* make faft the doore, and leave us, and give us notice if any body approach.

Vrin. What hafte this gull makes to cheat himfelfe in private, muft the muficke enter?

Exit. Vrin.

Fort. No by no meanes, weel call to them through the doore, varlet avoide. Now coz, to beginne our ceremony: firft, drinke to me.

Scon. I like it well when it begins with drinks, tis a figne twill end merrily; this cup is abominable too little, one can fcarce wet his whiftle out of it, it fhall be this goblet, a voftre grace, coz *Fortreffe*.

Fort. Sir *Pithagoras* we doe create you skinker, it fhall goe round my blades, you fhall dible in liquor of account; here brother *Make-fhift*.

Make. Gramercies Captaine.

Pirk. Choake you fir, learne manners, offer to drinke before betters, tis an affront to feniority, deftroy me if I can fuffer this, no forfake me Captaine I cannot.

Scon. There was a touch for you brother *Makefhift*, but good little *Pirke* be patient.

Mak. This Preface is very Cannonical my *Io*, nay, I fhal learn the phrafes inftantly.

Pig. Have you all had it brothers?

Pig. All but my felfe Sir *Holofernes*.

Scon. Who my coz *Pig*, off fup off thy wafh my Jo, at worft thou canft but be fwine-drunke; but coz, fhall we difpatch? I long to be inftald.

Fort. I now we'l to't, come hither Captaine, fing the hymne preparatory to Knight-hood, but wet your pipes firſt, Ganimed, they 'l ſqueake the better.

Scon. An admirable touch this, what 's next troe?

Song.

Fort. Now coz *Sconce*, our Order does conſtraine us to a frisk, a dance about you, as the Fairies tred about their great King *Oberon*.

Pirk. But can this muſicke play the Twibill dance, none elſe will ſatisfie.

Scon. Muſicke you muſt play the Twibill dance he ſayes, dance ſo while.

Dance.

They dance, the wine ſhall tread a ſink apace into my belly, you have loſt one of your beſt heels coſen.

Fort. No me Jo, twas off before the ceremony is halfe accompliſh'd, you are our wardrope keeper, brother *Knockedowne* have you brought the veſtments of our Order?

Knocke. Fuſe Captaine not I.

Pirk. Rot me ſir, you would be made to fetch them.

For. How, not our robes of honor the enſignes of our chevalry?

Knock. Sinke me, ſir you know they are in tribulation.

For. Hell take the Broker: we muſt perforce imploy one of our owne ſuits.

Knock. Take my Buffe Jerkin Captaine.

Make. Death keepe it on, you'll ſhew your dirty ſhirt.

Pirke. Found you ſir, you lye: I fathome in your guts, hee has none on.

Make. How, ſonne of foule Adultery, the lye?

For. What doe you blunder, whifflers Pigge, are you grunting too: ſhall I whet my Twibill on your bones nips of debility?

Scon. Nay, Cofen, Gentlemen rather than you ſhall fall out, Ile be content to bee dub'd in my own cloathes: nay pray you Gentlemen.

For. Tis againſt order, and we muſt obſerve ceremony.

Scon. O by all meanes Coz.

For. Firſt then receive this cap of maintenance.

Scon. Cap of Maintenance doe you call it? I will maintaine when this old Cap was new, 'twas a Dutch felt, but now tis nine degrees below a ſtraw Hat; I doe not like this touch: but Coz I ſhall have my Bever agen I hope?

Fort. How? ſuſpitious my *Io*: Brother *Knockdowne* diſroab his necke of this old linnen, favours of a winding-ſheet: this is *Decimo Sexto*, feares no rumpling: Now Cofen *Sconce*, you muſt difcuſſe your doublet.

Scon. That will be damn'd inſtantly; pray heaven my skinne ſcape.

For. Here ſir, receive this Military Caſſocke, 't has ſeene ſervice.

Scon. 'T has been ſhot through both the Elbowes; this Military Caſſocke has I feare, ſome Military hangbyes: this Twibill Knight-hood is but a louſie Order, would I had ne're medled with it.

Fort. Now you appeare ſomething above an Embrio: *Makeſhift* helpe to untruſſe his breeches.

Scon. I ſhall be whipt inſtantly: But Cozen *Fortreſſe*, is there no redemption for my Breeches?

Pirke. Sume me Captaine, tis not requiſite he ſhould put off his Breeches.

Scon. Thankes good Captaine *Pirke*, twas a friendly touch that.

Pir. May not his tranſitory money ſerve to excuſe his breeches?

Fort. To him it may.

Pir. A Twibill Knight ought to regard no money, but the gliftring fteele.

Scon. Well, fince it muft be fo, there take my money.

Knock. Paw fir, you lofe the priviledge of the Order, if you refpect your money.

Scon. Now doe I looke like —— as if I were new come from the Lottery : or what fay you Sir *Holofernes*, to the Picture of the Prodigal in the painted Cloath ? Sure I have now perform'd all the Ceremonies ; if not, Ime fure I have nothing elfe left to performe withall.

Fort. So, now kneeele downe, while thus I thee create : *Ieremias Sconce*, Knight of the order of Twibill. Now avaunt Chevaleire.

Omn. Health to our worthy Brother, *Ieremias Sconce*, Knight of the Twibill.

Fort. But brothers, there is Sacke yet to be drunke, in Celebration of this Knight-hood.

Scon. I like this drinking heartily; there's fome goodneffe in 't : will you beginne, my Captaine Generall ; Ile call you fo now.

Fort. Pythagoras, fill his Bowle up. Capt. *Pirk* this *Cornucopia* to my Leiftenant Generalls health ; Ile call you fo now.

Scon. A place of Marke and Charge that.

Pirke. Man of valour, refpect this Cup to the health of our Leift. Generall.

Mark. A vous brother *Knockdowne*.

Knock. Here Sir *Barrabas*.

Scon. Altogether gentlemen, a health Mufitians,

found.

Gentlemen all *tres humblement ferviture voftre* : I ha done you right.

Fort. Expect me *Jo* ; heart of my father, you muft for confummation of your inftallment, drinke a cup a piece to each of us.

Sconi Twas my intention Generall : to you all in

generall, helpe *Pith.* let it be two Captaine, tis pitty to put fo many worthy men in a pint pot.

Pirk. Soule of my valour, y'are fhip'd fir, you muft drinke five together.

Scon. Y'are wanton Captaine, a wag upon my Knight-hood, you meane to meafure the profundity of my belly, twill bee a hard taske to doe it to a Dutch-man——looke you Captaine.

Fort. Thou fhalt be my *Bacchus* Io, he drinkes as if hee had eaten Pickle Herring.

Scon. This Cup was as deepe as Fleet-ftreet Conduit. Sound me my *Io*, I ha' made a new River in my Belly, and my Guts are the Pipes: Tother cup good wreckling, vertue fhall be vertue ftill, fo long as I can ftand Captaine.

Fort. That will not be long I hope.

Enter Vrin.

Scon. This Coller fpoyles my drinking, or elfe this Sack has horfe-flefh in't, it rides upon my ftomacke. O *Vrinall*, Ime a Knight of the Twibill honeft *Vrinall*.

Vrin. Take heede you'll crufh me fir to pieces. Gentlemen yonder are the Conftables at the doore to apprehend Captaine *Fortreffe*.

Scon. Some more facke firrah, I fhall be married anon.

For. That's I, tis for the linnen brothers: Hell my *Io*, how fhall I fcape them?

Scon. More Sacke firrah, the tother touch fweet Pig, the tother touch.

Vrin. There is no way but one fir, they have befet the houfe; my Mafter is perfwading them. Follow mee, Ile by a backe way fet you fafely out with your company.

For. Noble *Vrinall*: come Blades here's purchafe for us.

Exit Vrinall cum Knights.

Scon. This is but foure Cups captaine Cofen Pigge. *Skinke* my parting Cup, and then Ime gone: ha! where be you Gentlemen, I am not blinde, or play you at Boe-peep? they are gone, this is a pretty touch, my touch my *Jo*, with my money and Cloathes, a pretier touch still, let me see, they have left some Sacke behind them, there's my comfort yet.

Ent. Poping. and Lovring in womans cloaths.

Who's this? my wife that must bee,
Come hither wife, thou seest the worst of me
I am but drunke: Kisse me *Borankee*: never feare, I will not spoyle thy gorget. Hark in thy eare my *Io*, shall I have a gentle touch? twill doe no harme, wee are to be married anon thou know'st; I shall get wife children on thee.

Lov. What wouldst thou ravish me libidinous Swine?
Strive, and thou dyest.

strikes up his heeles.

Scon. Twas an unkinde touch that, my *Io*, you might have falne under me, 't had beene the fitter place for a woman, pray helpe me up agen.

Lov. Yes, to thy death, if thou deny t' performe what I enjoyne thee.

Scon. How, kill a Knight of the Twibill, and in the Ensignes of his owne Order, ere it shall be said to the disgrace of Knighthood, that any of the fraternity was kild by a woman, Ile doe any thing: Lead on, Ile follow you.

Pop. Thus they must strive,
Who in loves subtle Merchandise will thrive.

Exeunt.

Explicit Actus quartus.

Actus Quintus, Scena prima.

Enter Doctor, Vrinall, Mris. Artleſſe, and Mris. Mixum.

Doct. THis ſtealth was unexpected, tis almoſt
Beyond beliefe, my daughter ſhould thus change
Her perverſe humour, and embrace his love
Which when I motion'd to her, the darke ſhade
Seem'd not a greater enemy to bleſt light
Than ſhe appeard to it : and that ſhe ſhould
Coſen my hopes, and without me her mother,
Or any friend reſigne her will to his,
And ſtrike the match up, puzzles my beſt faith,
Though I rejoyce at it.

Vrin. You have reaſons ſir to doe ſo, your daughter had more wit then you expected, tis the quality of maids, to deny what they deſire : had you but ſeene how nimbly ſhee trod over the threſhold, you would have ſworne ſhe had beene mad of the match: I ſtood and heard him aske her : ſhall wee goe to the Church? Church anſwerd ſhe, iſt not too late quoth he agen, never too late to doe well replied ſhe agen : (though it were at midnight) and then the Dutch younker tooke her up into a (what doe you call it) a ſedan (and heaven ſpeed) away they went, marry to what Church, he's gone I know not, only I heard him ſweare he would not come at Pencridge.

Mrs. Art. And why not ; tis an ancient Church, and all old things muſt not be caſt away, there has beene many an honeſt couple given to the lawfull bed there, ſo there has.

Vrin. No matter for that, he proteſted he would be marryd in a Taverne ere that Pencridge, there's no drinke nere it, but at the Pinder of Wakefield, and that's abominable, and he has vowd to ſeaſon their bargaine with a cup of Sacke ere they returne.

Miſt. Art. Hee will not bee drunke on's wedding night I hope; my daughter would have a ſweet bed-bellow of him, if he ſhould.

Vrin. There is another loving couple gone with them too for company, who will be man and wife if the Prieſt ſay Amen to it.

Doct. Who are they of our knowledge?

Vrin. O yes ſir, tis Maſter *Lovering*, the attendant to Maſter *Knoworth*, and Sir *Martines* Niece that came but yeſterday.

Doct. Is't poſſible? twas ſome ſlie policy of her Uncles to bring her hither, Maſter *Lovering* knew her before it ſeemes.

Vrin. Too well I feare ſir, they would not have marryd in ſuch poſt haſte elſe.

Mrs. Mix. Well Maſter Doctor, I hope my gloves ſhall bee better then the ordinary, I had no ſmall hand in this match, you know.

Doct. Tis nine a clocke at leaſt: twill not be long ere they returne, wife pray goe in and ſee all things in readineſſe for their lodgings.

Mrs. Art. They will have more ſtomacks to their beds then to their ſuppers.

Doct. To morrow we'l celebrate their nuptiall feaſt: *Vrinall* be you carefull of the doores; let none come in but our owne company.

Vrin. Ile locke them up, and keepe the keyes my ſelfe ſir, Mrs. *Mixum* your husband is with them, and in his abſence I would deſire a word with you.

Mrs. Mix. I love to talke with any man in my

husbands abſence; ſweet *Vrinall* I will fulfill your
pleaſure, will you goe Miſtris?

Ex. Vrin. Mrs. Art. & Mrs. Mix.

Vrin. So now have at her.
Doƈt. Have I not plotted finely? has my braine
Not won the lawrell garland the famd breath
That wafts the honor of deſerving wits
Among the humorous multitude (as lowd
As it ſpeakes conquering triumphs) ſhall proclaime
My politicke merit, who have raiſed my ſelfe
From worſe then to name in the judging world,
To an indifferent wealth, which though I've got
By wayes ſiniſter, ſuch as erre from truth :
Nay might incurre a puniſhment no eyes
Has ere diſcern'd them, but with wonder how
I ſhould atchieve ſuch fortune, now compleat
In this alliance.

Enter Lady Yellow and Knoworth.

Lady. Siſter let's to our chambers and to bed,
That time approaches.
Doƈt. Your good Ladiſhip (I hope) will honour me
ſo much
As for an houre to diſpenſe with reſt,
And ſee my bride in bed.
Lady. Your bride good Maſter Doƈtor, who ſhould
that be?
I underſtand you not.
Doƈt. My daughter Ladies, that to me
And all the houſe ſeem'd ſo averſe from marriage,
Is this night ſtolne forth with younker *Sconce*,
And is by this time wedded to him.
Lady. Beyond wonder, well ſir,
We'l have her bride garters, it ſhall goe

Hard elfe, fifter could you have thonght it?
  Doct. You may both credit it, inftantly they will
returne, and then Ile wait upon you.
                                    Exit Doctor.

  Lady. I pitty the poore girle
That fhe fhould be fo fuddaine in her choyce,
Enthrall her foule ith' manacles of fate,
(For fuch are nuptiall bonds) experience fifter
Inforces me to lament her.
  Know. How equally we two
Divide true forrow, fympathize in griefe,
As in our blood and nature : fifter you
When your affectionate fancy fix'd your heart
Upon your husbands love, had no fufpition
Of his unmanly jealoufie, and I
When I confin'd my love to *Freewits* breaft,
Judg'd him as void of falfhood, as the fpring
When it has refted in green robes, the Earth
Is of bare nakedneffe, but we are both
Deceiv'd by our credulity.
  Lady. For you,
Difcretion may releafe you from the care
Of his affection, you are free (as light)
(Which in the darkeft night retaines fome fplendor)
From the obedient flavery, due to marriage ;
But I no burne-markd captive is engag'd
With more officious zeale to ferve his Lord,
Then I my husband, I muft either perifh
Like the chafte ice, when from a Chriftall Rocke,
It feeles a fad converfion into fowle
Corrupted waters, by his jealous flames ;
Or breake thofe ties whofe diffolution
Would betray my innocent vertue to a ruine,
Sure and eternall.
  Know. But yet counfell me,
I love this man fo that if honour would
Difpenfe with his offence, I fhould forgive him,

And take him to my bofome.
 Lady. Alaffe you cannot,
What noble foule (though halfe ftarv'd) would be fed
With bafe reverfions, confcience too forbids
The fupplantation of another, fifter
Strive to forget him.

    Enter Vrin.

 Vrin. Mrs. there is a gentleman without, has knockt for entrance as if he had beene a Conftable, his bufineffe is with you, and his name *Freewit*; I told him you were in bed, and he fwore he would come to you through the doore, fhall I admit him?
 Know. This is his laft night, his bufineffe carryes weight, pray let him in. Be now propitious Love : is any with him?
 Vrin. There is enough of him, unleffe he made leffe noife. Ile fend him to you.
 Lady. Sifter, now give him his lateft anfwer, and refolve
Upon fome choife more happy : here he comes.

    Enter Freewit.

 Know. How, as a Bridegroome?
Deckt with the Enfignes of young Nuptialls,
A wreath of Flowers, and Bayes, and yet me thinkes
His hand difplayes a Willow; what fhould this Embleme?
Mafter *Freewit* we fcarce expected you thus late.
 Free. You'll pleafe to afford my manners an indulgent pardon,
For preffing to your prefence thus : but tis

Perhaps our extremeſt enterview, and ſo
May challenge the prerogative of excuſe,
For the audacious errour.
    Know. Would I could,
With as much ſafety to my honour, grant
Remiſſion to your other fault.
    Free. My thanks
Are humble debtors to you for it, Miſtris,
The nimble minutes have with crafty theft,
Stolne time away, reduc'd your limited houre
To an unwelcome period : I have ſought
With the ſame diligence good men ſeeke heaven,
What you injoyn'd me, but the raine that falls
In Summer time upon the parched duſt,
May eaſier be reſtor'd to the moyſt Clouds,
Then ſhe to my diſcovery. Wherefore ſince
Her loſſe is certaine, and the loſſe of you
Depends on her, to ſatisfie your ſoule
That I have man about me, I am come
With the ſame confidence your ſcorne has taught me,
To tell you, I as lightly prize your love,
As you have valued mine : nor can you blame me,
    ſince 'twas your owne deſire.
    Know. Credit me Ime very glad on 't : pray tell me ſir,
Why you come thus adorned with Nuptiall wreathes,
Into my preſence ? is 't to invite me to your wedding,
    or expreſſion
Of your contempt, I have not merited ſo harſh an uſage.
    Free. Neither : This branch of forſaken Willow I reſigne
To your owne wearing, that when after times
Shall know our mutuall parting ; 't may report,
That we were both forſaken, though we ſever
With the unwillingneſſe that flouriſhing trees,
Diveſt themſelves of greeneneſſe, yet no blemiſh
Of harſh unkindneſſe ſhall defile our thoughts :

                                          L 2

We'll part faire, though for ever.
   Lady. This gentleman feems fo noble, I repent that I advis'd her from him.
   Free. This Laurell wreath, that circles
My uncaptiv'd brow, I doe juftly challenge,
Since I have conquerd the greateft enemy,
Mankind can combate (paffion) yet the dew
(That on the red lips of blufhing Rofe
Beftowes a weeping kiffe) leaves not fo fadly
The amorous flower, that curles its purple leaves,
To hide it from the Suns enforcing Rayes,
As doe my thoughts your memory, which did once
Preferve it as inviolable, as heaven
Does the bright foules of innocents.
   Kno. You might
Have had fo much humanity, as to have kept
Your purpofe to your felfe : though your loofe finne
Conftraines my honour to renounce your love,
I would not have my eares difturb'd with this
Relation of your contempt, for fo
Truft me I take it *Freewit.*
   Free. Why, good Madam ?
Can you condemne my too officious truth,
Of a conceite of falfhood, when the fpring
Of my Revolt, derives its head from yours.
You for a triviall, and fcarce knowne offence,
Could without fcruple banifh me your heart,
When Angels fhould, for a defertleffe kiffe
From an impure lip, have renounc'd their bliffe,
Ere the moft urgent reafon of fufpect,
Should upon me have practis'd a contempt
Of you : Had not your breath expos'd a mift
Of infidelity before the eyes
Of my cleare feeing foule, and left it blinde
As the blacke Mole, that like a Pioner digs
A winding Labyrinth through the earth to finde
A paffage to the comfortable light,

He never has fruition of.
  Lady.   But ſir,
Suppoſe my ſiſter did it for a proofe,
Of your affection, and now ſhould reclaime
The harſh preſcription ſhe impos'd, you would not
Continue in this temper.
  Free.   Madam ever.
The Cedars juyce, whoſe bitter poyſon gives
The moſt ſtrong body unavoyded death,
Preſerves the Carcaſſe by its dying force,
Voyd of corruption : ſo has dealt her love
With me ; its reclamation ſtrucke me dead,
And ſince my Exequies has kept my heart
From entertaining a corrupt regard
Of future ſlavery.

Enter Doct. Vrin. Mris. Artleſſe.

  Vrin.   They are entred, ſir, I heard Mr. *Mix.* ſay as I let them in, that they were marryed.

Enter Mixum with a Torch, Popingaies in Sconce his cloaths, leading Dalinea : Lovering leading Sconce attired in Poping. womans cloaths.

  Mix.   Nay, come an end gentlemen and your wives, Mr. Doctor wil not be angry though I have uſurp'd his office, and beene the father to his daughter.
  Doct.   You are not a cunning baggage ? you would none forſooth when I propos'd it to you ; but when the fit came on you, you could then runne madding, and never let the Sexton ring the Bell to give us notice : had it beene any one but Mr. *Sconce,* you ſhould have fought a portion ; but ſince to him, we pardon it : take her ſonne, heavens give thee joy of her.

Vrin. You would fcarce fay fo, knew you as much as I doe.

Pop. We thanke you fir, and reft your dutifull children.

Lad. Ha! my Nephew *Popingay*!

Doct. Mr. *Popingaies*, Sir *Martins* Nephew! I am abus'd, undone, my daughter's coufend *Vrinall*, a tricke put on mee, Mr. *Popingay* to wed my daughter.

Pop. Twas with her owne confent Sir, and fhe my wife by your free gift.

Mrs. Art. Your wife, your whore fhe is as foone, fhe is Mafter *Sconces* wife, and that you fhall finde, fo you fhall, let me come to the baggage husband, Ile fcratch her eyes out.

Doct. Ere he fhall injoy her, Ile fpend the beft part of my wealth he fhall not have a penny portion with her, depart my houfe I charge you: *Vrinall* call in my neighbours, ere Ile be us'd thus.

Vrin. Harke you fir, you know I know you and your wayes.

Doct. What talk'ft thou varlet?

Vrin. Goe to, be patient, then give this gentleman your daughter; nay be friends, and love him too, or all fhall out.

Doct. Thou wilt not betray me villaine?

Vrin. But I fhall difcover you and your practifes, nay to the Juftice,

This gentleman is the fame Sir *Martin* brought hither as his Niece.

Doct. Plots upon plots againft me.

Vrin. But the great one is ftill behinde: if you will be friends quickly with them, fo; if not, your impoftures all come out.

Doct. Is it even fo? well fince I am ore-reach'd,
Better fit downe in peace, than with difgrace:
Mr. *Popingay* confideration of your juft defert,
Now his perfwafion has fupprefs'd my heat,
Enjoyns me to forgive your loving theft;

Accept my daughter with as good a heart
As ſhe is mine : come hither wife, ſay you ſo
   too ?
  Mris. Art. Nay, ſince you ſay it, it muſt be ſo.
  Pop. Humbly I thanke you : ſuch another gift,
Should Nature offer all her pretious ſtore,
Could not be given Mortality : but truely ſir,
I had much adoe to winne her.
  Dal. You have me now ;
But I profeſſe untill we came to be
Conjoyn'd ith' Church, I tooke you for Mr. *Sconce*,
   but now rejoyce
I was deceived ſo, I ſhall ſtudy to love you.
  Doɛt. Now you name, where is Mr. *Sconce* ?
  Scon. Tis my cue now. O father I'me here they have given mee a touch, a very ſcurvy touch, I am a brother of the Twibills, and I am married too, but I need not feare being a Cuckold.
  Vrin. Mris. you know the Gent.
  Know. My ſervant *Lovering* married to Mr. *Sconce* !
You'll get brave boyes I doubt not.
  Scon. I and wenches too ; come hither, we will be man and wife, that's certaine, nay and lie together, ſo we will, you ſhall behave your ſelf well enough like a woman : but that you have a ſtiff impediment for bearing Children : but give me thy hand, ſhal's be drunk together !
  Vrin. He is ſcarce ſober yet I thinke.
  Scon. Ile tell you father, ere I went to the Church I had gotten a touch in the Crowne, the Twibil Knights, confuſion on them my Jo, had made me drunke, and got my cloathes, and how I came by theſe I know not : But ha, let me ſee, this ſhould be my ſuite, tis it, by valour it is : doe you heare goodman Foxe, how crept you into this Lyons caſe ?
  Pop. What meanes this new married man ?
  Scon. Do you jeare me, with a touch of that ?

harke you husband, Though I be your wife, you shall
not hinder me from claiming my owne Breeches. Mis-
tris a word with you too, you put a gentle touch upon
me did you not? But I shall know you hereafter, Ile
say no more, and touch you boldly for it.

 Lov. Y'are very merrily dispos'd Sir: had it not
beene to have done Sir *Martines* Nephew, I should
not have beene fool'd so.
Ile trie his temper though.

 Know. No matter *Lovring* thou art a Gent.
And since I am resolv'd from Master *Freewit*,
That heele not have me now (though I were wil-
 ling)
To roote the least remembrance of him
Out of my breast, by this my happyer choyse,
Ile marry thee.

 Scon. But let him marry you though if he dare, Ile
sue the Statute of Bigamy upon him, he shall be
hang'd for being double marryed.

 Free. In this one act
She onely appeares woman, all the rest
Speake her a Saint. I did not thinke her heart
Could have resum'd (though 't had rejected me)
A baser choyse. Sir you've good Fortune: Mris
I will not wish you ill succeffe in your
So suddaine Love: but it was cruell in you
To give away your foule, (as in despight)
In my loath'd presence: yet to shew how much
I prize your satisfaction, I resigne
My interest in you to him, and thus freely
Bestow him on you: will you have him Lady?

   *Pulls of Loverings Periwigs, he is discovered to be
   Martha.*

 Lady. Heaven blesse me sister, this is the same
 maid
Whom Master *Freewit* is reported to have

Got with Child: this is ſtrange.

 Free. Nay, be not amaz'd Miſtris it is ſhe:
You had beſt call her to a ſtrict account
How long tis ſince I lay with her.

 Know. O *Freewit*, what meanes this mad deluſion?

 Scon. My wife turn'd a woman indeed: this is a touch indeed, I had beſt be gone, for feare ſhe challenge me.

 Vrin. O ſtay your patience good Mr. *Sconce*.

 Free. Now let heaven, and all that can be titled
 good beneath
Divinity, conjoyne to frame a piece
Of vertue great as this; yet be deficient
In the atchievement; for ſome cunning Artiſt
To draw her in this poſture (to be plac'd
(In Alablaſter, white as her owne figure)
Or ſome greene meade, or flowry valley, where
Poſterity of Virgins yearely might
Offer a teare to the bleſt memory
Of perfect feminine goodneſſe. Let me dye,
Gazing on you, and I ſhall flye to heaven
Through your bright eyes.

 Doct. Sir, what meanes this extaſie?

 Free. Ile tell you, and Mrs. truſt each word,
As the juſt accent of Oraculous truth:
Knowing your ardent love to me, I feard
It might embrace a change, and therefore ſhap'd
This woman in the habit of a man,
Got her unknowne to you, prefer'd to ſerve you:
(Which ſhe could not have bin without diſcovery,
In her owne ſhape) not to o're-looke your life,
Or watch your actions, but to raiſe report
That I had bin falſe: ſo to trye if that
Would ſtagger your reſolve, which I have found
So noble, that the happineſſe of Fates
Can give no more addition to my bliſſe.
Madam beg you my pardon.

Know. O sir you have it,
And I my best of wishes, but why did you
Employ a woman thus disguis'd, suppose
She had beene got with childe, you must
Have beene the father of it.

Free. I knew she was too honest, and beside,
I put her to the acting of't, because
She being the accuser of me for her selfe
Might without the least scruple of suspect
Free me from her owne calumny, nay here's another
Can witnesse this for truth.

Know. How *Vrinall* Master Doctor's man turnd to *Tristram* Mr. *Freewits* man, and *Marthaes* brother?

Vrin. So it appeares by the story Mrs. I am glad sir you put my sister in this disguise, she has got a good husband by the shift, take your wife sir, she is no worse a woman then my owne sister.

Scon. But let me see and feele you better, it is no periwigge this but are you my husband, a woman, wife?

Lov. I your wife am sir.

Scon. Master Doctor you wish me well I know, I have married here I know not whom, you have excellent salves and unguents sir.

Doct. They are at your service all.

Scon. Thanke you good Mr. Doctor, have you never a one that will eat off the wen of manhood, make all whole before, that will eunuchise a man, I would faine be a Hermaphrodite, or a woman to escape this match, I do not like it.

Enter Mrs. Mixum.

Mris. Mix. Help gentlemen, help Mr. Doctor, yonder is a man would ravish me whether I would or no, nay kild me, I thinke he has] puld out the longeſt naked weapon, O there he is.

Ent. S. Mar. drawne.

S. Mar. She ſhall not ſcape me where ſhe
Fenc'd with fire, ſtrumpet thou dieſt.
  Doɛt. Who's this, Sir *Martin*, what doe you meane ſir?
  Mris. I, this is he *Thomas* doe you ſee what a terrible thing hee has got? was that fit to uſe to a woman? I was but laid in the next roome, to ſleepe, and he would have done ſomething to mee ſo hee would, had not I beene the honeſter woman.
  Lady. Is't ſo Sir *Martine*? I have now juſt cauſe
To ſuſpect your loyalty, and that your fond
Jealouſie proceeds out of intemperate luſt,
Could I not ſerve, but underneath my noſe
You muſt be rioting upon another?
  Sir Mart. Shame and confuſion ſeaſe me.
  Vrin. You may ſee Sir what comes of your jealouſie, but feare not Sir, your wife will pardon it, there's no harme done.
  Mrs. Mix. But there might have beene, had not my honeſty been the greater.
  Lady. Well Sir *Martine*, though you have injurd
Me moſt infinitly, I doe remit all if you will proteſt
Nere to be jealous more.
  S. Mar. Amaſement and my ſhame hinders my utterance,
Let me breath in ſighes my true repentence,
And henceforth
That jealouſie in man if't be injuſt
Is ill, nay worſe then in a womans luſt.

Know. But pray you brother, who brought you hither ?
We ſhall rejoyce to have you at our wedding, And ſee this reconcilement.

Vrin. I Madam, I ; under pretence to have attempted his wife, but I ſent him in to *Mrs. Mixum,* who I knew would fit his turne.

Mrs. Mix. And ſo I could have fitted him as well as another woman.

Scon. Brother *Vrinall* you are a knave, brother *Vrinall,* and have ſhowd all a cozening touch.

Vrin. No ſir I ſav'd you from being cozend, my fiſter ſhall have ſome portion, here's a hundred pieces in this purſe.

Scon. Sinke me my Jo, my owne purſe.

Vrin. It is indeed Sir, I got it from your Twibill brothers, and this your watch too, and your cloths which Mr. *Popingay* weares, by locking them into a roome, and threatning puniſhment, if they denied, the blades ſhall now reſume freedome, this key will let them out, come forth gentlemen, here is your brother Maſter *Sconce.*

Enter the Twibill Knights.

Scon. Captaine generall, give thy hand bully, Captaine *Pirke,* my coſen *Pig,* and all of you ; though you would have cheated me tis no matter, you ſhall dance at my wedding, and be drunke too, my Joe, you ſhall.

Pirk. Confuſion rot the bones of *Vrinall* perdition ſhall ſlay him.

Free. Madam I hope we ſhall keepe our nuptiall feaſt with Maſter Doctor.

Know. As you diſpoſe it ſir, I have reſign'd my will to yours.

Pop. Unckle I hope you'l pardon me, that I de-

ceiv'd your expectation in watching my Aunt, she is too vertuous: father your blessing, and then we are happy.
   Doct. Take it.
Thus all are pleas'd I hope: what this night cannot
(For celebration of these feasts) performe,
To morrow shall, and from this minute I
Renounce all waies sinister to get wealth.
Things that ith' period prosperously succeed,
Though cros'd before, are acted well indeed.

FINIS.

WIT IN A CONSTABLE.

[1640.]

WIT IN A Conſtable.

A Comedy written 1639.

The Author
HENRY GLAPTHORNE.

And now Printed as it was lately Acted at the Cock-pit in *Drury lane*, by their Majeſties Servants, with good allowance.

LONDON:
Printed by *Io. Okes*, for *F. C.* and are to be ſold at his ſhops in Kings-ſtreet at the ſigne of the Goat, and in Weſtminſter Hall. 1640.

To the Right Honourable

his fingular good Lord

THOMAS
LORD
WENTWORTH.

My LORD,

SO many are the noble attributes inherent to *your* Heroicke *Nature,* that 'tis difficult to diftinguifh whither they be *divers,* or one intire *virtue,* but impoffible to define which ought to be accounted the Superlative in fo perfect a

The Epistle Dedicatory.

Harmony: to ascribe to *one* more then to *another*, were to derogate from the justice of *either*. I cannot therefore proclaime 'twas any particular, but *your* generall *Goodnesse* which has imboldn'd me to intrude this *Poem* on the Patronage of *your* Name, as honourable in *vertue* as in *Greatnesse:* nor shall I tender any excuse for the presumption, since I am assured *your Lordship* cannot conceive an anger from the true devotion of

Your humblest honourer,

Hen ; Glapthorne.

The PROLOGUE.

YOu need not feare me Gentlemen, although
   I come thus arm'd; tis but to let you know
I am in office; in my owne defence,
And to secure me from the violence,
Which might from you (who now my Iudges sit)
Be off'red to this Trophee of my wit:
And cause I know that you will obay
Authority, I doe charge you, like the Play:
Thinke who I am, how often I may catch
You at ill houres in Tavernes, or ith' Watch;
In Fraies sometimes; nay sometimes (not to trench
Too much upon you) with a pretty wench.
All this is possible, and Gentlemen,
Consider how my rage will use you then,
If you should now, as sure tis worth your feare,
Be in the censure of my wit severe,
Vext I'me implacable; and though the Tribe
Of Constables doe us't, Ile take no bribe
To let you passe: These sturdy knaves will take
Not the least mercy on you for my sake:
Nor will the Iustice free you: (to your smart)
You'le find, he and his Clarke will take my part.
I can but gently warne you to prevent
A danger, nay a certaine punishment,
Should you dislike: for if the Play doe fall
 Vnder your votes, Ile apprehend you all.

The Perſons in the Play.

Thorowgood, *a young Gentleman, ſutor to* Clare.
Valentine *his friend, a ſutor to* Grace.
Knowell *their friend.*
Sir Timothy Shallowit, *a Country Knight.*
Sir Geffery Hold-faſt, *a Knight of* Epping.
Jeremy Hold-faſt, *his Sonne.*
Alderman Covet.
Buſie, *a Linnen Draper, the Conſtable.*
Triſtram, *ſervant to* Jeremy Hold-faſt.
Formal, *ſervant to Alderman* Covet.
A Parſon.
Foure watch-men.
Clare, *neece to Alderman* Covet.
Grace, *his Daughter.*
Maudlin, *ſervant to* Clare.
Nel, *daughter to* Buſie.
   Fidlers boy, Drawer, Attendants.

The *Scene* London.

Wit in a Conſtable.

Actus primus, Scena prima.

Enter Holdfaſt, Triſtram.

Holdfaſt.

ID you ere we departed from the Colledge
Orelooke my library?
   Triſt. Yes ſir, I ſpent two dayes in
ſorting Poets from Hiſtorians,
As many nights in placing the divines
On their own chayres, I meane their ſhelves, and then
In ſeparating Philoſophers from thoſe people
That kill men with a licenſe: your Phyſitians
Coſt me a whole dayes labour, and I finde ſir,
Although you tell me learning is immortall,
The paper and the parchment, tis contayn'd in,
Savors of much mortality.
   Pold. I hope my bookes are all in health.

Trist. In the fame cafe the Mothes have left them,
    who have eaten more
Authenticke learning then would richly furnifh
A hundred country pedants; yet the wormes
Are not one letter wifer.
    Hold. I have beene idle
Since I came up from Cambridge, goe to my ſtationer
And bid him fend me *Swarez* Metaphyfickes,
Tolet de anima is new forth,
So are *Granadas* commentaries on
Primum fecundæ Thomæ Aquinatis,
Get me the *Lyricke* Poets. And ———
    Trist. I admire
How he retaines thefe Authors names) of which
He underftands no fillable, 'twere better
I bought the *Authenticke* Legend of Sir *Bevis*,
Some fix new Ballads and the famous Poems
Writ by the learned waterman.
    Hold. *Iohn Taylor*, get me his nonfenfe.
    Trist. You meane all his workes fir.
    Hold. And a hundred of *Bookers* new Almanacks.
    Trist. And the divell to boot,
Your fathers bookes in which he keeps th' accounts
Of all his coyne will fcarce yield crowns to afford
Your fancy volums: why you have already
Enough to furnifh a new Vatican,
A hundred country pedants can read dictats
To their young pupills out of *Setons* logicke,
Or *Golius* Ethicks, and make them arrive,
Proficients learn'd enough in one bare twelmonth
To inftruct the parifh they were borne in: you
Out of an itch to this fame foolifh learning
Beftow more money yearely upon bookes;
Then would for convert fifters build an almes-houfe.
    Hold. You will difpleafe my patience *Triftram*.
    Trist. I fpeake truth: if you fhud want, your
    learning fcarce would make you

Capable of being town Cleark, or at beſt,
To be a famous Tyrant unto boyes,
And weare out birch upon them: or perchance
You may arrive to be the City Poet,
And ſend the little moyſture of your braine
To grace a Lord Maiors feſtivall with ſhowes,
Alluding to his trade, or to the company
Of which he's free, theſe are the beſt preferments
That can attend your learning.
   Hold. I ſay *Triſtram,*
The ſpirit of my learning ſtirs me up
To give thee due correction.
   Triſt. Would you ſtudy?
As does young *Thorowgood* your noble Coſen,
Not bookes, but men which are true living volums:
You would like him, be held rich ith' eſteeme
Of all the illuſtrious wits that decke the city
When the extent of your admirers is
Confinde to freſh men: and ſuch youths as only
Know how to frame a ſyllogiſme in *Darij,*
And make the ignorant believe by Logicke
The Moones made of a Holland Cheeſe: and the
   man in't.
A ſwagbellied Dutch Burger.

      Intrat Thorowgood.

   Thoro. Coſen *Holdfaſt,* a good day attend
Thy learned piamater: prithee tell me
How doe the *Cabaliſts* and antient *Rabbins*
And thou agree? will they be ſociable,
And drinke their mornings draught of Helicon
With thee: have they inſtructed you to prove yet
That the world runs on wheeles? or that the ſea
May be drunke off by a ſhole of Whales? ſuch
   things
You know there are in nature.
   Hold. O far ſtranger.

Thoro.   Peace you booke-worme,
Fit only to devour more paper then
A thousand grand tobacco men or a legion
Of boyes in pellets to their elderne gunnes.
Dost thinke to live this life still? you're not now
Amongst your cues at Cambridge, but in London,
Come up to see your mistris beautious Clare,
The glory of the city: goe and court her,
As does become a gentleman of carriage,
Without your Tropes and figures Inkehorne termes,
Fit only for a Mountebanke or Pedant,
Or all your Physickes Metaphysickes and Meteors,
(Tomes larger farre and more replete with lies,
Then *Surius, Gallo-Belgcus,* or the welsh
Bard *Geffrey Monmouth*) shal be straight-way made
Pitifull Martyrs.
   Hold.   Why cosen I had thought.
   Thoro.   Thy selfe an errant ideot, that's the fittest
Thought for thy braine more dull then a fat Burgers,
Or reverend countrey justices, whose wit
Lies in his spruce clearkes standish, thou wert begot
Surely ith' wane oth' Moone, when natures tooles
Were at lame *Vulcans* forge a sharpening,
Thou art so lumpish.
   Trist.   He has already spoyld
His eyes with prying on Geneva prints,
And small dutch Characters: his watching makes him
Looke like a grand-child of old *Errapaters,*
Some leane Astronomer who to get ten shillings,
For that's a large price for an Almanacke,
Has wasted himselfe to the bignesse of his *Iacobs* staffe,
Which is so limber, 't cannot stand to take height of *Venus* rising.

Thoro. He fayes truth: befides your ftudy has
 attain'd already,
Learning enough to informe your minde the know-
 ledge
Of arts fit for a gentleman, wert not better
For you my fprightfull fenior to advance
Your bever with a hatband of the laft
Edition in the Court, among the nobleft.
Youthes of our nation, then to walke like *Fauftus,*
Or fome high German conjurer, in a cap
Fit for a Cofter-monger, to weare your purle
Or cut worke, band then this fmall fnip of linning
That's proper only for *Tom Thum* : or fome of queen
 Mabs gentlemen-ufhers.
 Tri. This Caffocke were a pretty garment for a for-
 tuneteller.
 Thoro. And this cloake of tinder comely for a
 ballad-feller,
Life fir, you are borne here to an ample fortune.
Your father abfent knowes not how you've altered
Your difpofition : I muft reclayme it,
Thou fhalt with me and court the beauteous
 Clare
Referv'd for thee, a purpofe ith' meane time,
Our chiefe companions, fhall be wits more pure,
Then your quicke fophifters, or flie logicians,
Wee'l talke of the bright beauties of the age,
Girles whofe each looke deferves to be a theme
For all the nimble poets, two dayes practife
In our brave arts will teach thee to forget
Philofophy as fruitleffe and abjure
All other Ethicks, but what's ufd mongft us,
As moft erronious.
 Hold. Well You fhall perfwade me,
Ile be an errant affe, or any thing
For thy fake coz, but fhall we have fuch wenches
As are at Cambridge, hanfom as peg Larkin.
 Thoro. O farre before her, cofen thou fhalt read
Aretins Politicks, and *Ovids* Art.

Shall be new read thee and wee will refine
Thy Academicke wit with bowles of wine.
 Hold. *Triſtram* ſhall toth' Colledge and ſell my
 bookes immediately.
 Thoro. Spoke like the ſon of *Phœbus* and my
 coſen.
 Triſt. My ſtudious maſter.
 Thoro. Sell thy Dictionary.
 Hold. Ile not keepe a prayer booke.
 Thoro. They are out of faſhion.
 Hold. Nor a Calender, to looke the age oth'
 Moone in, *Triſt.* be ſure
You burne *Greens* groats worth of wit; I ſcorne to
keepe
The name of wit about me.
 Triſt. Tis confeſt ſir,
But for the numerous Rhemes of paper, which
Are pil'd up in your ſtudy, give them mee,
I have a brother in law ith' towne's a cooke.
Ile give them him to put under his bake meates.
 Hold. Take them: I will not leave a pen within
 my lodging,
I will forget to write, or ſet my hand to any thing.
 Thoro. Unleſſe 't be to a bond.
 Hold. Ile goe put this bleſt deſigne in exe-
 cution,
Coſen, anon ile meet you at your chamber.
 Thoro. What in that reverend ſhape? the gentle-
 men
That I converſe with, will believe thee ſome Itine-
rant
Scholler, have thee whipt by th' ſtatute.
 Hold. I would be loath, now I am paſt a freſh
 man to bee had into the buttries.
 Thoro. Still theſe termes? ſtudy to forget them,
Ile ſend my man to you with a new ſuite of mine
I never wore yet,
Be ſure to put it on right, you mere Schollers

Know no degree of garment above Serge,
Or Satanifco: tie your band-ftrings neatly
And doe not eat the buttons off, put not
Your Cuffs both on one hand; twill tax your judge-
   ment
Of new inventing fafhions when accouftred,
Come to my chamber, and Ile furnifh you
With language fit to accoft your miftris.
   Hold. Rare, I've got more learning from him in
      halfe an houre,
Then in a whole lifes practice out of bookes.
Follow me *Triftram*, farewell deare cofen.

Ex. Hold. Trift.

   Thoro. How I could laugh now, were my fpleen
large enough: a hundred fuch lame ftupid Ideots
were enough, if marry'd,
To precife Burgers daughters to replenifh
The city with a race of fooles, and root
The ftocke of knaves quite out of it, he loves
   bookes:
Not that he has a fcruple more of learning
Then will fuffice him to fay grace, but like
Some piteous cowards, who are oft thought valiant
For keeping ftore of weapons in their chambers,
He loves to be efteem'd a doctor by
His volumnes: but I fhall fit his fchollerfhip: whofe
   thefe?
Alderman *Covets*, *Formall*, byth' proportion:

Ent. Formal and Clare.

That rib of mans flefh fhould be *Clare*, doft heare
My honeft Cadis garters: who for care
And clofe attendance on thy charge deferves
To be grand porter to the great Turkes *Seraglia*:
   how hight that vayl'd damfell?

Form. She has been at Brittains burse a buying
   pins & needles
To worke a night-cap for my master sir.
   Thor. Pox upon him, is not her name *Clare*, niece
      to Alderman *Covet*?
   For. Her father was a country Squire of large
      revenew and her mother.
   Thoro. I shall be forc'd to heare him blaze her
      pedigree,
Ide beat him, but that clubs and paring shovells oth'
   city
Would be so busie about my eares: they'd spoyle
My hearing two months after. Gentle Lady
Pardon my error if I doe mistake, are not you mistris
   Clare?
   Clar. *Formall* at last, would have resolv'd you,
      and I held my
Peace of purpose, cause I knew his slow discovery
   would vex
Your nimble patience.
   Tho. You are a Gipsie, but does thy unkles
      humour hold of wedding
His daughter to sir *Timothy*.
   Clar. Yes, or to young monsieur *Holdfast* whom
      he sayes is
Learned enough to make Cheap-side a Colledge,
And all the City a new Academy, but have you
Thorowgood perform'd what I advis'd you to?
   Thoro. Yes, my girle: good *Formall* use thy
      motion to convay
Thy ears a little a farther off, there's mony
To buy thee a new payre of garters: *Clare*
Thou shalt no more behold me in the garbe
And noble ornament I us'd to weare, my fashion shall
   be altred.
   Clar. To the schoolars,
Young *Holdfasts* likenesse.
   Thoro. O by all meanes girle, thou shalt behold
      this comely hat transform'd

To frugall brim, and fteeple crowne, this band
Of faire extent chang'd to a moderne cut,
Narrower then a precifians: all this gay
And gawdy filke I will convert to Serge
Of limber length: like fome fpruce ftudent (newly
Exalted for faying grace well, to be fellow
Oth' Colledge he had ftudied) I will
Salute thy reverent Uncles fpectacles,
And without feare of his gold chaine, ile woe thee
In metaphores and tropes Scholaftick till
The doting Senator with a liberall hand
Give thee his dainty darling to become
My fpoufe infeparable.
 Clar. This fuites well
With my directions.
 Thoro. True girle true, farewell *Clare*,
I kiffe thy white hand: Sir refume your charge,
I've done my errand: let not your old Sir *Amias*,
Know of this conference, if you doe, that twift
Of fpinners thred, on which your life depends
Shall be fhorne off like a horfe mane. Farewell.
 Form. Mans life indeed is but a thred, good day
  fir.

    Exe. Clare and Formall,

   Ent. Valentine & Sir Timothy.

 Thor. Attend your charge friend, *Valentine*, Sir
  Timothy.
You'r well incountred, may I inquire the affaire
Which happily has brought you up toth' City?
May I know it? is 't not to purchafe a Monopoly
For Salt and Herrings? for ftate bufineffe,
Unleffe it be to fee the great new fhip,
Or *Lincolns Inne* fields built: I'me fure you've none
 here.
 Tim. Very right fir.

    Thor. But for thee : my noble man of merit, thou
       art welcome,
Weel be as kind to one another boy,
And witty as brifque poets in their wine,
Weel court the blacke browd beauties of the time,
And have by them the height of our defires :
With eafe accomplifhed.
    Val. Noble *Thorowgood*,
Did I not owne you by the name of friend,
Already thefe indearments would ingage me
To beg that title.
    Tim. Very right, and me too.
    Thor. You fir, you've reafon,
I know you for the moft Egregious knight
In all the country.
    Tim. Very right, I am indeed efteem'd fo.
    Thor. One that lives on Onions and Corne-
       fallets.
    Tim. Right agen,
Sure he can conjure, I had one to my breakfaft.
    Thor. Nay no Herald
Can better blafe your pedigree. I've heard
Your father my moft worthy knight, was one
That died a knave to leave you fo.
    Tim. Paffing right ftill.
    Thor. And pray right witty, and right honor'd
       fir,
What may your bufineffe feeme to be ith' city,
Are you come up to learne new fafhions ?
    Tim. Exceeding right agen.
    Thor. To change this ancient garment to a new
       one
Of a more fpruce edition.
    Val. Yes, but before,
For I am privie unto all's intentions,
He means to fee and court his miftris.
    Thor. Who's that ? my doughty Impe of fpur and
       fword,
Some faire *Dulcinea de Tobofo*.

Val. No, tis *Grace*, daughter to Alderman
  Covet.
Thor. I doe commend thee my deare *Don*, and
  will
Be thy affiſtant, goe and ſee thy horſe dreſt,
And then approach my chamber.
  Tim. Very right, I kiſſe your fingers ends.

                              Ex. Timothy.

  Thor. Doe you, *Valentine*, know
The Lady he intends to Court.
  Val. Onely by report,
Which ſpeakes her moſt accompliſh'd.
  Thor. Oh ſhe 'll make
An excellent Aſſe of him : ſhe has a wit
More ſharpe and piercing than a Waſpes ſting, ſhe
  ſpeaks
All fire ; each word is able to burne up
A thouſand ſuch poore Muſhromes : had her mother
Not beene held honeſt, I ſhould have believ'd
She'd bin ſome Courtiers By-blow, or that ſome
Quicke Poet got her.
  Val. How's her feature?
  Thor. Rare, paſt expreſſion, ſingular, her eyes
The very ſphears of love, her cheeks his throne,
Her lips his paradiſe, and then her minde
Is farre more excellent than her ſhape.
  Val. You give her a brave Character ; is't poſ-
  ſible
To have a ſight of her?
  Tho. Yes, by my means, ſcarce otherwiſe wilt
    thou have her,
Speake but a ſyllable, 't ſhall be perform'd
As ſure as if *Don Hymen*, in his robes
Had ratifi'd the contract.
  Val. You are merry ſir.
  Thor. When didſt thou know me otherwiſe : yet
    now
In ſober ſadneſſe friend, couldſt thou affect

A woman, as there's few of them worth loving,
Thou canſt not make a nobler choiſe : Ile bring
  thee
On to the skirmiſh, but if thou retreat,
Beat backe by th' hot Artillery of her wit,
Which will play faſt upon thee : maiſt thou live
To be enamour'd on ſome ſtale Hay, or Matron
Of foureſcore, that may congeale thee to a froſt
Sooner than forty winters : or be wed
To an inſatiat Chamber-maid.
  Val. Defend me
From thy laſt curſe ; feare not my valour.
  Thor. This foole ſhall ſerve both her and us for
  ſport ;
Lets to our taske ; and if our project hit,
Ile ſweare all fortune is compris'd in wit.

                                      Exeunt.

              Explicit Actus primus.

Actus secundus.   Scena prima.

Covet, Clara, Maudlin.

Cov. YOu will provoke me.
    Clar.   No matter :
Although you be my uncle, and so nature
Binds me to observe you, ile not be oblig'd
To what the phlegmaticke humour of your age
Strives to enforce upon me : I was borne
Free, an inheritresse to an ample fortune,
Of which you doe pervert the use, and trust me,
Ile be no longer tame and suffer it.
  Cov.   Suffer what ? you're us'd
Too well : if you complaine of this, I shall
Study to be more harsh.
    Clar.   Doe ; you shall not, as you had wont,
Thinke to attire me in blacke Grogram,
Daub'd o're with Sattin lace, as if I were
Daughter, and heire apparent to a Tayler,
Who from the holiday Gownes of sixe neat fish-
    wives
Had stole the remnants made the thrifty garment.
Nor shal you sir (as tis a frequent custome,
Cause you're a worthy Alderman of a Ward)
Feed me with Custard, and perpetuall White-broth,
Sent from the Lord Majors, or the Shriefes feast,
And here preserv'd ten dayes, (as twere in pickle)
Till a new dinner from the common hall
Supply the large defect.
    Cov.   You'll leave this language ?
    Clar.   Leave to use me so then :

Y'ave made my felfe, your daughter, and my
  woman,
Sup with a penyworth of Lettice, under
Pretence 'twould make us fleep well: your full mor-
  fells
(Had not the vertue of Clay wall, and Oatmeale
Preferv'd my maid) ere this fhe'd bin fhrunk up
Toth' bigneffe of a Squirrill.
  Maud. Any Dwarfe
Might without ftretching his fmall fingers, have
Spand me about the wafte.
  Clar. Nor fhall you,
(As fure tis your intention) marry me
To th' *quondam* fore-man of your fhop, (exalted
To be your Cafh-keeper) a limber fellow,
Fit onely for deare *Nan*, his fchoole-fellow,
A Grocer's daughter, borne in *Bread-ftreet*, with
Whom he has ufed to goe to *Pimblico*,
And fpend ten groats in Cakes and Chriftian Ale,
And by the way has courted her with fragments,
Stoln from the learned Legends of Knights Errants,
Or from the glory of her fathers trade,
The Knight o' the Burning Peftle.
  Cov. Sure the Devill
Has entred her ith' likeneffe of an Eele,
Her tongue's fo flippery: Minion——
  Clar. Ile not be frighted
As are your Prentifes, with Little eafe,
Or fhewing them the Beadle. In plain termes,
I doe not meane to incorporate with a Salter,
Or any of thofe thriving trades, to have
My fhooes lickt o're each faturday night
By th' under prentife; they fhine fo brightly
With foot and kitching-ftuffe, that I next morning
May fpare my glaffe, and dreffe my head by their
Greafie reflection: yet let me tell you,
I muft be marry'd inftantly: a virgin
Of my full age, fetting afide all niceneffe
May juftly claime a husband.

Cov. Have but patience, ile wed thee to a
 Knight.
Clare. What is hee, one oth' Poſt ſir, or ſome
 ſuch
As was in the old famous Ballad mention'd :
He that has forty pounds *per annum*, by
Which Charter I ſhould be undutifull,
And take the wall of my ag'd Grandame : No,
Ile have a Courtly gentleman, whoſe wit
Shall equall his eſtate, and that ſo large,
As 't ſhall afford me a ſufficient joyncture.
 Cov. This Knight ſhall do 't, or if you like not
 him,
What ſay you to Sir *Geffery Holdfaſt's* ſonne,
The famous Schollar ?
 Clare. If he be a Parſon ;
And I his wife, I ſure ſhall make my friends
Lucky to horſe-fleſh ; No, I will have one
That ſhall maintaine my Coach, and foure faire
 horſes :
Not ſuch thin jades, nor ſuch a crazy Chariot,
As i've ſeene us'd by Citizens to convey
Their wives with leiſure to their Country houſes,
(For feare the late Plum-pudding they had eaten
Fryed to their Breakfaſt, ſhould with too much jog-
 ging
Broyle on their queaſie ſtomacks) One that ſhall
Maintaine me a Sedan, and two ſtrong varlets,
That ſo I may not need the Common men
 Mules,
With their wood-Litters, with nineteene at end of
 them,
The uſuall ſhelters, which the Gallants carry
Their wenches to their Chambers in : In briefe,
If you can find me any where a husband
That I can like, I will allow your choyſe ;
If not, ile take my owne ; ſo good day to you.
Pray meditate upon it.
                    Ex. Clare, Maud.

Cov. This is the maddeſt wench : would I were rid of her,
She vexes me more than her Portion's worth ;
But if ſhe ſtoope not to my Country Knight,
Sir *Timothy Shallow-wit,* or to young *Holdfaſt,*
(Whom I had rather marry to my daughter)
She ſhall ha graſing.

Enter Formall.

For. Sir, there are a brace of gentlemen without,
Deſire admittance to you.
Cov. Let them enter.
For. I ſhall denote your pleaſure.   *Ex. For.*
Cov. Some young heires,
To borrow money upon Morgages.

Enter Holdfaſt, Brave, Triſtram.

Hol. I ſhall obſerve my Coſens rule, nere fear me.
Cov. Save you ſir.
Hol. You do not think me damn'd ſir, you beſtow
That ſalutation on me.
Cov. Good ſir no.
Whom would you ſpeake with here ?
Hol. Sir, my diſcourſe
Poynts at one Alderman *Covet.*
Cov. I am the party.
Hol. Good Mr. *Covet,* I covet your acquaintance :
I underſtand you have a daughter is
Of moſt unknowne perfections.
Cov. She is as heaven made her.

Hold. She goes naked then,
The Tailer has no hand in her; may I fee
 her?
 Cov. I muſt deſire your name firſt.
 Hold. My name is *Holdfaſt.*
 Cov. Sonne to ſir *Geff. Holdfaſt.*
 Hold. His proper ſonne and heire, and I am
 come
To ſee your Daughter and your Neece.
 Cov. Came you from Cambridge lately.
 Hold. I come from *Cambridge*:
What do you ſee in theſe my looks, ſhould make
 you
Judge me ſuch a Coxecombe.
 Cov. Your father writ me word, his ſon that
 ſhould
Come up to ſee my Daughter and my Neece,
Was a rare ſchollár, wholly given to's bookes.
 Hold. My father was an arrant aſſe for's la-
 bour,
I ne're read book in all my life, except
The Counter ſcuffle, or the merry Goſſips,
Raynard the Foxe, Tom Thumbe, or Gargantua,
And thoſe i've quite forgotten: I a ſchollar!
He lyes in's throat that told you ſo.
 Triſt. On my Conſcience
You may believe him: he ſcarce ere ſaw booke,
Vnleſſe the Chronicle in an iron Chaine,
In's fathers Hall: for learning ſir, except
What's in a Horſe, a Hawke, or hownd, he knowes
 not.
How to expound your meaning.
 Cov. I mar'le ſir *Geff.* knowing my averſion
From any of theſe courſes, ſhould bring up
His ſonne to all of them: nay, write me word,
Knowing my love to learning, he had him
A ſchollar purpoſely: pray ſir reſolve me,
Are you ſir *Gefferies* ſonne?

Hold. I am a Baſtard elſe.
Cov. Sir *Gefferies* ſonne of *Eppinge* ?
Hold. Yes, of *Eppinge*,
One that will venture five hundred pounds upon his horſe,
Soone as the proudeſt hee that lives in *London*,
Ile play my Crop-eare 'gainſt my Lord Majors Steed,
And all his furniture : I doe intend
To ſcoure *Hide* Parke this ſummer. *Triſt.* didſt give him
His Oates this morning ? Shall I ſee your daughter.
Did he drink's water haſtily ? Your Neece
I'de be acquainted with.
   Cov. Sir, you muſt pardon me, you're not the man
I tooke you for.
   Hold. You did not take me for an Aſſe I hope.
   Cov. O by no meanes, but they cannot be ſeene
Conveniently this morning : another time,
At your beſt leaſure, I ſhall not deny you,
Pleaſe you walke in, and taſte our Beere ?
   Hold. I know 'tis but oth' fixes; and I hate
Liquor of that complexion : pray commend me
To both my ſweet-hearts. *Triſtram* come lets backe,
And, as my Coſen ſayes, drinke luſty ſacke.

     Exeunt Holdfaſt and Triſtram.

   Cov. There's ſome deceite in this, perhaps ſome gallant,
Knowing my purpoſe with Sir *Geffery Holdfaſt*,
Has tane his name upon him : ile diſpatch
A meſſenger ſtraight to him : whom have we here ?

Enter Thoroug. and Formall.

Form. Sir, that's the Alderman my Mafter.
Thor. Is this the venerable Man, to whom
This goodly Manfion is impropriate:
I fhould negotiate with his reverence
About authentick bufineffe.
Cov. This rather
Should be fir *Geff.* fonne, his words and habit
Speake him moft learned. I'me the perfon, pray
Let me be bold to crave your name.
Thor. My *appellation* or *pronomen*, as
It is tearm'd by the *Latins*, is *hight Ieremie*,
But my Cognomen, as the Englifh gather,
Is called *Holdfaft*.
Cov. This is he certainely; are you, I pray
Sir *Gefferies* fonne of *Eppinge*?
Thor. The Nominalls, the Thomifts, all the fects
Of old and moderne Schoole-men, doe oblige me
To pay to that Sir *Geffery* fillial duty.
Cov. I'me glad to heare it, tother was fome varlet,
I fhall finde out and punifh: Sir y'are welcome;
I geffe your bufineffe; tis about a match
Or with my Neece, or Daughter: which you like,
Shall be at your difpofe: if not, your bufineffe.
Thor. My bufineffe is of procreation, or as
The Civill Lawyers learnedly doe paraphrafe,
Is of concomitance, Cohabitation,
Or what you pleafe to terme it.
Cov. How am I bleft, that this rare fchollar fhall
Be match'd into my family? Within there;
Neece, Daughter, both come hither.
Thor. One at once fir

Twill satisfie ; the Canon does prohibit
Us Polygamy.

Enter Clara, Grace.

 Cov. Sir, this is my onely daughter, this my neece,
Pray know them better.
 Thor. Faire types, nay Orbs of beauty, I salute you,
Each in his proper altitude.
 Grace. Heyday, this is some Fortune-teller.
 Clare. Tis *Thorowgood*, you must not seeme to know him.
 Cov. Daughter and Neece, this is a gentleman,
My care has pick'd out, as a most fit husband
For one of you ; which he can soonest fancy,
Heare him but speake, and he will put you downe
Ten Universities, and Innes of Court,
In twentie sillables. Good Mr. *Holdfast*
Speake learnedly to th' wenches ; though I say't,
They have both good capacities.
 Thor. Most rubicund, stelliferous splendant Ladyes,
The ocular faculties, by which the beames
Of love are darted into every soule,
Or humane essence, have into my breast
Convey'd this Ladies lustre : and I can
Admire no other object ; therefore beauty
Your pardon, if I onely doe addresse
In termes Scholasticke, and in Metaphors
My phrase to her.
 Grace. I shall not
Envy my Cosens happinesse.
 Thor. Y'are full of Candor ;
If you will love me Lady, ile approach your eares,
Not in a garbe Domesticke, or termes vulgar,
But hourely change my language, court you now,

In the *Chaldean*, or *Arabicke* tongues,
Expound the *Talmud* to you, and the *Rabbines*,
Then read the Dialect of the *Alanits*,
Or *Ezion Gebor*, which the people ufe
Five leagues beyond the Sun-rifing, in ftead
Of pages to attend you, I will bring
Sects of Philofophers and queint Logicians,
Weel Procreat by learned art, and I
Will generate new broods of Schollers on you,
Which fhall defend opinions far more various
Then all the Sectaries of Amfterdam
Have ever vented.
    Covet. Learned, learned young man,
How happy am I in thee ?
    Thor. Doe but love,
Ile call the Mufes from the facred hill
To Enucleat your beauty: I my felfe
(After in loftier numbers I have fung
Your fam'd Encomiums) will convert to poet,
And for your fake Ile write the city annals,
In famous meter which fhall far furpaffe
Sir *Guy* of *Warwickes* hiftory : or *Iohn* Stows upon
The cuftard with the foure and twenty Nooks
At my Lord *Majors* feaft.
    Cov. How am I ravifht !
    Thor. Whofe brave fhow hereafter
Shall be no more fet forth with ftalking pageants,
Nor children ride for angels nor lowd actors
Pronounce bold fpeeches ; I will teach his Hench-
    boyes
Serjeants and trumpeters to act and fave
The city all that charges : Nay Ile make a new
Found engin ; which without fire fhall keepe his
Whitebroath warm til his return from Weftminfter
Nor fhall the Aldermens daughters, who have
Dreamt at leaft fix nights before of guilded
Marchpane, forfeit their ferious longing : Ile have
Horfes with their Saint *Georges* on them, that fhall
    gallop

Into their handkerchers.
 Clar. You promife wonders.
 Covet. Hold your tongue, hees able
To performe more by's learning.
 Thor. The croffe
And ftanderd in Cheapefide I will convert
To *Hercules* pillars : and the little conduit
That weepes in lamentation for the Church,
Remov'd that did leane on, it fhall be ftill
Like the great tun at Heidleberge fild with wine,
And alwayes running, that the prentifes
Shall not on Sundayes need to frequent Tauerns,
And forfeit their indentures.
 Covet. Still more miraculous.
 Thor. The great conduit
Shall be a magezin of facke, and Smithfield
A Romifh Cirque or Grecian Hippodrom,
My Lord Maiors gennet fhall not die without
An Elegy, nor any cittizen breake,
But have a dolefull ditty writ upon him.
 Val. Save you gentlemen.
 Covet. Noble fir *Timothy*, and your friend both
Welcome, this is my neice, & that my daughter,
  pray
Be pleas'd to know them, Sir honor me to walke,
I'de have fome private conference with you,
The hour fir *Timothy* is at your command.
 Grace. Cofen what would thefe gentlemen?
 Clare. Truth I know not,
Ile venture my difcretion to his nofe there,
And that appeares a rich one, they are two
Country Ideots whom thy father would
Put upon us for husbands.
 Grace. Very likely,
Pray gentlemen your bufineffe.
 Tim. Speake for me *Valentine.*
 Val. La. es wee'r come to fee you, fame does
  give yo
The attribut. of faire and witty.

Clare. Yet
Our wits you ſee ſir will not ſerve to keepe
Fooles from our company.
  Tim. Very right yfaith.
  Val. That tartneſſe
Becomes you prettily, and might ſerve to fright
Young linnen-drapers or ſome millaner
That does with gloves and bracelets ſtolne from's
    Maſter
Court you, a haberdaſher would have ſhak'd
His blocke-head (as if he had beene trying a Dutch
Felt out) and with a ſhrug departed, but we are
Gentlemen Ladies, and no city foremen
That never dare be ventrous on a beauty,
Unleſſe when wenches take them up at playes
To intice them at the next licentious Taverne
To ſpend a ſupper on them, we are creatures
Deſerve you at your beſt and nobleſt value,
And ſo expect you'l uſe us.
  Tim. Very right, this is
A countrey gentleman my neighbor I
A truſty and coragious country knight.
  Clare. I doe believe you ſir, your face does
    tel me,
You'r one that feed on bacon and bagpudding,
Your noſe by its complexion does betray
Your frequent drinking country Ale with lant in't,
Have you no hobnayls in your boots, driven in
To ſave the precious leather from the ſtones
That pave the ſtreets of London.
  Grace. Is not ſir
Your cloake new turn'd, the aged three pil'd velvet
Was not your grandams peticote this jerkin
Made by your grandſire at his firſt tranſlation
From Clowne to Gentleman, and ſince reſerv'd
An heire loom to the family, and this ſword
The pariſh weapon ?
  Tim. Very right agen.
  Clare. Now for you ſir.

Who of two fooles doe yet appeare the wifeſt,
Can your ingenious noddle thinke that we
Bred in the various pleaſures of the city,
Would for your ſake turne beaſts and graſe ith' country,
We cannot milke, make wholſome cheeſe, nor butter,
And ſell it at next market and lay up
Out of the precious Income as much coyne
In thred bare groates, mill-ſixpences, and pence,
As will ſuffice to finde the houſe in Candles
And Sope a twelvemonth after.

 Grace. Nor can wee
Spin our owne ſmockes out of the flax which growes
Behind your Dovehouſe, no, nor card the wooll
Muſt make us peticoates things (to ſay truth)
Not worth the taking up.

 Val. They've Magicke in their tounges
They have ſo daunted me, I thinke I ſhall
Turne foole and get me 'hem without reply.

 Clare. All the company,
We can injoy there is each day to walke
To the next farmers wife, whoſe whole diſcourſe
Is what price Barly beares, or how her husband
Sould his laſt yoake of Oxen: other meetings
We cannot have, except it be at Churchales,
When the ſweet bag-pipe does draw forth the Damſells
To friſque about the May-poles, or at Weddings,
Where the beſt cheare is, wholſome ſtewd broth made
Of legs of porke and turnips.

 Grace. Yes, at Chriſtnings,
Where the good wives, ſtead of burnt Wine and Comfets,
Drinke healths to th' memory of all chriſtian ſoules
In Ale, ſcarce three houres old: eat cakes more tough
Then glew or farthing gingerbread: then talke
Of the laſt Blaſing Starre, or ſome new monſter:

Then drinke, and cry heaven bleſſe us from the Spaniard,
While the learn'd Vicars wife expounds the Ballad
Of 'twas a Ladies daughter in *Paris* properly,
And ſo breakes up the wife aſſembly.
   Val. And you
That are the precious paragons of the City,
Who ſcorne theſe harmeleſſe ſports: can have your meetings
At Iſlington, and Green Gooſe faire, and ſip
A zealous glaſſe of Wine till the parch'd floore
Be moiſtned with your virgin dew, then prattle
How that you dreamt laſt night that *Iohn* the Mercer,
Or *Tom* the Drapers man at London-ſtone
Was in your bed, and what ſweet work he made there.
   Tim. Very right, and kis'd you oftner
Then ere the good man did his Cow, and hug'd you
As the Divell hug'd the Witch, that's right now.
   Val. When you'r married
(For that you will be, or elſe run away
With Coſtermongers, Mountebankes, or Taylors)
Your husbands are more ſubject to you then
Their bondmen are, whom by profuſe expenſe
You breake beyond redemption from the Indies,
The ſtraights, or Barbary, ſee them lodged in Ludgate,
And then turne pricking ſemſters, till that trade
Fayling, you take your ſelves (as to the laſt refuge)
To the old occupation; till the Marſhall
Carry you to Bridewell, of which you'r free,
Even by your fathers charters that have beene
Sometimes the maſters of it, there Ile leave you,
So farewell wild cats.
   Tim. Very right as I am a gentleman.
   Grace. I like his ſpirit well *Clare*, ſuch a fellow
Or none ſhall be my husband.

Enter Thorowgood.

Thor. Helpe me to laugh good wenches, I haue talk'd
Thy Unkle *Clare* into fo free an humour,
That hees refolv'd ftraight to take forth the licence,
And marry us ith' morning.
   Clare. What od fellow's this ?
Know you him Cofen *Grace*?
   Thor. Prethee good wit noe more, we've overcome
All forraigne enemies, and tis unfit
To war among our felves.
   Grace. This is the pedant
My father brought to mocke us, good thine ftuffe,
Get thee home to thy parifh and inftruct
Thy people wholefome Doctrine, for us,
We have no zeale to learne.
   Thor. Life they'l perfwade me out of my felfe,
Clare, Grace, know you not me, not *Thorowgood.*
   Amb. Thorowgood, pray put your trickes on fome body,
More eafie to be wrought on, *Thorowgood,* Ha ha, ha.

                                 Exe.

   Thor. What fhould thefe wenches meane, the five and fheares
Cannot refolve this myftery : they know me
Better then I can know my felfe : 'twas fhe
Advis'd me to this habit to deceive
Her uncles prying eyes, and why then

Should they abuſe me thus? the reſt were made
But fooles in Quarto, but I finde my ſelfe
An aſſe in Folio : Ile away, and if
   I quit them not with an abuſe as fine,
  Ile ſay there is no quickning ſpirit in wine.

                                          Exit.

              Explicit Actus Secundus.

Actus Tertius. Scena prima.

Enter Thorowgood, Valentine, Knowell.

Know. ARE they so witty sayst thou?
Val. You'd best try
The acutenesse of their intellects.
   Thor. You may endeavor
With the large talent of your masculine wit
To exceed their female sharpnesse you shall finde,
Though you [be] firme and stiffe in your defence,
These city lasses able to take downe
Your most couragious fury: pray endeavour't.
   Know. That gentleman, were to usurpe your pre-
fence,
I finde no inclination, yet I thanke you,
To rest a foole upon record as you doe.
   Val. How's that, my impe of understanding?
   Know. By being so egregiously abus'd
By two poore City infants, things that never
Have heard wit nam'd, unlesse 'twas when their father
Has cal'd his *Formall* foreman witty varlet,
For cheating hansomely; had they been some
Illustrious dames, the glory of Cheape-side,
Stars of the City, that are daily haunted
By this great Lord that courtly kisse their gossips,
It had beene possible their conversation
Might have instild into them so much language
And wit sufficient to withstand the assaults
Of some young Innesacourt man.
   Thor. Yes, who never

Had mooted in the hall or feen the revels
Kept in the houfe at Chriftmas.
  Know. Some fuch gamfter might have
Come oft with credit, though hee'd ventur'd
His whole eftate of wit on them and loft it,
But you the rookes oth' age to be oredone
At your owne game by city girles.
  Val. Thou art an affe,
A very coxcomb, there are girles ith' City
Able to oredoe at their owne game a hundred
Such feeble fellows as thy felfe, but *Thorowgood*,
Leaving this infidell to his mif-beliefe,
Are you refolved that I fhall undertake
The new defigne we plotted?
  Thor. With what fpeed
Can be convenient, fir *Timothy*
Shall be our inftrument.
  Know. If there be wit in 't,
Honour me to affift you.
  Thor. A revenge
Upon thefe peevifh wenches, one of them
Loves me intirely, nay has vow'd me a marriage,
And did advife me to affume this fhape,
To cheat her uncle.
  Val. And for the other,
By many a fhrowd caft of her eye upon me,
I doe fufpect for all her queint diffembling,
She's taken with my good parts.

Enter Maudline.

  Thor. Thy face I muft confeffe,
Is full of choyce allurements, fee their maid,
How fares it with your witty miftris,
My gallant type of beauty, is the ftomach,
Come down, I'm fure you are furnifh'd
With fome excufe or lamentable epiftle,
To reconcile me to them.

Maud. Sir I am
As ignorant of the interpretation of your words,
As of your perſon.
  Thor. Shee not know me neither?
  Maud. But if there be one *Valentine* among you,
A well accompliſh'd gentleman.
  Val. That's I, that's I.
  Maud. Then ſir,
I would require your privacy ſome minutes.
  Val. Weel be as private as thou wilt, my girle,
Your patience gentlewoman.
  Know. I wonder *Thorowgood* what buſineſſe
She can have with him.
  Thor. Heel declare it.
See they are parting.
  Val. Tel them Ile adviſe ont.
  Maud. You will be ſpeedy.

                              Exit Maudline.

  Val. Yes, yes, nere doubt my haſte, ſay Ime their ſervant.
  Thor. The buſineſſe *Valentine.*
  Val. Doſt not thou know it,
Euen by inſtinct?
  Know. We cannot prophecy.
  Val. Thou art a foole then,
Does not the harmony of my good parts
Speake me the conqueror of all beauties *Thorowgood.*
The wenches are on fire for me.
  Tho. Their bloods
Are always hot ith' Dogdayes: but good *Valentine*
Be ſerious, did their maid bring newes of love
From either of them?
  Val. From both, from both, now wert not for the ſtatute,
'Gainſt Bigamy my tender conſcience
Would not much be oppreſs'd to have two wives,

But one of them thy Pinnace, thou ſhalt man her :
But I delay too long, I muſt goe meete them ;
I long to be a kiſſing, pray heaven their breath
Smell not of Marmalade, 'twill turne my ſtomacke.
 Tho. You'll practice our deſigne I hope.
 Val. Methodically : farewell boyes.

Ex. Val.

 Tho. Pray be you Sir *Timothy*, know his en-
  trance :
Tis ſuch another mad-cap my Scene is.

Enter Holdfaſt.

 Hold. Nay, come forward Land lord Spoild elfe.

Triſt. Buſ.

Tis my Coſens lodgings, pray be bold in 't,
As is my Chamber. Coſen this is a Conſtable.
 Tho. He comes not with a warrant.
 Hold. No, Ile warrant you,
I brought him Sir to ſee you ; he 's a wit,
A very wit, or as the modernes terme it,
A ſparke, a meere ſparke, ſuch a one as I am,
Since I left off thoſe idle toyes cald books,
He'll take Tobacco too, and with a grace
Spit ith' rub'd chamber, though his teſty wife
Crye fie upon him : he's a very ſparke,
And worthy your acquaintance.
 Trif. Come forward ſir, you ſtand as if you'd
  coſen'd
One of them with bad linnen ; pray advance,
My Maſter is your Leader.
 Buſ. Save you gentlemen.
 Tho. Y'are very welcome Sir, my Coſen ſpeakes
  you
A Citizen of ranke.
 Know. That you beare office

Of honour in your parifh.
Tho. That y'are witty,
Or as he fayes a fparke.
Know. Nay, a good fellow.
Buf. Tis granted gentlemen,
This is my Character, I am by trade
A Linnen Draper.
Tho. Would truft me
For forty ells of Holland?
Buf. Ha, how's that fir?
I have more wit I thanke you: caufe you feeme
A Gentleman of quality, I care not
To venture as much Cambricke as fhall make
Your Crufh a gorget, but no farther, fir,
There is no wit in't: how's that Mr. *Holdfaft*?
Hold. You are a fparke ftill Landlord.
Know. Ile fweare in this he's witty.
Buf. Tis my humour,
My wit has halfe undone me long ere this;
But for my wit Ide beene an Alderman,
And twirld a pondrous chaine upon the bench,
With as much grace as can the formalft of them:
I fhould have fin'd for Sheriffe, but all *Guild* Hall
Hearing I was a wit, cry'd out upon him,
Twill breed an alteration in the Senate,
To have a wit amongft them. How's that fir?
Know. And fo you mift preferment.
Tho. And continue
Ith' ftate of wifedome ftill, an humble Conftable?
Hold. Yes, and an honeft one, ile fay that for him,
He ne're ftop'd wench in's watch.
Buf. How's that? I fcorne it,
I've ftopt a hundred in my time: how's that fir?
You relifh wit I fee.
Know. Tis fo acute,
No pallat but muft tafte it; fhall's to th' Taverne?
Y'are for a cup I hope?
Buf. For now fir,

It is my frequent ufe, when I have fet
My watch, to view the Taverne, drinke a quart,
And then backe to my bufineffe, and there wit in 't.
 Thor. Tis granted fir : Come gentlemen, an houre
Is our extent of time : good Mr. Conftable
It fhall be yours. Cofen I have fome bufinefle
Concernes your knowledge, as we paffe along
I fhall informe you.

Exeunt.

 Enter Valentine, Grace, Clare, Maudlin.

 Val. You fee Ime come
Vpon your fummons.
 Clar. Sure you miftake,
There 's none here is fo fond of you to court
Your cheap and vulgar prefence.
 Val. Here's a Letter
Speaks other language, you might cloath your dif-
 courfe
In the fame phrafe, or I fhall laugh your folly
Into a milder temper, and then leave you.
 Clar. You'r very confident.
 Val. No, you're too coy,
Ime now ith' humour to be tempted to
Love any of you : take me while the fit
Is on me, for ime fure twill not endure
Longer than does a wealthy widdowes griefe
For a loath'd husband. Speak, ha you a mind to me?
Speake quickly, or for ever more hereafter
Be fure to hold your peace, and that 's a taske
Farre worfe then death to any of your fexe.
 Clar. Her blufhes does betray her, wer't to me,
He fhould finde other ufage. Sir my Cofen,
I know not how tranfported by her love,

Above her reafon, has enthrald her heart
To your difpofe.　I hope fir you'r fo much
A Gentleman, you will make civill ufe
Of her affection ; twill be worth your care fir.
Befides the rich endearements of her youth,
She's Miftris of a fortune that may challenge
A noble retribution for her love.
Weele not difturbe your conference.

Ex. Clar. Maud.

　Grace.　Cofen, cofen, you will not leave me thus?
I pray let me goe fir.
　Val.　Thus farre into my armes girle, that's the place
Thou oughtft to reft in : you expect I warrant
That I fhould court you now, and with an armie
Of oathes, ftuft with as many finicall falfehoods,
Proteft I love you : by this light I know not,
Tis folly to diffemble, whether or no
I can affect thee ; yet thou feemft to weare
That pretty harmleffe innocence in thy lookes,
It wins my credulous thoughts to believe
Thou maift be vertuous.
　Grace.　Sir, I hope my owne
Too forward zeale, in tendring you my love,
Will not in your good thoughts beget an ill
Opinion of my modefty.
　Val.　Never fear't :
That freeneffe more engages my juft faith
To embrace thy affection.　I have feene fome Ladyes,
Coy as a Votereffe below their fuiters,
Yet with a tough-backt groome, have knowne them fin
With moft libidinous appetite in private ;
But Ime as feareleffe girle, that ought amiffe
Can ftaine thy foule, as thou wert confident
In fetling thy moft conftant choife upon

A ſtranger; yet I muſt deſire the reaſon
Why you did love me: for my owne good parts,
Certaine they're not ſo attractive as to conquer
A beautie at firſt ſight.

   Grace. Since I have
Diſclos'd my affection to you, (although love
Oft times admits no reaſon) ile endeavour
To ſatisfie your queſtion; the firſt cauſe
Moov'd me to love you, was my father.

   Val. Hang thy father
In 's owne gold chaine: but ſuch another word,
And never hope to have me; doſt thou thinke
Ile be beholding to an eight ith' hundred,
To ſuch an empty caske as is thy father,
(Who ſoon did get his wealth by the old proverbe,
Of fooles have fortune) for a wife; but that
I have ſome mercy in me to believe
Thou maiſt be virtuous; I would not match
With any of my ſqueamiſh Ants of *London*,
For all the wealth ith' Chamber.

   Grace. Sir, you ask'd,
A queſtion of me, and will not permit
Me give a civill anſwer; as I ſaid,
My father——

   Val. Father agen, farewell; my eares doe bliſter
At the harſh found: would thou hadſt beene a Baſtard,
So thou hadſt no title to his blood:
Another father, like a whirlewind, blowes me
Hence from thy ſight for ever.

   Gra. Pray heare me.
Intends to match me to Sir *Timothy
Shallow-wit*, a creature onely fit for ſcorne;
Which to prevent, and taken with the fulneſſe
Of your true worth, I rather chuſe to caſt
My reputation on your noble pitty,
Than ſtand the deſperate hazard of my ruine.

   Val. She loves me by this light, this is no tricke.

Now to my *Thorowgoods* project: th'art a good
 wench,
A harmleffe wench, and I believe a found one,
And I will have thee; give me thy hand: yet
 ftay,
Ere I doe caft my felfe away upon thee,
You here fhall promife Miftris, to become
A moft obedient wife, and not according
To th' ancient tricke inherent to the City,
Raile till you be my Mafter.
 Grace. Never feare me.
 Val. Nor fhall you, when you're at my houfe ith'
 Country
Be niggardly, or fpoyle a dinner for
Want of the tother ounce of Sugar, nor
Repine to fee me merry with my friends,
Or curfe my brothers, when they fojourne with
 me,
Nor ftarve my fervants when I am from home,
I muft be drunke fometimes too, then you muft
 not
Whine and cry out, were I a maid agen,
Ide never marry any that does take
This wicked Herbe Tobacco. Thefe injunctions,
And fome few hundreds more of the fame nature,
Seald and deliver'd to me by your promife,
I may be wonne to wed thee, nay to bed thee,
And get a race of fuch Heroicke children,
As fhall intice pofterity to conceive
Some good came from Cheapfide. Your lip fhall
 feale this.
 Grace. You fee your ftrengths upon me.
 Val. Tis my good girle:
Thy father, armed with the trained bands o'th
 City,
Shall never pull thee from me: to confirme thee
How much I love thee, ile difclofe a plot
I had to gaine thy affection.
 Grace. Tis fome good one,

Pray let me heare it.

Val. You fee my youth and feature will admit
A womans Character; if I were cloath'd
But in the habit, fhould I not appeare
A bouncing *Mary Ambree.*

Grace. Some fuch creature; but to your project.

Val. I have prepar'd mee
A handfome female fhape, my man without
Has them under his cloake; and I perfwaded
Sir *Timothy*, in hope that I would court thee
In this behalfe, to have prefented me
Here for his Neece; you marke me.

Grace. Very well; but now
This thy defigne is ufeleffe.

Val. By no meanes;
It muft be put in action; come goe in,
And helpe to dreffe me: Sir *Timothy* expects
To meete me in that fhape here: and befides
In that difguife, fecure I can at any time
Steale out with you, and marry you.

Gra. Your reafon
Shall governe my obedience.

Val. Come let's in then.

Enter Timothy, Covet, Formall.

Tim. Tis very right that fir, but yet methinkes
A wholfome fong, fung to a fine new tune,
Should not be much amiffe: my boy here has one,
And Ide be very loath, although I cannot
Sing, as they fay, my felfe, that fhe fhould heare
What thofe, I keep, can doe; is not this right now

Cov. Your pleafure fhall prevaile, 'though to fay truth,

Sonne *Shallow-wit*, for fonne I ftill fhall call you,
I never lik'd a Song, unleffe the Ballad
Oth' famous *London* Prentice, or the building
Of *Britaines* Burfe: for Muficke, leffe the Vir-
　ginalls,
I never car'd for any. Does but cloy
The eares, but never fills the purfe fonne.
　Tim. Very right indeed ; tis too light
For fuch a purpofe.
　Form. With your leave fir,
Muficke is moft delightfull, and young Miftris
Grace, and her Cofen furely will receive it
With thankfull Equipage.
　Tim. Honeft *Formall*,
Th'art in the right ftill ; come exalt thy voyce
My little Impe of gut and haire : My Miftris
Shall know there's fomething in me.
How doe you like it ? 　　　　　　　　*Sings.*
　Form. Tis very odoriferous.
　Cov. I fhall beginne
To love it better then I have done ; tis a good
　boy,
A very pretty boy, and ile reward thee.
There's a threepence for thee.
　Tim. Very right.
Father you are too bountifull.
　Cov. He fhall take it,
Indeed he fhall ; tis manners to receive
Mony from your betters boy ; but here's my Neece.

　　　　　　　Enter Clare.

　Tim. Very right, I had almoft forgotten, pray
　　where's mine ?
　Cov. Why, have you a Neece Sir *Timothy* ?
　Tim. Yes, yes, I've two or three, but one I
　　fent

Hither, to view my Miſtris in a Coach
An houre agoe at leaſt.   Sure ſhe is come.
   Cov.   *Clare* did you ſee the gentlewoman ?
   Clar.   None ſuch came hither yet Sir.
   Tim.   That's not right though,
A poxe upon her for her paines.

Enter Maudlin.

   Maud.   Mrs. your Coſen does deſire ſome conference with you.
   Cov.   *Maudlin*,
Did there a Gentlewoman arrive here lately,
To ſee my daughter ?
   Maud.   There is one within,
In buſie conference with her.
   Cov.   Very right that, he's pleading for me now.
Faire Damſell that's my Neece; pray tell her, here's
A Knight, a ſimple Uncle of hers, or ſo, deſires her
Company.   But here ſhe comes, my Miſtris with her; Neece
Tis well done, ile give thee the tother thouſand to increaſe
Thy portion for't : Miſtris, and how, and how do yee like my Neece, a plaine Country girle, or ſo.
   Cov.   A very handſome woman, I could love her,
Did I but know her portion.   Miſtris welcome.
Whats in that houſe is yours ?
   Grace.   Sir *Timothy*,
You have much grac'd me by the ſweet acquaintance
Of this good gentlewoman.   Pray Coſen know her;
She's worthy your endearment.

Clare. I shall be proud
To doe you service.
　Val. I most fortunate
To be esteem'd your creature.
　Tim. Very right
Shees a poore niece of mine, yet she can speake
You may perceive or see.

Enter Thorowgood, Holdfast, Tristram, Knowell.

　Cla. Life *Thorowgood* with young
Holdfast, pray heaven my folly
Has not undone me.
　Thor. You'l please to pardon
Our rude intention sir, we have some businesse.
　Cov. Please you declare't.
　Thor. This gentleman and my selfe,
Come to informe you that this sparke my Cosen,
Is sonne and heire to sir *Geffrey Holdfast,*
And since I heare you have dispos'd your daughter
To that good knight, I in his fathers name,
Desire your niece should be his wife.
　Cla. Pray Sir speake
In your owne cause he needs no advocate.
　Cov. I've beene abus'd,
Is this Sir *Geffreys* son the scholler?
　Thor. The very same sir.
　Hold. I am the sparke sir.
　Know. *Valentine,* ith' name
　　　　　　　　　　puls off his periwig.
Of madnesse: man why in this shape?
　Thor. *Valentine,* Ha, ha, ha.
　Tim. Very right, my niece is *Valentine.*
　Thor. And how ist bully, hast not found these
　girles

Of a hot appetite, how often ha?
  Val. Has my Land-lady
Provided me a cullis, life my backe
Does needs a fwathband.
  Cov. What meanes this gentleman?
  Thor. Nothing fir,
But to informe you what ftrange things your neice,
And daughter and, nay never blufh he has
Perform'd it better then your uncles foreman.
I know he has.
  Covet. Timothy this abufe muft not be thus
    put up,
Did not you fay I was your Neice.
  Tim. Very right, but it was *Valentine.*
  Know. He has beene here all night too.
  Grace. Cofen we are bafely betray'd.
  Cla. Take courage.
  Thor. Doe you thinke fir, my Cofen fhall mixe
    with fuch
Stale ware that keepe their gamfters in their chambers.
  Know. Or this knight have *Valentines* reverfions?
  Tim. Very right, I fcorne it.
  Thor. Keepe them, they'l ferve to fet up fome
    twife
Broken Merchant, or undone Linnen-draper, come
  away
Valentine, thou haft made a brave difcovery. Farewell,
My witty virgines, you are payd now.   *Exeunt.*
  Cov. Ile be reveng'd for this, and if it coft me
Halfe my eftate. *Formall* fend poft for fir *Geffrey*,
The whole towne fhall know of this abufe.
Ile make you faft enough.

Explicit Actus tertius.

Actus Quartus. Scena prima.

Grace, Clare, Buſie, Luce.

Buſie. They are both ſparkes, that's certaine, if ere
I take them in my watch, Ile make them ſtoope
Under my ſtaffe of office, Miſtris *Clare.*
Though I'me a Citizen, and by my charter,
Am not allowed much wit, as being free
Oth Linnen-drapers, and a man in office,
Yet if my counſell, if you pleaſe to follow it,
Doe not revenge you on theſe ſawcy mad caps,
May taking up of Holland at deare rates,
Be quite abjur'd by courtiers: and I canvas'd
Out of authority, how's that now?
   Clare. Maſter *Buſie,*
You ſeeme of ſage diſcretion: and to ſay
Truth, I conceive you have the ſtocke of wit
Belonging to the city in your cuſtody,
You are the chamber of London, where that treaſure
Is hoarded up, and I doe hope you can
Be true and ſecret.
   Buſie. How's that Lady?
I were unworthy elſe to thrive by linnen,
Could I not keepe ſmocke ſecrets for your uncle,
Your father miſtris *Grace,* I care not for him,
Although he be right worſhipful and an Alderman,
As I may ſay to you he has no more
Wit then the reſt oth' bench: what lies in's thumbe-
   ring,

Yet I doe love you deerely for the kindneſſe
Shown to my girle here, and becauſe you have
Some flaſhes in your braines: and ſince you have
Opend the caſe to me, ere we proceed
To ſentence, tell me ſeriouſly doe not you two
Love *Valentine*, and *Freewit*?
　Grace.　For my owne part,
And I dare ſay as much too for my coſen,
Their memories are as diſtant from our hearts,
As civill honeſty from theirs.
　Clare.　And though
I well could like that *Freewit* for a husband,
Yet in mere ſpight becauſe he ſhal not have me,
Ile wed the next mans offered me.
　Buſie.　How's that?
I would my wife were dead; two comely laſſes,
Such as ſometimes I light on in my watch,
Would make fit wives for ſuch rude ſparks, and t'ſhal
Goe hard but I will for your ſakes ſweete beauties,
Number a brace of ſuch ſound cuttell to them,
If you'l give way to it.
　Cla.　And crowne thee for
The king of witty Conſtables uſe our names,
Or any thing to draw them forward, that
Wee may in triumph laugh at their diſgrace,
And weel procure a pattent, to continue
Thy office to thee, during life: and after
Hire ſome ingenious poet that ſhall keepe
Thy fame alive in a brave Epitaph
Grav'd on thy marble.

Enter Covet, Sir Geffrey Holdfaſt, Sir Timothy,
young Holdfaſt.

　Geff.　What varlet ſhould that be trow?
　Cov.　Truth I know not,
Nor can conjecture, yet I did believe

Him to be truely yours, becaufe attird
Ith' habit and the phrafe of a right Scholler,
And for your fonne, pardon me mafter *Holdfaft*,
I tooke you for fome lewd audacious varlet,
That had ufurpt that title.

 Hold. I imagine
It was fome baftard of my fathers, gotten
In youth upon his Taylors wife or Landreffe,
He has good ftore of them, but mafter Alderman
You now conceive Ime fon and heire apparent
Unto the *Holdfafts*, whofoever got me,
That's not much matter.

 Buf. How's that, anon before I fet my watch,
Ile vifit you agen : meane time, pray give
My daughter *Luce* leave to come home, her fifter
Poore wretched, is troubled with a paine ith' bottome
Oth' body, pricks even to her very heart,
And I would have *Luce* goe toth' Pothecaries,
And get fome Befar ftone, they fay 'twill cure her.
Farewell good Ladies, you'l be fure to come *Luce*.

        Ex. Bufie.

 Geff. Are thefe the maidens, I promife you mafter
Alderman the'r virgins of good feature, and I fhall
Be well apaid if my fonne match to either,
Which lik'ft thou beft boy ?

 Hold. Both of them good father,
Be not fo troublefome, but let me take
A view of them : Sir *Timothy* which doe you
Like beft of thefe two Ladies ?

 Tim. Which doe you
Like beft good Mr. *Holdfaft.*

 Hold. Yours fhall be
The choyce noble Sir *Timothy.*

 Tim. Yours indeed,
Magnanimous Mr. *Holdfaft.*

 Hold. On my gentility yours.

 Tim. Yours on my knighthood.

Cov. Good sir *Timothy*,
No striving, they are free for you, and for
The staine those idle gallants put upon them,
Twas on my credit gentlemen to keepe
All other suitors off, in hope by that meanes
To obtaine them for themselves.
   Tim. Tis very likely
That *Valentine's* a wagge.
   Cov. Daughter and neice,
This hopefull gentleman, and this good knight
Are by my care provided for your husbands,
Pray use them as befits their worth, and take it
As a fatherly admonition ; either resolve
To marry these or none.
   Cla. Tis a hard choyce sir,
Yet rather then our maiden-heads shall starve,
Weel feed on this course fare, young wenches uncle,
Are like young hungry Hawkes : they'l stoope at
Jack-daws, when they can meet with no better prey,
Draw neerer thou doughty knight, and thou good
Squire oth' damsells, Uncle these youthes are bash-
   full in the
Presence of you two their grave Elders : your grim
   beards,
And azure notes able are to fright
Their precise love to silence.
   Tim. Shees ith' right,
Ime such a fearefull foole I cannot speake,
If any body looke on me.
   Geff. Let's withdraw,
Now plye thy businesse boy.

   Exe. Sir Geffery and Covet.

   Clare. So now the game
Will begin presently : I pray you tell me
Which of you is the valiant Rosicleer,
Dares breake his Launce on me.
   Tim. Marry that would I
If I durst be so bold, mine is a stiffe one,

And will pricke forely.
    Clare. A fooles bable ift not?
But come in briefe toth' purpofe: is it you
Sir knight of the ill favored face,
That would have me for your Dulcinea?
    Tim. Very right,
You know my minde as well it feemes as if
You'r in my belly.
    Grace. So then you are fped:
This gentleman's my comely fpoufe that muft be,
T'were fitting Cofen *Clare* ert be a bargaine,
They know on what conditions they doe caft
Themfelves away upon us.
    Hold. Twas difcreetly
Thought on, I would doe nothing rafhly.
    Clare. Marke then
You men that will transforme your felves to monfters,
Wretches that will become fo miferable,
You'l hang your felves: & think it a faire riddance,
Marke what youl come to, if you be fo mad,
So defperate mad to wed us, you muft firft,
Refolve like patient gulls to have your nofes
Twingd if ours chance to itch: your eares like afles
When they grow lafie cropt, leaft they oreheare
Our chamber fecrets, for our recreation,
And leaft with too much eafe we fhould grow refty,
Weel beat you daily: while you like tame Spaniells,
Shall fawne and licke our fhooe-ftrings.
    Grace. Nor expect,
To get a good word from us in a twelvemonth,
Hourely revilings and perpetuall noyfes
Shall be as favours taken that we would
Vouchfafe to fpend in fuch regardleffe trifles,
Wee'l be as proud as ere our mother was,
When fhe was Lady Majoreffe, and you humble,
As her trim hench-boyes: whatfoever fervants
You kept before, although they were your grandfires,
You fhall turne off and limmit your attendants,

As tis the city fashion to a woman
Butler, that shall not dare without our licenſe,
To let you have a penny pot of ſacke
To give a frugall entertainment, to
Your viſiting friends.
    Clare. If you have a brother,
Kinſeman, or friend, that does in pitty grieve at
The tyranny you live in, him it ſhall
Be felony to converſe with, we in tiſſue
And pluſh will brave it while you walke in fuſtian,
Weel when we pleaſe have our faire coach and horſes
To carry us up to London to aske counſell of
Our mothers and our goſſips how to abuſe you.
You ſhall be ſtill obedient, we commanding,
And if a Lord or courtly gentleman,
Whom we ſtile ſervant, out of love ſometimes
Gives us a viſit, you ſhall not repine :
If we forſake your bed to goe to his.
    Gra. And if you chance, as fooles will oft be peeping
To ſpye us coupling, with reſpective ſilence,
You ſhall depart, not daring to bedew
Your eyes with tears for grief that you are cuckolds,
Nor to exalt your honors above your neighbours,
But big with joy triumph that you have wives
That are in ſo much credit, as to have
Perſons of quality, take the paines to get you
Heires to your large revenewes.
    Tim. Very right,
Tis not the faſhion now adayes for knights
To get their owne ſons, tis ſufficient for us
If we can leave them lands, no matter who
Were their true fathers.
    Cla. Say ſir *Timothy*
If upon theſe conditions you can like
The match is perfect : but faith take my counſell,
Make not your ſelves meere raskalls : the reproach
To boyes and ſchollers, ſubjects fit for ballads,
Not worthy M Ps name to them, good Sir *Timothy*,
Have pitty on your ſelfe, and marry rather

In your owne tribe, some damsell that can churne,
Make Cheese and Apple pies with Currants in them,
And Mr. *Holdfast* twere far better for you
To match with some grave doctors impe at Cambridge
Or else as twas your use when you'r a student,
Lye with your bed maker.
   Tim. Very right,
Yet I doe know all this is but in jest,
To make us love you better.
   Hold. True sir *Timothy,*
Speake as it were to let us understand
By an Irony as we the learned call it,
How well they meane to use us : therefore in
My judgement it were requisit with all speed,
While the're in this good humour
To strike the match up.
   Tim. Very right, we are
No Jackdawes to be fright with these Scar-crowes,
Mistris your hand, and if you'l have me so,
If not so likewise : but you will repent it,
You'l scarcely meet two that will offer fairer
Then we have done.
   Cla. But doe you meane performance,
Truely of these conditions.
   Hold. As sincerely
As 'ere we meane to eate.
   Tim. Or drinke good Ale
At mother *Huffs* a mornings.
   Grace. You'll confesse this
Before the Priest and witnesses.
   Hold. Before
The Congregation, or at a Commencement
Before the University.
   Clar. That you'll be
Honest contented Cuckolds, beare your heads
As peaceably, and with as much obedience,
As the tam'st beast ith' City.

Tim. On my Knight-hood.
Hold. On my gentility.
Clar. Why then ſtrike hands on 't ;
Since you will needs undoe your ſelves, 'twere
  folly
To indeavour to redeeme you : but this night
We will be marry'd, and in private,
Not yours nor our friends being acquainted with it.
Weele meet you any where, procure the licenſe,
And weele be ready ; ſo farewell : to night,
Or not at all lets heare from you.
                    Exeunt Clara, Grace.

Hold. And feele us too ere morning, 't ſhall goe
  hard elſe.
Sir *Timothy*, was not this wiſely carryed :
To let them have their ſayings ? but we will not
Be ſuch ſtarke fooles to doe what we have pro-
  mis'd ;
When they're ours once, we may rule them eaſily
At our owne pleaſures.
  Tim. Very right ; and uſe them
At our owne pleaſures : But ſee here's your Mr.
And Mr. Conſtable your Landlord.

          Enter Grimes, Buſie.

Hold. Landlord, welcome
On my Gentility, to my houſe that muſt be.
Thou thoughtſt, becauſe I did weare Lokram ſhirts
Ide no wit : but harke thee, I have got
The wench of Gold : Sir *Timothy*, and I
Have ſtrucke the ſtroake old boy : to night's the
  night,
Thou ſhalt know more of it ere twelve of Clocke,
And then believe me : *Grimes* goe you to th'
  office :
There's mony, fetch a Licence.

Tim. There's more money,
Bring me a Licence too; fure as we woo'd
Weele wed together.
　Bufie. How's this? Gentlemen
I fhall have gloves I hope.
　Hold. And favours too,
Thy daughter *Nell* fhall have my Bride garters,
And thy fore-man my poynts: But honeft Landlord,
I know th'art excellent at a device,
This matter muft be private, not my father,
Nor Mr. Alderman muft be acquainted
Till all is finifhed: Could thy wit but helpe us
To plot this finely: *Clare* and *Grace* will meet us,
At any place where weele appoynt.
　Buf. How's that?
Ile fet you prefently ith' way; my houfe
Shall be your randevous: foone after ten,
The houre of meeting: there Ile have prepar'd
For the two Ladyes a Sedan: that fhall
Carry them thence unfeene through the watch
At Ludgate, where I exercife my office,
Into white-Friers, there fhall a little Levite
Meet you, and give you to the lawfull bed.
With much celerity: give me your mony,
And ile take out the licence. How's that now?
　Tim. Very right.
　Buf. Meane time my daughter *Luce* fhall give them notice
How all's contriv'd, they'll be willing,
When they fhall know the managing's committed
To my difcretion; but about your bufineffe;
It will grow late oth' fuddaine.
　Hold. Come Sir *Timothy.*

　　　　　　　Ex. Hold. Tim. Grimes.

　Buf. So, fo, as I would have it: if I doe not

Doe something to exalt the fame of Constables,
May I be hang'd upon my staffe of Office.
Ha! *Valentine* and *Freewit* with my daughter!
They must not see me.
                                        Exit.

               Enter Valentine, Free-wit, Luce.

   Luce. Tis certaine Mr. *Freewit* they are con-
     tracted,
And this night to be marryed: I am sorry
You should be thus supplanted, by two such
Dull witlesse ideots: but they are so bent on't,
That when I speake in your behalfes, my Mistris
Stopt my mouth with a blow oth' lips: see here

                   Ent. Clar. Grace.

They are themselves; if you doe any good,
It must be now or never.
                                      Ex. Luce.
   Clar. Grace. Ha, ha, ha.
   Free. What doe the Monkyes laugh at?
   Clar. To behold
Two such trim gallants as your selves, like Asses,
Shaking your empty Noddles ore the Oates
You faine would eate, but must not lick your
     lips at.
You thought to have wonne us by your wit, where
     lyes it?
In your gay cloaths; perhaps so, if you can
Out-sweare the faithfull Tayler, that's unpaid yet,
Or cheat your Sempstresse. Troth make safe retreat
Into the Suburbs, there you may finde cast wenches,
Who will in pitty have you: and for dowry,
Bring you an ampler stocke of hot diseases,
Than you are already furnish'd with. We Orphans
Oth' City have more charity to our selves,

Than to wed Surgeons boxes.
   Grace. When our portions
Shall be confum'd in Pothecaries Bills,
Or giving Doctors fees ; or at beft ufe,
Serve but to purchafe Sacke ; or be as tribute
Paid toth' three Kings ; or pioufly beftowed
Upon *Jerufalem.*
   Free. No, you'd beft referve them
Till thofe you wed be beg'd for fooles ; and then
They will be feas'd to better ufe. You think now
You have broake our gulls with anger that you have
Refolv'd on other husbands : who would have you ?
But two fuch ideots, fit to be the ftyles
To the vaft pride and luft lurkes in your blood,
Derivative from the City : for our felves,
Why fhould you have a thought we could defcend
So much from gentries honour, to mixe with you ?
Tis true, you appeare handfome, but you paint
Worfe then a Bawd, or waiting-woman, in love
With the fpruce Chaplaine.
   Val. For your haire let's fee
Your eye-browes badge : oh tis not your owne ;
Be modeft and confeffe it : tis a Peruke,
I faw it at the French-mans in the Strand,
The other day : and though you hold your head up,
It is fuppos'd it growes too neare your fhoulders,
And you weare iron bodyes, to keep downe
And rectifie the crooked paths that are
In this fame hill your body.
   Free. Nay, befides
Y'are infinitely lafcivious, tis reported
Y'ave kild the reverend Alderman at leaft,
Ten Prentifes, befides foure journy-men,
With too much labour : That you will be drunke
Our felves can teftifie : and with thefe imperfec-
   tions

This inexhaufted Magazin of vices,
Could you imagine we would have you? no,
Heaven give you joy, with your well chofen fpoufes:
May they be patient Cuckolds, that's all the harme
Weele wifh them: the more fooles, more fit for husbands
To fuch hot wild cats.
   Clare. Well Mr. *Free-wit*,
I thought how ever we, in mirth, or madneffe,
Could have tranfgreft civility, that you
Would not have made fuch a fevere conftruction
Of our intentions: how i've lov'd you, heavens
Can beare me righteous witneffe; but mans faith

                                  weeps.

Is fickle as his fhadow, never feene,
But when the Sunne fhines.
   Grace. And that you, whom I
Even at the firft view lov'd, and fixt my heart on:
Should not alone contemne me, but with thefe
Abufes wound my fame, torments my foule
Beyond the ftrength of patience, heaven forgive you.
   Free. They are our owne, deare *Valentine*: our owne as furely,
As if the officious Prieft had put the Ring
Upon their pretty fingers; why you need not
Take words with fuch unkindneffe *Clare*, yourfelves
Being the occafion.
   Clar. Such difcourtefies
From friends; nay, fuch beloved friends as you were,
Wounds deeply Mr. *Freewit*.
   Free. Prethee *Clara*
No more remonftrances of this unkindneffe,
Drye thy faire eyes, or I fhall elfe grow childifh,
And weep for company: poore heart i'me forry

Th'art thus diftemper'd; prethee fweet forgive
  me;
We will be friends, and inftantly fteale hence,
And end all difference in a happy marriage.
  Clar. Ha, ha, ha: hold the mans head, heel
    fwowne
I feare oth' fuddaine: marry you; goe boaft
How you've abus'd us, and doe not forget
Tis part oth' ftory, twill much grace the action,
That you were foold agen into beliefe
That we could love you: ha, ha, ha.

Ex. Clare, Grace.

  Val. We have made our felves fine fooles, a poxe
    upon them:
I knew their teares could not be ferious:
They onely fell from their left eye, as wealthy
Young widowes weep for their old husbands. *Free-
wit*
They're loft, paft all recovery.
  Free. Who can helpe it;
There are more wives ith' Kingdome; yet Ime
    vext
That two fuch gulls fhould carry them: lets goe
    feeke
Sir *Timothy* and my Cozen *Holdfaft* out,
And geld them, then proclaime them to be Eu-
    nuchs.
That courfe may fpoile their marriage.

Enter Bufie.

  Buf. I have o're-heard them all, and it con-
    duces
Much to my purpofe: now, or never *Bufie*
Shew thy felfe a true fparke, that Conftables
Hereafter may be thought to have fome wit,

More than is in their ſtaffe. Good day to you
  gallants,
I have ſome buſineſſe with you.
  Val. Your name is *Buſie*?
  Buſ. The ſame body,
Your friend, although a Conſtable; there were two
  Ladyes
Went lately from you.
  Free. What of that?
  Buſ. They told me, as I am of their councell, that
  they lov'd you.
And though ſome words of courſe had paſt between
  you,
As oft does among friends: you know the Proverbe
  put lately
In a Ballad, where I learnd it, that *amantium iræ
amoris redintegratio eſt*: yet that was but in jeſt, and
in all haſte,
Wiſhed me to aſſure you, that if you would ſpeedily
Take out the Licences this very night, twixt nine
  and ten, at my
Houſe they would meet you, and joyne with you in
  Matrimony.
  Free. Is this truth?
  Buſ. How's that? upon the faith ſir of a man in
  office,
You may believe me: for a Prieſt, leave that
To my care gentlemen, ile have one ready
Privately in White-Friers, the houſe anon
I will enforme you, and what way to take
To miſſe purſuit, if any ſhould endeavour
Your apprehenſion.
  Val. How may we deſerve this kindnes from
  you?
  Buſ. When tis done, then thanke me; meane
time make haſte, and get the licences.

Ex. Free. Val.

I will purfue the reft, and if I fit not fome body,
Let me be held as other of my fellows are, Affes in office.

Ent. Luce.

Luce thou art come as aptly as I could wifh : be fure at nine of Clock to be at home, and if you can bring with you two of the gentlewomens gownes, queftion not why ?
But on my bleffing doe it; if this hit,
Time fhall report fome Conftables have wit.   *Ex.*

Explicit Actus Quartus.

Actus Quintus, Scena prima.

The Watch.

1 *Watch.* IT is a cold night neighbour,
And tis likely we ſhall have froſt,
That will make Sea-coales deare; heaven helpe poore
    people.
Is no newes ſtirring neighbour?
    Men. 2 *Wat.* Yes, to day
I heard ſuch newes, heaven bleſſe us, as would
    make
A man's heart quake in's belly; ſtrange, and true,
It came up in a Carret Boat from Sandwich
Laſt tide; an Oiſter wife, a good old Woman,
Heard it at *Billingſgate*, and told my wife on it.
    3 *Watch.* What is it? pray lets heare it.
    Men. 2 *Wat.* Marry, that twixt *Deale*
And *Dover*, one fiſhing for Flounders, drew
A Spaniards body up, ſlaine ith' late ſea-fight,
And ſearching him for monie, found ith' ſets
Of his great Ruffe the—I ſhall think on't preſently,
Tis a hard word—the Inquiſition.
    1 *Wat.* O monſtrous, what's that?
I have not heard of ſuch a Beaſt before.
    Men. 3 *Wat.* You've heard nothing then:
It is a Monſter very like the Man-drake
Was ſhewen at Temple Barre.
    2 *Wat.* You have heard nothing neither:
The Monſter's no ſuch Monſter: neighbor *Mandivell*
You are a zealous brother, a Tranſlator,
Tis ſuch a Monſter as will ſwallow thee,

And all the Brethren at *Amſterdam*,
And in new *England* at a morſell: verilies,
Your yeas, and nayes will not appeaſe its ſtomacke,
Twill ſup them up as eaſily as a Tayler
Would doe ſixe hot loaves in a morning faſting,
And yet dine after.

Enter Buſie and Parſon.

Buſ. There is the Licence ſir for Mr. *Holdfaſt*,
And wife Sir *Timothy*; you have inſtructions
How things ought to be carryed: when I have
Diſpos'd my Watch, I will be there my ſelfe;
Meane time good Sir be carefull.

Parſ. Doubt me not,
Good Mr. Conſtable; tis not the firſt time
I have eſpouſed couples of as much worſhip,
Behinde the Brickhills: when tis done, tis done,
And ſurely conſummate.

Ex. Parſon.

Buſ. Well ſaid neighbours,
Y'are chatting wiſely o're your Bils and Lanthorns,
As becomes Watch-men of diſcretion: pray you
Let's have no wit amongſt you: no diſcourſe
O' the Common-wealth; I need not neighbours give you
Your charge to night: onely for faſhion ſake.
Draw neare and be attentive.

3 *Men.* I have edified
More by your charge I promiſe you, than by
Many a mornings exerciſe.

Buſ. Firſt then,
You ſhall be ſure to keep the peace; that is,
If any quarrell, be ith' ſtreets, ſit ſtill, and keepe
Your ruſty Bills from blood-ſhed; and as't began
So let it end: onely your zeales may wiſh
The Devill part them.

1 *Wat.* Forward Mr. Conſtable.

Buf. Next, if a thiefe chance to paſſe through your watch,
Let him depart in peace; for ſhould you ſlay him,
To purchaſe his redemption he'le impart
Some of his ſtolne goods, and you're apt to take them,
Which makes you acceſſary to his theft,
And ſo fit food for Tiburne.
   Men. Good adviſe,
I promiſe you, if we have grace to follow it.
   Buf. Next if a drunkard or a man diſguiſd,
Deſire to paſſe the gate, by all means open't,
You'l run your ſelves into th' premunire,
For your authority ſtretches but to men,
And they are beaſts by ſtatute.
   1 *Wat.* Such as we are,
Horn'd beaſts he means.
   Buf. How's that; you carry lanthornes,
Thou haſt wit, and Ile reward't, there's foure tokens
To buy the cheeſe: next for the female creatures,
Which the ſeverer officers ith' ſuburbs
Terme girles, or wenches, let them paſſe without
Examining where they been: or taking from them
A ſingle token: laſſe good ſoules, they get
Their mony hard, with labours of their bodies,
And to exact on thoſe were even extortion
Beyond a brokers.
   Men. Yet they doe't
Without the City, I have heard a brewer,
Being one yeare in office, got as much
From theſe good ſoules as bought him a new maſh-fat,
And mended all his coolers.
   Buf. How's that? we are bidden
Not to take ill examples, for your ſelves you have
Free leave for th' good oth' common wealth to
Sleepe after eleven: meane time you may play at
Tray trip, or cockall for blacke puddings,
So now your charge is finiſh'd.

*Enter Sir Timothy, Grimes, Holdfaſt,
with a Sedan.*

1. *Wat.* Stand, who goes there ?
Men. Come before Mr. Conſtable.
Hold. Tis I Landlord,
There's ſixteenpence to buy thy watch ſome Ale,
Prithee tie up their tongues.
Tim. And there's foure groates
To purchaſe toſts to it.
Buſ. How's that, pray ſtay my maſters,
You'r ſober men and fit to be examin'd :
Whither goes all this carriage ? cloſe conveiance,
Theſe are the cunningſt wodden bawdy houſes,
Were ere invented, and theſe blew coate men mules,
The moſt authenticke pimps : ſet downe and open
Your chaire of ſinne you varlets.
Hold. Why good Landlord,
You will ſpoyle all, doe you not know your tenent,
Not *Ieremy Holdfaſt* ?
Buſ. How's that ? not my father
Upon a watch, Ile lay my life they've ſtolne
Some city orphane, they'r ſo loath to have
Their load diſcover'd.
Hold. There's ten ſhillings Landlord
To buy thee ſack : although it be thy office,
And thou art ſworne to't, for a friend tis lawfull
To breake an oath : I will forſweare my ſelfe
A hundred times to doe thee good.

Exeunt Holdfaſt, Timothy, Grimes, and Sedan.

Buſ. I am
Appeas'd, march on : looke you remember my
Inſtructions : ſo this money was well gotten,
And 'tſhall as merrily be ſpent, you need no
More, club your halfe pence ſparkes to purchaſe
    Ale,

You've an exchequer : ha! another chariot, *Int.*
This fame fhould be fome Lady from a labor,
Her waiters fmell of groning cheefe : good night
Gentlemen, pay the Porter, what ift twelve pence?
Share it amongft you.
 Men. Mr. Conftable
Tis very late, a fire and a browne toft now,
With fome of mother *Trundles* Ale, I promife you
Would comfort much the inwards.
 Buf. How's that? hang it,
It is hereticall : Sack's the Orthodoxall
Liquor : and now I thinke ont, you two, and
 Mendwell
Shall with me to th' Saint Johns head : there is
A cup of pure Canary, and weel have it,
Twill breake your heads, your owne bills,
And weare your Lanthornes in your nofes bullies :
My mafters, you that ftay behinde obferve
My charge with ftrictneffe, and if any bufineffe
Be of importance, call me.

    Exit cum Cæteris.

 1 *Wat.* Now my mafters,
Shull I expound a motion to you, fhall wee
Share, and fhare like this mony?
 4 *Wat.* With all our hearts. *Omnes.*
 1 *Wat.* Lets fee what comes it to a peece : there's
  eleven groats,
And we are five of us, that is —— that is, let me fee,
  feven pence a piece.
No, no, I lye, tis eight pence, and fix pence over.
 4 *Wat.* Right, right, this it is to be booke-
  learn'd,
He's a good Arimetician : but ftay neighbours,
Here comes more company : come before the Con-
  ftable.

Enter Covet, Sir Geffery, Formall with a Linke.

Cov. This is the government the city keepes,
How doe you lik't Sir *Geffery?*
Geff. Very well,
I doe not thinke all Chriſtendome affoords
The like for formall diſcipline.
 1 *Wat.* Leave your prating,
And come before the Conſtable, though he be not
Here himſelfe, theres thoſe that can examine you?
 Cov. You doe well maſters to keepe diligent watch,
Theres many varlets at theſe houres commit
Diſorders in the City: Wheres the conſtable?
 1 *Wat.* Good maſter Alderman, I cry your worſhip mercy,
Becauſe your worſhip wanted your worſhipfull horſe,
We did not know you: Mr. Conſtable
And pleaſe your worſhip is but at next doore
Drinking a pint of ſacke.
 Cov. How at a Taverne?
 1 *Wat.* At the Saint Johns head,
And pleaſe your worſhip, where if your worſhip pleaſe,
You may have excellent ſacke, and pleaſe your worſhip.
 Cov. This is the fowlſt enormity I ever
Heard on ith' city, that a Conſtable,
Who ought to ſee good orders kept, ſhould be
At theſe unlawfull houres, breeding diſorder,
And in an open Taverne. Good Sir *Geffery*
Beare me but company, Ile make the knave
A faire example to all men in office,
How they come nere a buſh: watchmen looke well
To the charge committed to you: for your Conſtable,
Ile make him kiſſe the counter, light on *Formall.*

Exit Covet, cum cæteris.

1 *Wat.* A ſhrewd man this, if ere he live to be
Lord Major, ha mercy upon us ; neighbours ſurely
Tis very late, and I was up till twelve
Laſt night a mending my wives bodies, ſhall we
Each to his bulke and take a nod?
   Omnes. Agreed, agreed.   *Exe. Watch.*

      *Buſie, Mendwell, watchmen as
           in a Taverne.*

   Buſ. Set downe your truſty Bills my ſparkes, and
   let us
Watch ore a cup of Sacke, here tis will make you
Each one an Alderman : a bigger glaſſe boy,
I doe not love theſe thimbles, they are fit
For none but preciſe Taylors, that doe ſip,
In zeale, and ſweare cuds nigs over their wine,
To cheat their cuſtomers : ſo this is ſomething.
A ſcore or two of theſe my ſparkes, will ſet
Our braines a floate, and then weel talke as wiſely,
As all the common Counſell, how's that now?
   Men. Mr. Conſtable
Y'are in the right I promiſe you : I feele
My ſelfe already growing from a watchman
Into a head-borow.
   Buſ. How's that? thou ſhalt be
A Conſtable within this halfe houre *Mendwell*,
Carry thy ſtaffe with the red Croſſe and Dagger
In as much ſtate, as the beſt goldſmith,
That ere bore office in Cheap-ſide ; here's to thee,
Hang care and Coſenage ; let mercers uſe it
In the darke ſhops : I am a Linnen Draper,
Love wit and Sacke, and am reſolv'd to thrive by't,
When they ſhall break like bottles : Here lets
   canvas
This quart, and then will bumbaſte off another,
And drinke a health to *Holland*, and the mad
   boyes

That traile the puiffant Pike there : how's that ; doe
you peepe ?

Enter Fidlers Boy.

 Boy. Pleafe you hear a good fong Gentle-
men ?
 Buf. Thefe fqueakers, doe claime more
Priviledge in a Taverne,
Then a man in office ; into every roome
They thruft their frifled heads ; and Ide bin at it
With fome diftreffed Damfell, that I had taken
Late in my watch, thus Ide bin ferv'd : ile have
An Edict made againft them at *Guild Hall*,
Next fitting certainely.
 Boy. A very new fong and pleafe your worfhips
gentlemen.
 Buf. There you lye boy ;
I doubt it is fome lamentable ftuffe,
Oth' Swine-fac'd gentlewoman, and that youle grunt
out
Worfe than a parifh Boare when he makes love
Unto the Vicars fow ; her ftory's ftale boy,
'T has beene already in two playes.
 Boy. An't pleafe your worfhips,
My fong is of a Conftable.
 Buf. How's that ? a Conftable,
Tis not my felfe ; I hope ime not exalted
Into a ballad : Dare you firrah abufe
Officers in your Madrigalls ; you deferve,
And fo does he that made it, to be whipt for't.
 Boy. Pray heare it fir : tis no fuch matter on my
credit.
 Buf. How's that ? Well on thy credit I will
heare it.
Call in your company ; welcome my Mafters :

Wit in a Conſtable.

Ent. Muſicians.

Here : wet your weſands firſt, then thunder forth
Some lofty Sonnets in the praiſe of Conſtables :
And never feare the whipping-poſt hereafter.

Conſtables 2. Song.

SIng and rejoyce, the day is gone.
  And the wholſome night appeares,
*In which the Conſtable on Throne
Of truſty bench, does with his Peeres
The comely watch ; men ſound of health,
Sleep for the good oth' Common-wealth.*

*Tis his office to doe ſo,
Being bound to keep the peace,
And in quiet ſleep all know
Mortall jarres, and lewd brawles ceaſe :
A Conſtable may then for's health,
Sleep for the good oth' Common-wealth.*

*Vnleſſe with Nobler thoughts inſpir'd,
To the Taverne he reſort,
Where with Sacke his Sences fir'd,
He raignes as fairy King in Court ;
Drinking many a luſty health ;
Then ſleepes for th' good oth' Common-wealth.*

*With a comely girle, whom late
He had taken in his watch,
Oft he ſteales out of the gate
Her at the old ſport to match,*

Though it may impaire his health,
He sleeps with her for th' good oth' Common-
  wealth.

Who then can Constables deny
To be persons brave and witty,
Since they onely are the eye,
The Glory, the delight oth' City,
That with staffe, and Lanthorne light
Are like blacke Pluto *Princes of the night.*

  Men. An excellent Ditty I promise you.
  Busie. Well done boy.
There's twelve pence for you Knaves, and tell the Poet
That made it, if heele come to me, ile give him
A quart of Sacke to whet his Muse.

Ent. Drawer.

  Draw. Sir, below there's one enquires for you, and I suppose him
To be at least an Alderman.
  Buf. And if he be
The Major and his horse, let them come up.
Flinch Squeakers into another roome : Good Mr. Alderman

Ent. Cov. Sir Geff. Formall.

Tis strange you are abroad so late, wil't please you
To taste a cup a Sack, twill warme your stomacke
After your walking.
  Cov. No Sirrah, ile not be
Partaker of yout riot : this the watch
You keep good Mr. Constable? introth

The City's much beholding to your care,
And they shall understand it, in a Taverne
A fit place for an Officer: but ile send you
To one fitter for you to the Counter.
Lay hands I charge you, beare him hence,
Ile have you all laid fast else.

Buf. How's that? I hope youle let us
Drinke off our sacke first: twere farre better sir,
In my poore judgment, that you sate down in peace,
As does befit your gravity, and drinke
A friendly cup or two: then for the first
Offence to send your neighbour to the Counter:
Pray sir be not so fierce; a glasse, or two
Will mollifie your hard heart.

Cov. Will you not stirre knaves?
Where is the Master of the house? ile make
This *Busie* an example.

Buf. Pray doe not sir:
Perhaps y'are bashfull sir, and will not drinke,
Cause you want coyne to pay: ile lend you some;
Or if you scorne to borrow, you may dip
Your chaine; a good pawne never shames the
    master.
Pray sit downe sir; we just now had Musicke,
Ile call them in agen.

Cov, Within, the master of the house, ile have
These knaves indicted for this bold contempt,
And whipt about the City.

Buf. You may see sir,
My Watch-men know their duty, they'll obey
None but the Constable, and ile experience,
If they'le know me for one: My masters, take
This Alderman and his company I charge you,
And carry them straight to th' Counter, ile secure
    you
'Gainst all the harme that followes.

   Seife on the Alderman and Sir Geffery.

Men. Come, come, come along sir.

Cov. Dare you doe this firrah?
Buf. Yes, and anfwer't too fir.
Y'ave met a Conftable that has the wit,
To know the power of's office: neighbour *Mendwel*,
Becaufe they'le take him for a Rat ith' Counter,
And Ide be loath to have his reverend beard
Be twitch'd off for his Garnifh, to my houfe
Convey him, and that comely Knight, and bid
My maid fhew them a Chamber; ile deale kindlier
With you, then you'd have done with me: there
    watch them
Till I come home: how's that now?
Cov. Sirrah, firrah, ile make you fmoak for this.
Mend. Come, we lofe time fir.
Buf. Let him have
A good fire pray you. So, all works as't had bin
Molded afore in waxe: boy there's your reckoning.
Now to my fparkes, Ive done that will be talkt on
    ith' City,
And regiftred, a Conftable was witty.

    Freewit, Thorowgood, Valentine, Luce, Clare.

    Clar. You thinke you have us fure now. This
    fame *Bufie*
Is a meere cheating Rafcall.
    Thor. Come, your rage
Is ufeleffe now: he has done better for you,
Than I by th' circumftance perceive you had
Intended for your felves: what would you've done
With two fuch March-pane husbands? I believe,
For all you fet a good face on the matter,
Twas your owne plot.
    Clar. Ours? then may we dye Virgins,
And thefe fame trufty youths, now cald our hus-
    bands,
Be fuddainly transform'd to Eunuchs; we
Had thought young *Holdfaft*, and Sir *Timothy*

Had bin the Squires had ufher'd us, and them
We had refolv'd to couple with.
 Free. Sweete *Clare*
No more of this; for all your queint diffembling
I know you love us, better than to part
For a flight quarrell; now we're man and wife,
And we will love you, if you'll be obedient,
And get fuch Boyes upon you, as fhall people
Cheap-fide with wit five generations after us.
 Val. Feare not thy fathers frownes: fweet *Grace*
  I have
An *Aldermans* heire a joyncture.

    Enter Bufie.

 Buf. Bleffe you my hearts of gold, and give
  you joy.
Frowne not good Miftris *Clare*, I knew your minde
And fo fulfild it.
 Free. Conftable, ile have
Thy *Annalls* writ, in a farre larger volume,
Than *Speed* or *Hollingfhed*.
 Clar. Well Mr. *Bufie*,
Y'ave ferv'd us fweetly.
 Buf. How's that? I hope your husbands
Anon will ferve you fweetlier: faith I thought
There was no wit in't, that you two fhould caft
Your felves away on two fuch gulls, your por-
 tions
Deferv'd more noble husbands: therefore finely
After you were gone downe, to take your Chariot,
In ftead of them, when ith' meane while my
 daughters
Held in difcourfe, I fent thefe, now your hus-
 bands,
To exercife their office: Now you are marryed,
I fhall have Gloves I hope?
 Clar. Yes, and fuch favours

As thou ſhalt weare in triumph: but what have you
Done with our other ſweet-hearts?
   Buſ. How's that? matcht them
To two will hold them play: Come will you travaile?
Your father Miſtris *Grace* is at my houſe,
Thither you ſhall, and if he will be angry,
Let him be pleas'd agen: Advance my ſparkes,
Ile be your valiant Leader.   *Exeunt.*

Sir Geffery, Covet, Formall, Watchmen.

   Geff. Storme not ſo Mr. Alderman, the man
Has done no more beleev't, than what his office
Will beare him out in.
   Cov. Ile ſpend a thouſand
Pound, but Ile be reveng'd: a ſawcy raſcall
In my owne Ward to ſerve me thus?

Enter Timothy, Holdfaſt, Grimes, Luce, Nell.

   Hold. Nay, come forward Ladyes,
Although your father ſweet-heart, be in our ſearch,
Be not abaſh'd; come forward, though you kept
Your tongues in peace, ere ſince our going forth,
And nere ſpake word, unleſſe before the Parſon
When we committed Matrimony, yet now
Pull off your Maskes and Vailes, and ſhew your faces,
Be not aſham'd of them.
   Cov. Who's here? Sir *Timothy* and your ſonne, Ile lay
My life on't they have ſtruck a marriage up
Without our knowledge.

Geff. Very likely *Jeremy*.
Hold. No more words fir, tis done, I and fir *Timothy*
Have hit the white: Good father *Covet* be not
Ith' angry mood now I have wed your daughter,
And he your Neece, weele ufe them kindly: pray you
Bid give us joy; vour daughter is fo fearefull,
She dares not aske you bleffing.
Cov. This qualifies all anger, I forgive them.
Luce. Forgive us fir? you doe not heare us aske it,
Nor need we your remiffion.
Cov. Ha! who are thefe! Sir *Geffery* we are cheated
Abhominably, cheated by this Conftable,
This rafcall *Bufie*, thefe are his daughters.
Luce. Nor are we afham'd
To owne him for our father, that has provided
Us two fuch wealthy husbands.
Hold. *Nell*, I did not thinke you would have ferv'd me thus
Unkindly, gentle *Nell*.
Nel. Unkindly fir, in what? to make you mafter
Of all I have. Ile ufe you kindly truft me;
When you come drunke a nights home, in the morning
Ile make you amber Caudles.
Hold. Saift thou fo;
Give me thy hand: Father pray be not angry,
My Wife's my wife, and fo I will maintaine her
Gainft all the world. Sir *Timothy*, your fpoufe
Is not to be contemn'd, fhe's a good girle.
And therefore pray regard her.
Tim. Very like; for your fake
I will doe much: Although I find my felfe
Made a ftarke Affe. Come hither *Luce*.

Enter Clare, Grace, Thorougood, Freewit, Valentine, Busie.

 Grace. Your pardon Sir, and bleffing.
 Clar. We have done fir
What cannot be undone, now if you will
Be foolifh now, and vexe your felves, you may
Be laught at for your labour; they're our husbands,
And we no caufe now to repent our choyce,
Nor you Sir to repine at.
 Free. Our duties
And after carriage, fhall deferve your love,
Nor are our fortunes Sir fo meane, but may
Merit their portions.
 Cov. Well, you fhall not
Report me cruell; you have my confent,
And bleffing with it; neighbour *Busie*, Ile
Be friends with you, and at my intreaty
Sir *Geffery* fhall be reconcil'd.
 Buf. How's that?
Give me thy fift good brother Knight, my daughters
Shall not come without portions; they fhall have
Each one a Bolt of *Holland*, that's enough.
Sonne Knight give me thine too; and fonne
 Holdfaft
Weele be as merry boyes, and drinke old Sacke
In plenteous glaffes, till we all grow witty,
As humorous Poets; to your beds, the're ready,
Your wedding dinner fhall be mine, weele dance,
And have the Song oth' Conftable: March faire,
And get each one a chopping boy by Morning;
I and my Watchmen here will drinke your healths,
Though we doe lofe our owne by it.
 Free. Mr. *Busie*,
Wee're all beholding to you, and 'tis fit,
We fhould confeffe this Conftable had wit.

FINIS.

EPILOGUE.

ARe you refolv'd yet Gentlemen ? I am
In earneft hafte of Towne-affaires, and came
To know your minds : how's that ? there's one I
   fpye
That will diflike, to th' Counter inftantly
With him ; intreats Sir, fhall not prevaile,
Nor fhall you thinke to come out upon baile.
For in this cafe (believe it) I'de not fpare
(Though the fword were borne before him) my
   Lord Major;
Nor fhould the Court of Aldermen reprieve
For fuch a faƈt, my good friend Mafter Shreive.
If fo fevere to them then, who by vow,
Are my owne bretheren ? what will become of
   you ?
I have confider'd ; and will now commit
To your free votes the Cenfures of my wit.
For though their dulneffe (whom I've threatned)
   may
Diflike (you 'ave wit) and will allow the play.

NOTES AND ILLUSTRATIONS

NOTES AND ILLUSTRATIONS.

PAGE 1.

ARGALUS AND PARTHENIA. 1639.

This ſtory (originally taken from *The Countefs of Pembroke's Arcadia*) had been verſified by Francis Quarles ten years before the date of Glapthorne's play (1629). Our dramatiſt was probably indebted to both his predeceſſors for the outlines and incidents of his work. Of Sir Philip Sidney's romance, and of Quarles's poem, there were various editions current in the earlier half of the ſeventeenth century.

PAGE 65.

Happy Arabians, when your Phœnix dies, &c.

Theſe lines are ſubſtantially the ſame as the *Elegy upon the death of his Siſter Mrs. Priſcilla Glapthorne* (printed in Glapthorne's Poems).

In the comedy of *The Hollander* (at p. 102 of this volume) is another alluſion to the Phœnix, expreſſed in almoſt ſimilar words:—

> "The Phœnix whofe fweetneff
> Becomes her fepulcher, afcends agen
> Vefted in younger feathers from her pile
> Of fpicy afhes.'

In *Argalus and Parthenia* again, at p. 12, we read o

> "aromatique winds
> That fing the Phœnix Exequies."

The allufion feems to have been a favourite one with Glapthorne. It occurs feveral times in his *Poems* (*e.g.*, pp. 179, 182, 185).

PAGE 85.

one in the confpiracy with Barnevet, *at whofe hanging he fled ore hither.*

The execution of John of Barneveld took place on a fcaffold erected in the Binnenhof, at the Hague, on May 13, 1619. The whole ftory of his life and death has recently been told, with an accuracy of refearch and a graphic power alike admirable, by Mr. Motley (*The Life and Death of John of Barneveld, Advocate of Holland, with a View of the Primary Caufes and Movements of the Thirty Years' War.* By John Lothrop Motley. In Two Volumes. Lond. Murray, 1874).

PAGE 93.

Aurelius Bombaftus Paracelfus, *was the firft inventer of this admirable Unguent.*

Philippus Aureolus Theophraftus Bombaftus Paracelfus was born in 1493 at Einsiedeln, a little town in the canton of Schwitz, fome leagues diftant from Zurich. His father, who exercifed the profeffion of medicine at Villach, in Carinthia, was nearly related to George Bombaft de Hohenheim. It appears that his elementary education was much neglected, and that he fpent part of his youth in wandering from country to country, predicting the future from the infpection of the ftars and the lines of the hand, evoking apparitions, and repeating the different operations of magic and alchemy, in which he had been initiated by his father.

As Paracelfus difplays everywhere an ignorance of the rudiments of the moft ordinary knowledge, it is not probable that he fhould ever have ftudied ferioufly in the fchools: he contented himfelf with vifiting the Univerfities of Germany, France, and Italy; and in fpite of his boafting himfelf to have been the ornament of thofe inftitutions, there is no proof of his having legally acquired the title of Doctor, which he affumed. It is only known that he applied himfelf long, under the direction of the wealthy Sigismond Fugger of Schwatz, to the difcovery of the Magnum Opus.

Paracelfus travelled among the mountains of Bohemia, in the Eaft, and in Sweden, in order to infpect the labours of the miners, to be initiated in the myfteries of the oriental adepts, and to obferve the fecrets of nature and the famous mountain of loadftone. He profeffes alfo to have vifited Spain, Portugal, Pruffia, Poland, and Tranfylvania, where he communicated freely, not merely with the phyficians, but with the old women, charlatans, and conjurors of thefe feveral lands. It is even believed that he extended his journeyings as far as Egypt and Tartary, and that he accompanied the fon of the Khan of the Tartars to Conftantinople, for the purpofe of obtaining the fecret of the tincture of Trismegiftus, from a Greek who inhabited that capital.

The period of his return to Germany is unknown: it is only certain that, at about the age of thirty-three, many aftonifhing cures which he wrought on eminent perfonages procured him fuch a celebrity that he was called in 1526 to fill a chair of phyfic and furgery at the Univerfity of Bafil. There Paracelfus began by burning publicly in the amphitheatre the works of Avicenna and Galen, affuring his hearers that the latchets of his fhoes were more inftructed than thofe two phyficians; that all the Univerfities, all the writers put together, were lefs gifted than the hairs of his beard and the crown of his head; and that, finally, he was to be regarded as the legitimate monarch of medicine.

But at Bafil it was fpeedily perceived that the new Profeffor was no better than an egregious quack. Scarcely had a year elapfed before his lectures had fairly driven away an audience incapable of comprehending their emphatic jargon. That which above all contributed to fully his reputation was the debauched life he led . . . . At length, fearful of being punifhed for a ferious outrage on a magiftrate, he fled from Bafil towards the end of the year 1527 and took refuge in Alfatia. We find him at Colmar in 1528; at Nuremburg in 1529; at St. Gall in 1531; at Pfeffers in 1535; at Augsburg in 1536; at Villach in 1538. Finally from Mindelheim, where he was in 1540, Paracelfus proceeded to Salzburg, where he died in the Hofpital of St. Sebaftian, Sept. 24, 1541. (*Abridged from a tranflation of the account in the Biographie Univerfelle, appended to Mr. Robert Browning's poem of Paracelfus,* 1835.)

Paracelfus is alfo mentioned by Ben Jonson in *Volpone* (act II. fc. 2), and by Butler in *Hudibras* (Pt. 2, canto 3).

PAGE 122.

Then Mandrakes *groanes doe a conceite of death
In perfons refolute.*

The mandrake was the Englifh name of the plant *mandragoras,* concerning which fome very fuperftitious notions prevailed. An inferior degree of animal life was attributed to it; and it was commonly fuppofed that, when torn from the ground, it uttered groans of fo pernicious a nature, that the perfon who committed the violence went mad or died. To efcape that danger it was recommended to tie one end of a ftring to the plant and the other to a dog, upon whom the fatal groan would then difcharge its whole malignity.

Thefe ftrange notions arofe, probably, from the little lefs fanciful comparifon of the root to the human figure, ftrengthened, doubtlefs, in England by the accidental circumftance of *man* being the firft fyllable of the word. The ancients, however, made the fame comparifon of its form:

Quamvis *femihominis,* vefano gramine fœta,
Mandragoræ pariat flores.
                    Columella, *de Cult. Hort.* v. 19.

The white mandrake, which they called the male, was that whofe root bore this refemblance.

Glapthorne alfo alludes to the "mandraks grones" in *Argalus and Parthenia*, at page 48 of this volume.

PAGE 123.

Time fhall depend like fummer on your brow, &c.

The laft feven lines of this fpeech were, we prefume, confidered by the author as peculiarly good, for he has alfo introduced them in *The Lady's Privilege*.

PAGE 152.

Ile fue the Statute of Bigamy *upon him, he fhall be hang'd for being double marryed.*

See alfo *Wit in a Conftable*, page 198:

"now wert not for the ftatute
'Gainft Bigamy my tender confcience
Would not much be opprefs'd to have two wives."

1° Jac. I. c II. (A.D. 1603), "Forafmuch as divers evil difpofed perfons being maried, runne out of one Countie into another, or into places where they are not knowen, and there become to be maried, havinge another husband or wife livinge, to the greate difhonour of God and utter undoinge of divers honeft mens children and others; Be it therefore enacted by the Kings Majeftie, with the confent of the Lordes Spirituall and Temporall, and of the Commons in this prefent Parliament affembled, That if any perfon or perfons within his Majefties Domynions of England and Wales, beinge maried, or which hereafter fhall marie, doe at any tyme after the ende of the Seffion of this prefent Parliament, marrye any perfon or perfons, the former husband or wife beinge alive, that then everie fuch offence fhalbe Felonie, and the perfon and persons fo offendinge fhall fuffer death as in cafes of Felonie; And the partie and parties fo offendinge fhall receive fuch and the like proceedinge triall and execution in fuch Countie where fuche perfon or perfons fhalbe apprehended, as if the offence had bene committed in fuch Countie where fuch perfon or perfons fhall be taken or apprehended."

PAGE 169.

*Did you ere we departed from the Colledge
Ore looke my library?*

Under the heading of "Books," this fpeech, and a few lines of Triftram's anfwer, are quoted by Charles Lamb in his Specimens (ed. 1835, vol. ii., p. 164). It is the only paffage he gives from our author.

PAGE 170.

*the famous Poems
Writ by the learned waterman.*
    HOLD.   *John Taylor, get me his nonfenfe.*
    TRIST.   *You meane all his workes fir.*

All the Workes of John Taylor the Water Poet being Sixty and three in number, collected into one volume by the Author, had been publifhed in large folio form in 1630.

Ib.

a hundred of Bookers *new Almanacks.*

John Booker (ftudent in Aftrology) publifhed Ephemerides or Celeftiall Obfervations about our author's time, and for many fuccceding years.

PAGE 178.

Some faire Dulcinea de Tobofo.

It is fcarcely neceffary to remind the reader that Dulcinea de Tobofo was the name of Don Quixote's innamorata. This allufion (which is repeated at p. 214) proves the popularity which the now claffic novel of Cervantes muft have enjoyed in England even at this early date. The tranflation by Thomas Shelton had appeared in 1612—1620.

PAGE 178.

Svbjects fit for ballads,
Not worthy M. P.'s name to them.

M. P. [Martin Parker] was a celebrated writter of doggerel ballads in Glapthorne's time. Some of thefe are figned with his initials and fome with his full name. Many of thefe are preferved in the firft volume of the Roxburghe Ballads (Ancient Songs and Ballads written on Various Subjects, and printed between the years 1560 and 1700, chiefly collected by Robert Earl of Oxford and purchafed at the fale of Weft's Library in 1773).

PAGE 190.

Like the great tun at Heidelberge *fild with wine*
And alwayes running.

See alfo *Albertus Wallenftein* (Vol. II. p. 75):
   "And 'twere the Tun of Heidelberg, I'd drink it."

In a large under room in the caftle or palace of the Princes Palatine of the Rhine at Heidelberg, the eccentric traveller Thomas Coryat found this vaft veffel, in its original form, of which he has given a picture reprefenting himfelf as perched on its top, with a glafs of its contents in his hands. To him it appeared the greateft wonder he had feen in his travels, fully entitled to rank with those seven wonders of the world of which ancient authors inform us. Its construction was begun in the year 1589 and finished in 1591, one Michael Warner being the principal fabricator. It was composed of beams twenty-seven feet long, and had a diameter of eighteen feet. The iron hooping was eleven thousand pounds in weight. The cost was eleven core and eighteen pounds sterling. It could hold a hundred and thirty-two fuders of wine, a fuder being equal to four English hogsheads, and the value of the Rhenish contained in it when Coryat visited Heidelberg (1608) was close upon two thousand pounds.

"When the cellarer," says Coryat, "draweth wine out of the vessel, he ascendeth two several degrees of wooden stairs made in the form of a ladder, and so goeth up to the top; about the middle whereof there is a bung-hole or venting orifice, into the which he conveyeth a pretty instrument of some foot and a half long, made n the form of a spout, wherewith he draweth up the wine and so poureth it after a pretty manner into a glass." The traveller advises visitors to beware lest they be inveigled to drink more than is good for them. (*Chambers's Book of Days.*)

PAGE 205.

A bouncing Mary Ambree.

A famous Amazon frequently alluded to by our old Dramatists. *The valorous acts performed at Gaunt by the brave bonnie lass Mary Ambree, who in revenge of her lovers death did play her part most gallantly*, may be found in Percy's *Reliques*, vol. ii., p. 240, ed. 1812.

PAGE 226.

Bus. *First then*
You shall be sure to keep the peace, &c.

Busie's charge to the watchmen was obviously suggested by that of Dogberry in *Much Ado about Nothing*.

Page 232.

I doubt it is some lamentable stuffe
Oth' the Swine-fac'd gentlewoman; . . . *her story's* stale
   boy,
Tḥ*as beene already in two playes.*

A pamphlet was published in London in 1641, entitled *A Certain Relation of the Hog-Faced Gentlewoman.* From this production we learn that her name was Tanakin Skinker, and that she was born at Wirkman on the Rhine, in 1618. In a contemporary Dutch work, which is either a translation, or mayhap the original of the English one, she is said to have been born at Windsor on the Thames. Miss Skinker is described as having "all the limbs and lineaments of her body well-featured and proportioned, only her face, which is the ornament and beauty of all the rest, has the nose of a hog or swine, which is not only a stain and blemish, but a deformed uglinefs making all the rest loathsome, contemptible, and odious to all that look on her." Her language, we are further informed, is the only the hoggish Dutc̣h *ough*, *ough !* or the French *owee*, *owee !* Forty thousand pounds, we are told, was the sum offered to the man who would consent to marry her, and the author says: "This was a bait sufficient to make every fish bite at, for no sooner was this publicly divulged, but there came suitors of all sorts, every one hoped to carry away the great prize, for it was not the person but the prize they aimed at." Gallants, we are told, came from Italy, France, Scotland, England, and Ireland, to carry away the prize; but, when they saw the lady, they one and all refused to marry her. There is a very characteristic woodcut on the title-page of this work, representing a gallant, gaily attired, bashfully addressing her; while bowing, his hat in his hand, with the words—"God save you, sweet mistress." She, on the other hand, is most magnificently dressed, and coming forward to meet him with the greatest cordiality, can only reply with the words, "Ough, ough."

What the "two plays" were to which Glapthorne alludes, I am unable to inform the reader.

END OF FIRST VOLUME.

www.ingramcontent.com/pod-product-compliance
Lightning Source LLC
Chambersburg PA
CBHW031336230426
43670CB00006B/344